Validating a Best Practice

Validating a Best Practice

A Tool for Improvement and Benchmarking

Yves Van Nuland
Grace L. Duffy

A PRODUCTIVITY PRESS BOOK

First published 2021
by Routledge
52 Vanderbilt Avenue, New York, NY 10017

and by Routledge
2 Park Square, Milton Park, Abingdon, Oxon, OX14 4RN

Routledge is an imprint of the Taylor & Francis Group, an informa business

ISBN: 9780367443979 (hbk)
ISBN: 9780367443917 (pbk)
ISBN: 9781003009436 (ebk)

Typeset in Garamond
by Deanta Global Publishing Services, Chennai, India

Excellence is not an act, it is a habit.

–Aristotle

Contents

Foreword

As an expert in Excellence models, it is an honor for me to introduce this book to you. It provides practical guidance for leaders who want to use Best Practices as benchmarks for their own organizational Journey to Excellence. The BEST-method provides tools to identify which of the many Good Practices they are offered are indeed Best Practices – good enough to use as a benchmark for process excellence.

I have always preferred simple methods and tools in my work with diverse organizations around the world. Simple tools can be easily explained on the basis of common sense. There has never existed a test to assess a Best Practice until now. So, I am very happy to present to you this simple but very effective BEST-method.

The BEST-method and associated tools help leaders decide in a direct and structured way which Best Practices they can use to improve their business or organization. Comparing their organizational performance with real Best Practices allows them to identify key improvement opportunities immediately on a strategic level by validating strategies and strategic targets, and key processes and related key measurements of performance and benefit for stakeholders. On the operational level, the tools are valuable for identifying areas for process improvement and related operational measurements.

Chapter 1 explains how the BEST-method can be applied: if the Quick Scan – which takes only about 20 minutes – provides positive results, the detailed BEST-tool can be applied to further explore the potential benefit of Best Practices. To improve the benefit for the reader, the second part of the book provides concrete application examples from real case studies. The authors, who have many years of experience in Quality Management, include references to each case study analyzed through the BEST-tool and the BEST Quick Scan.

The BEST-method can be easily used as a universal approach for any profit or not-for-profit organization in any sector, country, or culture. This makes the BEST-method a unique and indispensable tool for every leader around the world to ensure their Journey to Excellence is sustainable.

Dr. sc.nat. Christian G. Forstner
Founder and CEO of CFyouradvantage.com
Dr. Forstner *is a Nuclear Physicist with a PhD from the Swiss Federal Institute of Technology in Zurich. He has more than 25 years of experience in supporting organizations around the world to achieve Excellence, on a sound basis of industrial expertise and corporate experience.*

Acknowledgments

We thank our families for their patience and support. This project took much more time than we expected. We worked hundreds of hours over the span of two years to provide just the right information and materials for our readers. We are proud of the outcome. We offer the management community a new and valuable tool with which to objectively assess a Best Practice. As we apply the BEST-method to multitudes of espoused Best Practices, we are convinced of the added value of this method to all types of processes across companies and organizations worldwide.

We wish to thank Ms. Cheryl Boglarsky, PhD, Human Synergistics and other Lion Nathan representatives for gaining agreement to feature Lion Nathan as a Best Practice process.

A special thank you goes out to: Mr. Preston Boyce, Area 7 Manager Community Health Florida Health Department, Mr. Willie T. Brown, Operations & Management Consultant Manager Orange County STD Office Florida Health Department, and Mr. Vicente Alberto Araujo, Quality Manager, Office of Strategic Planning, Florida Department of Health in Brevard County, for their data analysis of current trends in process improvement toward Best Practice in fighting the syphilis epidemic in Orange County, Florida.

Thanks also go to Ms. Janet Wells, PhD candidate, Florida Southern University, for her documentation search on definitions of Best Practice and search for best practice case studies.

We thank Norman Hughes who pointed out that there are not only Best Practices, but also Good Practices. We adapted the text so that the reader can discover how the BEST-method also applies to Good Practices. Paul Adriaenssens and Ken Somers helpfully informed us that the BEST-method is not applicable to technological and medical products and their Best Practices. These are very technical processes and have their own Best

Practice criteria. Nevertheless, the BEST-method is valuable for all other processes in companies and organizations.

We are most grateful to Katherine Kadian and Michael Sinocchi at Taylor & Francis, and Michelle van Kampen and Christine Selvan at Deanta Global for recognizing the importance of an effective Best Practice both in performance excellence and as a foundation for benchmarking. Their faith in our work product made all the difference.

Finally, we must confess that although many people know the acronym TEAM and more specifically the word with dots, T.E.A.M. (Together Each Achieves More), we have experienced the true value of this concept over the last two years. We (Grace and Yves) exchanged hundreds of e-mails as we worked across the Atlantic Ocean to create this work for our readers. Each time we revised a chapter, it became better. This work has been a never-ending story. We are so proud of the outcome of our collaboration.

As the deadline approached, we were obliged to stop the Kaizen process. Hopefully, the book will be a success, so that we can further improve the BEST-methodology for the next edition. We look forward to the input of multiple readers who will share their Best Practices with us.

We thank our readers, and people who apply the BEST-method, in advance. Send your comments, questions, suggestions, and, hopefully, your Best Practices to the authors or upload them to our website www.comatech.be. We will consider your input for the next edition.

Yves Van Nuland
Blanden, Belgium

Grace L. Duffy
Eustis, Florida, USA

Authors

Yves Van Nuland, PhD

After earning a PhD in Chemistry at the University of Leuven, Belgium (1977), Yves worked at the Belgian FDA (1978). Next, he was laboratory and quality manager at PRB (chemical industry) (1979–1988) and quality manager at UCB Chemicals in Brussels (1989–1994). As a self-employed consultant-trainer, he gives support to his customers on subjects like excellence models (EFQM and MBA), Business Process Management, KPIs and company culture. He is coauthor and editor of the book *Excellent: A Guide for the Implementation of the EFQM Excellence Model.*

Grace L. Duffy, President, Management and Performance Systems

Grace provides services in organizational and process improvement, leadership, quality, customer service, and teamwork. She designs and implements effective systems for business and management success. She is author of *The Quality Improvement Handbook, The Executive Guide to Improvement and Change, Executive Focus: Your Life and Career, The Public Health Quality Improvement Handbook, QFD and Lean Six Sigma for Public Health, Modular kaizen: Dealing with Disruption, Tools and Applications for Starting and Sustaining Healthy Teams, The Encyclopedia of Quality Tools, The Quality Improvement Pocket Guide*, and *Modular Kaizen: Continuous and Breakthrough Improvement.*

Ms. Duffy has over 40 years of experience in successful business and process management in corporate, government, education, healthcare, not-for-profit, and small business. She is a renowned specialist in leadership and executive performance. Grace uses her experience as President, CEO, and senior manager to assist organizations and individuals in performance excellence. She is a frequently requested keynote and conference speaker on organizational and professional performance. She is an active coach and mentor to senior leaders in large corporations as well as entrepreneurs, focusing on strategic alignment of individual skills to organizational outcomes.

Grace holds a master's degree in Business Administration from Georgia State University and a bachelor's degree in Archaeology and Anthropology from Brigham Young University. She is an American Society for Quality (ASQ) Certified Manager of Quality/Organizational Excellence, Certified Quality Improvement Associate, and Certified Quality Auditor. Grace is a Certified Lean Six Sigma Master Black Belt, and Manager of Process Improvement. Grace is a member of ASTD, ISPI, and ASQ. She is an ASQ Fellow and Past Vice President within the ASQ Office of the President and 2014 recipient of the ASQ Distinguished Service Medal.

DESCRIPTION OF THE BEST-TOOL

Chapter 1

Introduction

Sharing Best Practices across industries and functions is an accepted approach to continuous improvement. The Benchmarking trend of the 1990s has evolved with the help of competitive analysis, performance excellence awards, and other corporate recognition programs into an ongoing documentation of what works. Bob Camp introduced benchmarking against a Best Practice based on his work at Xerox in the 1980s. Case studies abound documenting Best Practice functions and processes. Some case studies use the words "Best Practice" without evidence that the process, results, or methods are, indeed, superior. What is missing is a comprehensive model for *assessing* and *writing* a Best Practice that provides sufficient information to use as an effective benchmark. This book provides that comprehensive model.

Not every process performs as well as desired. Perhaps the process is not designed or measured properly. Perhaps the process is not documented in a way that ensures consistency of results. Having a good example can be a source of inspiration. There is no need to reinvent the wheel if someone else has already identified potential improvements. The challenge is to find a Best Practice that provides enough material to conduct a useful gap analysis for subsequent improvement.

Best Practices are tools for designing processes more effectively. They guide us to better and even excellent results. There is a pitfall, however: you must learn from the Best-in-Class, not from the average. Implementing Best Practices minimizes mistakes while often achieving remarkable improvements. Developing a Best Practice within your own organization is one step on the journey toward excellence.

Today's consumers expect products and services to be of high quality, reliable, and user-friendly. This is the result of years of continuous improvement and innovation by producers. Although many organizations strive for excellent results, there is still room for improvement. Unfortunately, leaders don't always have methods and tools to measure or assess that degree of excellence. If a leader could use a tool to discover how good his approaches and methods are, and how excellent his achieved results are, he could plan further improvements. The goal is to achieve excellent results. The tool described in this book guides leaders to achieve that excellence.

No one is born knowing the best method to achieve great results. Outstanding achievements are the result of a long learning process, great perseverance, hard work, and inspiration. Each of us has learned much in our lives and will still learn more. But it is an illusion to think we can know everything that is already known, much less individually know all that is yet to be discovered. Working together in highly motivated teams increases our capacity for knowledge, but even this option has its limits.

To speed up the process, we can also learn from others, namely those who have already achieved significant progress. Learning from Best Practices (also known as Best-in-Class, excellent methods, and excellent results) allows us to shorten the learning cycle drastically to achieve excellent results.

In reality, the better these Best Practice approaches are structured and documented, the more robust and reproducible the methods, and the better the outcomes achieved. Well organized and documented Best Practice examples can be a true source of inspiration for others wishing to improve their operations.

1.1 Why a Book on the Subject of "Best Practice"?

- The BEST-tool is a new and unknown approach. It is not a software solution, although it employs Microsoft Excel. We offer our readers, managers, and anyone who wants to realize systematic progress in their key functional processes, a tool that allows them to plan improvement actions. Using the BEST-tool in the short term achieves breakthrough improvements. Consistent use of the BEST-tool achieves excellent results.
- Quantifiable data: the user of the BEST-tool receives a Likert-scale quantification of how close his process is to a Best Practice or World Class performance.

- Proof of need: when you search for "Example Best Practice" in Google, you get more than 2.7 billion hits. If you analyze a small number (100), you'll discover that only a very few are really Best Practices. Why is this so? No writer of a Best Practice had a tool until now to assess whether their Best Practice really is one. With the BEST-tool they can make an accurate assessment for the first time.

1.2 What Are the Advantages of the Application of the BEST-Method and BEST-Tool for the Reader?

- You have a handy tool to assess your *Good Practice* and your *Best Practice.*
- You'll know when you have reached the level of Best Practice and how others can study your process as a real Benchmark.
- Applying the BEST-tool contributes a further step in your journey to excellence.
- You get confirmation that you have indeed reached the highest possible degree of maturity for your Best Practice.
- You'll discover opportunities for improvement in your approach (enabler).
- The application of the BEST-tool reveals how your process results could be improved.
- You gain a higher level of collaborator involvement by discussing the description and assessment of your Best Practice.
- You give the collaborators a reason to be proud of what they have achieved.
- When you compare your own Best Practice with that of another organization, you'll receive confirmation of the strengths already inherent in your own process. You will also see the differences and what you can learn from them.
- You'll verify how well process approaches and results are deployed throughout the organization.
- You'll better understand the segmentation of process results.
- You'll discover the involvement and commitment of the other organization's leaders in the Best Practice you are benchmarking.
- The Best Practice can be used as training material within your organization.
- Actively use the Best Practice as a way of introducing a new collaborator within the organization.

- Use the Best Practice and BEST-tool in your own organization as a way to make improvements in other departments and services.
- In a multinational company, the Best Practice can be used as an internal benchmark. It allows colleagues from other plants and divisions to learn from each other.
- The BEST-tool provides a data-based platform from which you can set ambitious improvement goals.
- The BEST-method allows you to check the effectiveness and efficiency of your key process.
- The BEST-tool supports the establishment of ambitious goals by providing an innovative vision of the future.

1.3 But There Is More …

- As far as we know, there is no other book specifically addressing the assessment of a Best Practices.
- There has not in the past been a *method* or a *tool* to assess a Best Practice.

1.4 Additional Applications of the BEST-Tool

In many companies and organizations, managers want to know and measure how good their enablers, results, and processes are, without doing lengthy and difficult research for a good benchmarking company or organization. By applying the BEST-tools, they not only know whether they have a Best Practice, but will discover to what extent it is a Best Practice and where they need to make action plans for improvement.

Are you not yet convinced? The authors asked a PhD candidate in research science to interrogate the Internet for examples of Best Practice methods. Her search was extensive, although the results were dismal. There were a lot of hits for Best Practice, but very few survived scrutiny.

1.5 The Book Focuses on Two Potential Audiences for Three Major Purposes

- Members of the management team who could conduct an assessment of a Best Practice within the organization (this is the first and most important objective of the book). This approach allows management to measure and assess the degree of excellence of a so-called Best Practice, either in the reader's organization or when searching for an external benchmarking example.

- The Quality department or Organizational Development department who can use the BEST-tool and methodology to discover the gaps for their Best Practice. This leads the user to opportunities for additional improvement.
- The Quality department or Organizational Development department who can use the BEST-method as a guideline for writing the description of a Best Practice.

1.6 Benchmarking, Best Practices, and Excellent Results

It is not necessary to look at an identical operating environment and/or the same products and services. Much can be learned through examples from completely different sectors. Functional benchmarking is a very effective technique. *Functional benchmarking* compares processes to other organizations with similar processes in the same function, but outside the industry. For example, a process for responding to customer complaints is found in almost every organization; so, choose an organization that has an excellent process for complaint handling and learn from it.

Make no mistake: benchmarking Best Practices is not about industrial espionage, but to examine the methods and results of others that allow businesses to make similar and rapid progress. These others can include departments or entities (plants, sites, service centers, entrepreneurships, etc.) within larger organizations, or companies and organizations that are known for one or more Best Practice characteristics.

Granted, there are limits to the amount of information one company is willing to share with another. Confidentiality and competitive advantage must be respected. That is the boundary of industrial espionage. Most US performance excellence programs at the state level encourage companies to share Best Practices as part of the learning and improvement journey for all participants. These state-level awards feed into the US Malcolm Baldrige Performance Excellence Awards process. One of the authors is past President and CEO of a Community of Excellence that brought senior executives around Charleston, South Carolina, together once a month to share business and process improvement techniques. The use of such networks of executives and board members allows a whole community or industry to gain access to valuable Best Practices.

The quality specialists in the Community of Excellence delighted in sharing general process flows for administrative functions. The team was bogged down when it got to documenting measurements and results. There was no consistent format to gather and report data. Executives became concerned that competitive data might be shared while attempting to provide enough information for the benchmarking activity. Had the BEST-tool been available at the time, the criteria within the tool would have assured senior management that *consistent* boundaries would keep sensitive data out of the reports.

Best Practices are tools for designing *processes* more effectively. They guide us to achieve better, hopefully even *excellent results*. However, there is a pitfall; you must learn from the Best-in-Class, not from the average. There can be multiple Best Practices for performing a process. The better these Best Practice approaches are structured and described, the more robust and reproducible the methods, which achieve better outcomes. It is incumbent upon the organization to adjust a Best Practice to its culture and management style. The BEST-tool guides this customization through a series of criteria to help design the right fit for the organization and its culture.

There are three important aspects of achieving excellent results:

1) We need to apply excellent *approaches* (enablers),
2) We want to achieve excellent *results*, and
3) We assure ourselves of a well-managed *process*.

The BEST-tool described in this book assesses these aspects. The tool applies to a *process* in every type of organization: private or public, large or small, service or manufacturing. The BEST-method is a *universal approach* to identifying the characteristics of a process that delivers excellent and sustainable results.

1.7 Objectives, Benchmarking, and Definitions

The objective of the BEST-method is to offer the reader a *quick* and *user-friendly* tool to assess his Best Practice. One component is the written description of the Best Practice. We want to stress that the objective is not to create lengthy documents. On the contrary, we expect to see a brief text that reflects the main criteria and characteristics of a Best Practice under examination. This description obliges the author to be *factual* and to prove that the characteristics are real. The authors want to discourage the reader from falling into the trap of the early 1990s, i.e. ISO 9000 lengthy and non-productive descriptions.

Bob Camp refers to Best Practices without providing a specific definition in his 1989 text. In his introduction to benchmarking, he states:

> The focus is on practices. It is only (through) the change of current practices or methods of performing the business processes that overall effectiveness will be achieved. It stresses practices and the understanding of practices before deriving a benchmarking metric. Benchmarking metrics are seen as a result of understanding Best Practices, not something that can be quantified first and understood later.*

Bob Camp defines benchmarking as "the search for industry Best Practices that lead to superior performance."† David T. Kearns, Chief Executive Officer of Xerox Corporation in 1989, referred to benchmarking as "the continuous process of measuring products, services, and practices against the toughest competitors or those companies recognized as industry leaders."‡

Using the synonym of Best Practices, quality guru Dr. Joseph Juran provides the following definition:

> Organizations that attain superior results by designing and continuously improving the quality of their goods and services are often called World Class, Best Practices, vanguard companies, and most recently, performance excellence. We define this as an organization that has attained a state of performance excellence because its products and services exceed customers' expectations; they are regarded by their peers and have superior, sustainable results.§

---

* Camp, Robert C. *Benchmarking: The Search for Industry Best Practices That Lead to Superior Performance*, ASQC Quality Press, Milwaukee, WI, (1989) p. 13.

† Ibid: p. 12.

‡ Ibid: p. 12.

§ Juran, Joseph M. and De Feo, Joseph A. *Juran's Quality Handbook*, 6th ed., McGraw Hill, New York, New York, (2010) p. 4.

The authors suggest the following as a comprehensive **definition of a Best Practice**:

> A Best Practice is a *process* which is regularly reviewed and improved, monitored by KPI's, and incorporating lessons learned. A Best Practice contributes to the concretization of the strategy of the organization and leads to excellent and sustainable results.

These definitions agree on one point: look for that approach or result that is really the best and that guides you to increase your achievements.

The concepts of Best Practices and benchmarking are often used as synonymous terms. This is not accurate. Effective benchmarking depends upon reliable and complete Best Practice descriptions. Only when benchmarking teams identify an existing Best Practice can they perform a reliable self-assessment and perform the gap analysis that feeds their own process improvement. The authors provide a clear and sequential structure for writing a Best Practice that can be used for benchmarking comparison and continuous improvement. Offered in this text is a framework of characteristics with which to identify and describe a Best Practice.

Best Practice identification and adoption is crucial to the survival of companies in the Information Age. We can no longer afford slow evolution as industries are being disrupted – the trick is to be quick or be dead. Well-honed and focused meaty documentation is a requirement – the centerpiece of an effective approach to smashing through barriers to Best Practice adoption, but not the complete answer. Nothing in the Information Age gets adopted more widely than the meme – an idea, behavior, or style that spreads from person to person within a culture. These cultural artifacts can be shared through Tweets or in picture form. Somehow the Best Practice must come over in a fashion which makes it easy to implement locally but where the value and application of the Best Practice is as clear as a picture of a gorgeous sunset or the warmth of a fire on a cold evening. A Best Practice must become a vision for the benchmarker using the practice as a framework for their own improvement.

1.8 BEST-Method and BEST-Tool

The BEST-method is an approach that explains what is necessary to assess or write a Best Practice. It contains definitions, explanations of criteria, characteristics, how to use and interpret the assessment checklists, examples, tips, and tricks.

The BEST-method is also a valuable tool to assess your Good Practice. The outcome of this assessment will help you confirm that you have a Good Practice and identify where you can make further improvements to achieve a Best Practice.

The BEST-tool is a series of checklists (Excel-tables), enabling the reader to assess his Best Practice (Chapter 3) or to be used as a guideline for writing a Best Practice (Chapter 4). There are two tools: the **BEST-tool** (a *detailed checklist* consisting of four Excel segments) and the **BEST Quick Scan** (a summary of the BEST-tool in one checklist). Both tools are described in detail in this book. You can download these BEST-tools, for free, from the website www.comatech.be.

The BEST-tool provides an application-level approach to assessing whether a Best Practice exists. The initial intent of the tool is to apply it to a Best Practice a company wishes to emulate. It can also be used from a different perspective to make sure that a new Best Practice is written in a complete and consistent way, so others can implement it, or have it used for continuous improvement by the writing organization itself.

Some people like to visit other companies and organizations to compare their situations with others. We want to stress that an external comparison is only useful and necessary under the condition that the visitor improves his own approaches after the visit. There needs to be real improvement in the visitor's targeted processes, or the benchmarking visit or anything that has occurred is just another case of "industrial tourism."

With the BEST-tool at hand, the visitor knows very well what he wants to know (identified gaps in the BEST-tool) and to improve. He will look for precise details for several aspects in the *process* under investigation.

1.9 Structure of the Book

In Chapter 1 we explained the proof of the need, i.e. the motivation for a new management tool, the BEST-method. In Chapter 2 we present briefly the principles of the BEST-tool, while in Chapter 3 we provide a detailed description of the BEST-tool. In Chapter 4 we explain how to write a Best Practice. In the next chapters we give concrete examples of the application of the BEST-method. Chapter 5 illustrates the application of the *detailed* BEST-tool on three case studies, while Chapter 6 illustrates the use of the BEST *Quick Scan* tool on ten case studies. Finally, in Chapter 7 we describe the experience of a Best Practice that was published 15 years ago and adapted and improved thanks to the knowledge of the BEST-method. In the appendix we also answer some frequently asked questions.

Chapter 2

The BEST-Method

Today's consumers expect products and services to be high quality, reliable, and user-friendly. This level of performance is the result of years of continuous improvement and innovation by producers. Although many organizations strive for excellent results, there is still room for improvement. Unfortunately, leaders don't always have methods and tools to measure that degree of excellence. If a leader could use a tool to discover how good his approaches and methods are, and how excellent the achieved results are, he could plan further improvements. The goal is to achieve excellent results. The method and tools described in this book guide leaders to achieve that excellence in their processes.

When you are too busy, it is easy to lose sight of the fact that every activity should be focused on achieving business objectives. People get comfortable in their roles, form habits, and do things the way they always have done them, without questioning whether a particular activity is still the best use of resources.

A best practice approach asks why. It questions *what* you do and *why* you do it, at both the strategic and operational level. The goal is to constantly seek the most effective and efficient ways to deliver the best results for the business and organization.

2.1 Definition of Best Practice

A Best Practice delivers excellent and sustainable results based on the systematic management of a key process.

This short definition needs further clarification: see Table 2.1.

Table 2.1 Explanation of the definition of Best Practice

Excellent results	These include results for all the stakeholders of the organization (customers, employees, partners, contractors, suppliers, society, local community, etc.) which exceed the expectations of these stakeholders. These results are positive compared with benchmarks and organizations recognized as Best-in-Class.
Sustainable results	The results are lasting and show a positive trend for a long period (e.g. 10 years).
Process	A chronological order of activities and decisions transforming an input into an output and outcome.
Key processes	These are the most important processes of an organization. These are "key" for success. These contribute in a positive way to the achievement of the strategic goals and business plan of the company/organization. The results produced by the key process are mainly output and outcome results.
Systematic	Regular improvement, review, and monitoring of the process.
Management	Use of indicators (KPI), objectives, audit, learning, and sharing experiences, and prevention and strategy.

2.2 Key Concepts in the Definition of a Best Practice

- Technique, working method, or activity

  Often interpreted freely by the user, this element defines the process and describes how the outcome is achieved. These activities also include measurement methods, calibration methods, procedures, audit methods, evaluations, etc. Each can individually be a Best Practice.
- More effective and better outcomes

  There is only one best method. You compare yourself against the best and not the average. The aim is to obtain the best result and outcome.
- Comparison

  A comparison with the best for a given subject prevents complacency and provides opportunities for further learning.

Although our definition is very short, it includes the characteristics to be put into practice before a key process can be considered as a Best Practice. The remainder of this book describes the required characteristics and shares a proprietary set of tools with which to assess whether a process can be declared a Best Practice.

The terms described as part of the Best Practice definition above focus on an approach and result that propels your organization to the highest level of achievement.

2.3 Characteristics of a Best Practice

Complimentary to our definition of Best Practice are some additional attributes of a Best Practice:

- It produces consistent, measurable, reliable, and excellent results for the organization.
- It is executed effectively within the organization.
- It improves the organization's performance.
- It places the company in a top percentile ranking within its industry.
- It leverages and takes advantage of technology and innovation.
- It improves quality and speed, thereby lowering costs.
- It gives management more control and influence.
- It is led by the leaders of the organization, usually, the owner of the key process.

2.4 Best Practice versus Best Technical Product

To clarify our target for Best Practices, we are not referring to the use of Standard Operating Procedures (SOPs) which serve to provide a very specific written procedure used to perform a job function, whether that is an assembly of a product or a machine or an administrative procedure. These functions might collectively be part of a larger system within the company and therefore part of a process, but they are not targets for our pursuit of Best Practices in the scope of this book.

There is often confusion between the concepts of Best Practice (*process based*) and Best Technical Product (*product based*). In the former, we look at the whole process and how this process delivers excellent and sustainable results in line with the strategy of the company. In the latter, the product or installation remains the center of interest. The focus is now put on exceptional technical characteristics and performances. In this book, we describe only Best Practices, i.e. the *processes* that are the best available and that deliver excellent results.

A Best Practice is always clearly linked to a *process*, i.e. management of a key process. "Key" means those processes which contribute in a positive way to achieving the strategy and which deliver excellent results.

High-performance products, procedures, and standards are a part of the success of the company. Quite often, high-performance products are produced thanks to modern, reliable, and sophisticated machines. This doesn't mean that the whole process and organization are managed at its optimum. You can comply completely with standards (think about the ISO 9001 standard) and not be at a Best Practice level for the processes audited.

2.5 BEST-Method and BEST-Tool

The BEST-tool, described in detail in Chapter 3, provides a stable structure supporting fluid content. The BEST-method is a *universal approach* to identifying the characteristics of a process that delivers excellent results.

The remainder of this chapter includes the following topics:

- BEST-method and BEST-tool
- Documenting a Best Practice
- Measurement of Excellence (Enablers and Results)
- Enabler
- The Plan-Do-Check-Act (PDCA)-method
- Results
- Organizational maturity
- Benefits of the BEST-tool
- Use of case studies for demonstrating the BEST-tool
- Why we use older case studies
- Conclusion

BEST is an acronym for: "a **B**etter way to **E**xcellent results and **S**uccess through the application of an appropriate **T**ool."

The BEST-method is an approach that explains what is necessary to assess or to write a Best Practice. It contains definitions, explanations of criteria, characteristics, how to use and interpret the assessment checklists, examples, tips, and tricks.

If the BEST-method is correctly used, it allows management to make gradual improvements in their journey to excellence, i.e. the **achievement of excellent and sustainable results**.

Skeptical people could argue that the BEST-method isn't realistic. On the contrary, it is only through a structured, consistent set of criteria that process owners can verify that their process is truly a Best Practice. With no standardized instrument, tool, or method to identify a Best Practice, any process can be touted as one. Therefore, there must be a *measurement instrument* to verify to what extent a Best Practice is a true Best Practice.

2.6 Documenting a Best Practice

It is important to understand why Best Practices need to be documented. Identifying and properly documenting a Best Practice eases its adoption by other areas and by other teams. This facilitation of benchmarking with a comprehensive Best Practice is an unmet need in business today. Chapter 4 describes the process for writing a Best Practice that contains enough information for a benchmarking partner to gain insight for their own improvement efforts.

A *documented* Best Practice is also necessary for the following reasons:

- To make a distinction between intention and fact-based evidence.
- To see quickly (see the application of the BEST-tools in Chapter 3) where you can make further improvements.
- To use the Best Practice for internal training purposes.
- To compare the process with external benchmarks.

An example of a *standardized format* for documenting a Best Practice is given in Figure 2.1.

An overall summary of 13 items for a standardized format of a Best Practice is:

1. Enabler (the method for developing the process)
2. Results (measures of effectiveness)
3. Process (the flow of the activities to be improved)
4. Format (the structure of a Best Practice description: the format is the organization of components 1, 2, and 3)

1	Title
2	Subject
3	Author (name, title, company, contact)
4	Context (sector, country restrictions)
5	Description of the method and results
6	Measurement method
7	Process description and maturity
8	KPIs (Key Performance Indicator) and results
9	Distribution of the results
10	Cause and effect
11	Measurement
12	Conditions
13	Date and Revision Level

Figure 2.1 Best Practice – example standardized format.

The detail of these *four building blocks* is described in Chapter 3 of this book.

When a Best Practice is written effectively, it becomes a well-honed and focused document – the centerpiece of an effective approach to smashing through barriers to Best Practice adoption. It is not the whole journey to a successful benchmarking activity. However, a Best Practice is the basis for the **gap analysis** that offers the benchmarking partner an opportunity for improvement. A Best Practice and a gap analysis are the planning portion of benchmarking. Implementation is up to the benchmarking partner. This book provides details for **assessing a Best Practice**. The benchmarking process itself is beyond the scope of this work and is adequately covered in other materials, beginning in 1989 with the works of Bob Camp and others.*

2.7 Measurement of Excellence

A Best Practice is a model – a reference to a specific area of performance. But we still have questions: What is an excellent method? What is an excellent result? If we can determine the degree of excellence, a Best Practice will be more readily accepted by others as being excellent. You can then better assess objectively what method or outcome offers the best results.

* See also: Camp, Robert. *Global Cases in Benchmarking; Best Practices from Organizations Around the World*, ASQ Quality Press, Milwaukee, WI, (1998).

2.8 Enabler

The degree of excellence for an ***enabler*** (method, approach) is evaluated among organizations ascribing to the EFQM-model* by using the RADAR tool.† The US Department of Commerce has developed the Malcolm Baldrige Performance Excellence Model. Another common approach is through the PDCA improvement cycle. Since not all organizations are familiar with either the European or US performance excellence models, the authors have chosen to use a more universal Plan-Do-Check-Act (PDCA)-approach.

The key steps involved in the implementation and evaluation of quality improvement efforts are symbolized by the PDCA-cycle. The goal is to engage in a continuous endeavor to learn about all aspects of a process and then use this knowledge to change the process to reduce variation and complexity and to improve the level of process performance. Process improvement begins by understanding how customers define quality, how processes work, and how understanding the variation in those processes can lead to wise management action.‡

This text suggests the PDCA-approach§ for documenting an original Best Practice, and then it uses a freeform approach to assess a Best Practice for improvements. There are many *improvement methods* available, such as Six Sigma,¶ Lean Enterprise,** Quality Function Deployment,†† Quality Management Systems,‡‡ and others. The PDCA-approach is used as it offers a more universally recognized, simple way to organize thoughts around an improvement sequence.

---

* EFQM stands for European Foundation for Quality Management. The EFQM Excellence Model allows Managers and Leaders to understand the cause and effect relationships between what their organization does and the results it achieves.

† RADAR stands for Results, Approaches, Deploy and Assess & Refine. RADAR-method is part of the EFQM-Model. The RADAR logic is a dynamic assessment framework and powerful management tool that provides a structured approach to questioning the performance of an organization. Van Nuland, Yves, Broux, Georges, Crets, Luc, De Cleyn, Wim, Legrand, Jan, Majoor, Guy and Vleminckx, Gaston. *Excellent: A Guide for the Implementation of the EFQM-Excellence Model*, Comatech, Belgium, (1999) p. 31.

‡ Westcott, Russell T. and Duffy, Grace L. *The Certified Quality Improvement Associate Handbook*, 3rd ed., Quality Press, Milwaukee, WI, (2015) p. 78.

§ https://en.wikipedia.org/wiki/PDCA.

¶ https://en.wikipedia.org/wiki/Six_Sigma accessed 12/23/2019.

** https://en.wikipedia.org/wiki/Lean_enterprise accessed 12/23/2019.

†† https://en.wikipedia.org/wiki/Quality_function_deployment accessed 12/23/2019.

‡‡ https://en.wikipedia.org/wiki/Quality_management_system accessed 12/23/2019.

Table 2.2 PDCA-method

Plan	Is the method fully described? What must happen for the method to be effective? What are the plans? What is the relationship with strategy and business plan?
Do	Is the methodology used daily? Is the method applied in line with the plan? What happens in reality? What is being done? How is the method applied in practice? Is the methodology applied everywhere?
Check	What are the differences between the planned results and the results achieved? How important is the progress? What can we learn from this? Are the results aligned with the proposed plan?
Act	How are the processes revised and reconditioned considering the findings made in the Check phase? Do the resources (workforce, staff skills, facilities and equipment, budgets, etc.) need to be adjusted?

2.9 The PDCA-Method

The four steps in the PDCA-cycle are described in Table 2.2.

The criteria for implementing and documenting Best Practice approaches using the PDCA-approach are described in detail in Chapter 3.

2.10 Results

Assessing the results of a Best Practice process is done by a completely different set of criteria. The checklist in Figure 2.2 is designed to estimate the **degree of excellence of the results** obtained through the implementation of a Best Practice process(es). This checklist consists of seven criteria.

Results are outputs and outcomes achieved by your organization. Results are evaluated based on current performance; performance relative to appropriate comparisons; the rate, breadth, and importance of performance improvements; and the relationship of measures of results to key organizational performance requirements.*

Of the 13 recommended components of a Best Practice as shown in Figure 2.1 the Measurement component deserves strong focus. Many writers of a Best Practice do not know where to begin to quantitatively describe the

* Baldrige Performance Excellence Program, Criteria for Performance Excellence, 2013–2014, p. 49, National Institute of Standards and Technology (NIST), United States Department of Commerce, January 2013.

	Criteria and characteristics
1	**Scope and Relevance** * The results are aligned with the expectations and needs of the relevant stakeholders * The results are aligned with policy and strategy of the organization * The most important key results are identified and prioritized * The relation between the results is understood
2	**Integrity of data** * Results are timely * Results are reliable and accurate
3	**Segmentation** * Results are segmented in a suitable manner o By region, country, o By department, business line, division, unit o By product and service type
4	**Trends** * Trends are positive for 5 years or more * Results are sustainable and show good performance
5	**Targets** * Targets for core results are set * Targets are suitable * Targets are achieved
6	**Comparisons with targets and benchmarks** * Comparisons for core results are made * Comparisons are suitable * Comparisons are favorable
7	**Cause-effect** * The results are clearly achieved through the chosen approach (cause-effect) * The relations between results achieved and the approaches are understood * Based on the evidence presented, it is confident that the positive performance will continue in the future, i.e. the results are sustainable

Figure 2.2 Criteria for the evaluation of the results of a Best Practice process.

results of their process excellence and why their approach should be classified as a Best Practice.

Companies and organizations are different, and the context where a Best Practice is implemented is also different. Therefore, a quality manager can argue that he has a Best Practice in his situation. The questions remain: How does he know, and can he measure that Best Practice? How can he objectively assume that his approach is an excellent method? The BEST-tool gives the answer to these questions.

Measures and indicators are numerical information that quantifies the input, output, and performance dimensions of processes, programs, projects, services, and the overall organization (outcomes). Measures and indicators might be simple (derived from one measurement) or composite.*

It is important to measure and verify the results of a Best Practice and the way these results are achieved, i.e. process description. Everyone who is familiar with Total Quality Management (TQM) knows that process management is essential in the journey to excellence. There needs to be a clear linkage between strategy and business plan as well as process management and the corresponding results. This is something we do not see in the description of many case studies written as Best Practices.

The authors assessed more than 30 so-called "Best Practices" with the BEST Quick Scan tool. They have noted that the majority of so-called Best Practices give only a description of their enabler (method or approach). They didn't give the corresponding results or a process description. The only thing that can be deduced is that the case study is a nice method but not a Best Practice.

The strength of Chapter 6 is that it illustrates how the BEST Quick Scan tool serves as a pragmatic method to quickly screen whether a case study is a true Best Practice. All ten case studies we assess in Chapter 6 purported to be a Best Practice. Chapter 6 illustrates the importance of writing clearly about the target process and how results are measured. The BEST-tool is, as far as the authors know, the only method that provides a measure for the degree of excellence of a Best Practice. As a result of our assessment of numerous case studies, we now look first for whether the document includes a description of results before diving into the other criteria for a Best Practice.

Note that an excellent result is one that simultaneously meets *all seven criteria* described in Figure 2.2. If you can prove a 75% performance level for each of the seven criteria, it can confidently be said that the process provides a Best Practice result. It is difficult to achieve 100% compliance to all characteristics, i.e. that it can be shown how this approach is put into practice with many concrete examples. When a Best Practice has a 75% score for (nearly) all criteria (Quick Scan) and all characteristics (detailed BEST-tool), we can safely say that it is a Best Practice. We are not looking for the ideal world where everything is perfect. That does not exist. Furthermore, if a company scores itself at a full 100%, this might suggest a

* Baldrige Performance Excellence Program, Criteria for Performance Excellence, 2013–2014, p. 47, National Institute of Standards and Technology (NIST), United States Department of Commerce, January 2013.

defensive company culture where management is trying to manipulate the data.

Organizational culture has a tremendous impact on the way we think and behave. Human Synergistics developed a method to measure these thinking styles. There are basically two different thinking styles: defensive and constructive. In a defensive mode, people might readily assume that they have a Best Practice without being factual and precise. In a constructive culture, they are in a learning mode, i.e. they are open to feedback and they learn from others (benchmarking) and from other sources. In the constructive mode, they are eager to apply the BEST-method to investigate the degree of excellence of their approach. Only when they have confirmation that their approach is excellent, they will call it a Best Practice.*

In a constructive company culture, a supportive environment exists, i.e. leaders help their subordinates to learn and improve their processes. In a defensive culture, Best Practices are used to impress others.

2.11 Organizational Maturity

This is item 7 of Figure 2.1. It is important to note that the BEST-tool is presented in its most rigorous form. Most organizations are not at the level of development to experience the total benefit of implementing all the criteria or characteristics of the full-blown BEST-tool. Best Practices and benchmarking should be scaled depending upon the maturity of the organization.

Watts Humphrey's original Process Maturity Framework and most additional maturity models focus on transforming the organizational environment in which Best Practices are performed.† The original Capability Maturity Model (CMM) was a roadmap of Best Practices in software engineering accompanied with Best Practices in project and organizational management required to sustain them. Such descriptions give the reader a sense of how a collection of Best Practices might grow over time. Most of these models give little guidance on the specific steps to be taken to progress up the maturity levels.

---

* www.humansynergistics.com (Subject: *Organizational Culture Inventory*) accessed 2/19/18.

† Curtis, Bill and Alden, John, *BPM and Organizational Maturity*, BPTrends Column, October 2007.

Levels	Description
0	**Non-existent** Within the organization there are no or very little management measures. Control awareness is rather low and only few actions are taken to achieve an adequate system of organizational management (internal control system).
1	**Ad-hoc basis** Only ad-hoc management measures are in place within the organization. The awareness of the need for appropriate management (internal control) is growing, but there is still no structured or standardized approach present. The system of organizational management (internal control) is more focused on people than on systems.
2	**Structured start** A structured impetus is given to the development of management measures. The management tools are therefore being developed but are not yet applied (Plan)
3	**Defined** (= level 2 + ...) Control measures are provided. These are standardized, documented, communicated and implemented (Do).
4	**Management system** (= level 3 + ...) The control measures are internally assessed and adjusted (Check & Act). There is a "living" adequate and effective system of organizational management.
5	**Optimized** (= level 4 + ...) The control measures are continuously optimized through benchmarking and obtaining quality certificates or external evaluations (PDCA).

Figure 2.3 Example of maturity levels of a process. Interne Audit Vlaamse Administratie, *Annual report 2008*, p. 63.

Figure 2.3 shows the progression of the five maturity levels, including characteristics of each level. This model provides a useful tool for organizations to understand their current level of maturity and progression, leading to higher levels of business maturity.

A similar model can be applied to better understand levels of maturity of an organizational system and can help companies develop an improvement plan based on their current level of maturity and desired future state:

- The maturity of the company's business environment will have an impact on its ability to successfully implement process improvement efforts (either incremental or radical).

- Similarly, an effort to improve processes is probably futile if the very basic elements that are needed to support effective process management are not in place.

Companies need to implement effective quality management and process management systems before any serious improvement initiative is considered.*

Process improvement models are examples of specific steps to improve and move from one maturity level to another. Just as process improvement approaches require different levels of knowledge about process, information, people, technology, and systems integration, so do the evolving levels of organizational maturity.

The characteristics of process improvement models from simple PDCA and problem solving through increasingly more complex models, such as Cost of Quality,† Lean,‡ Six Sigma,§ Balanced Scorecard,¶ and Best Practice Recognition,** align effectively with the different levels of organizational maturity. Senior management must select appropriate process improvement models based on their company's level of maturity and leadership style.

It is important to recognize that companies are at different levels of maturity in implementing process improvement concepts. It does not make sense to take a huge jump from a low level of maturity to a very sophisticated approach. This comment is not a slight on the intelligence of the senior management. It is an approach that recognizes that some companies put major efforts into different parts of the business, depending on their corporate culture or their customer requirements.††

Matching different process improvement models to the level of organizational maturity described by CMM is illustrated in Figure 2.4.

---

* Ibid.

† Douglas C. Wood, *Cost of Quality* is described well by the American Society for Quality in Principles of Quality Costs, 4th ed.: Financial Measures for Strategic Implementation of Quality Management, ASQ Quality Management Division, 2013, ISBN: 978-0-87389-849-2.

‡ Manos, Anthony and Vincent, Chad, editors. *The LEAN Handbook: A Guide to the Bronze Certification Body of Knowledge*, ASQ Quality Press, Milwaukee, WI, (2012).

§ Pyzdek, Thomas and Keller, Paul, *The Six Sigma Handbook: A Complete Guide for Green Belts, Black Belts, and Managers at All Levels*, 3rd ed., McGraw Hill, New York, (2010).

¶ Kaplan, Robert S. and Norton, D. P. *The Balanced Scorecard: Translating Strategy into Action*, Harvard Business School Press, Boston, MA, (1996). ISBN 978-0-87584-651-4.

** www.apqc.org/ accessed 12/23/2019.

†† Duffy, G. L., *Bridge the Gaps*, Quality Progress Magazine, July 2017.

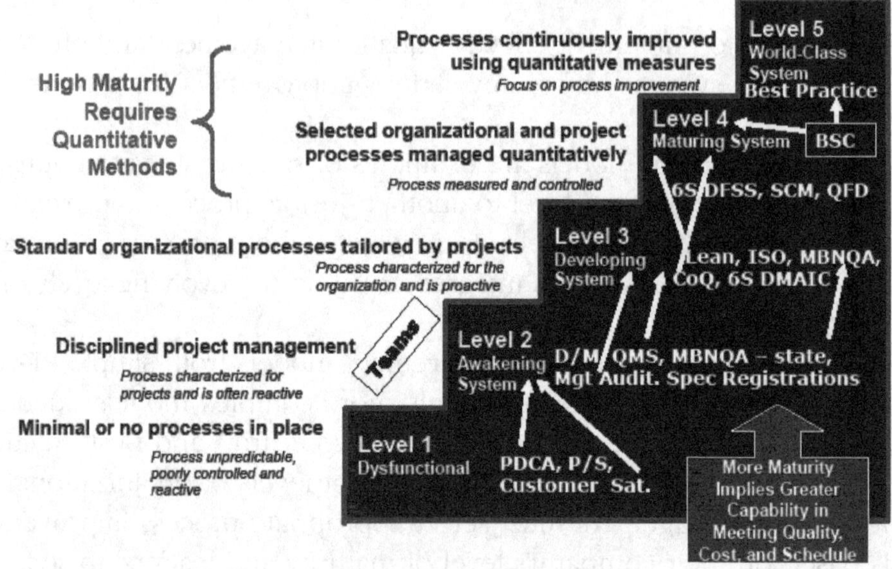

Figure 2.4 Process improvement models mapped to capability maturity model levels. Duffy, G. L., *Leveling Up, Achieve Higher Levels of Excellence through the Capability Maturity Model, ASQ Quality Progress magazine, June 2016.*

In Figure 2.4 Level 1 is described as dysfunctional with minimal or no processes in place. At this stage, the organization experiences unstable processes that are poorly controlled. The organization is functioning in a reactive mode. At Level 2, appropriate process improvement models are Plan-Do-Check-Act (PDCA), Problem Solving, and Customer Satisfaction.

The PDCA-cycle is a simple approach to address corrective action in the workplace. This model encourages observation and planning to identify the root cause of an error, plan a response, pilot the solution, measure the results, and then document the changes and new processes to hold the gains. This tool is a good beginning approach for an initial process definition in a Level 2 environment. The authors use the PDCA-cycle as the basis for the BEST-tool Enabler process because of its universal applicability across all levels of business maturity. Although improvement is not only a result of corrective action, the PDCA-cycle can be used for corrective action, general process improvement, and achievement of planned business objectives.

A legend for the tools identified in Figure 2.4 for improving Best Practice:

PDCA	Plan-Do-Check-Act
P/S	Problem solving
D/M	Decision making
QMS	Quality Management System
MBNQA	Malcolm Baldrige National Quality Award
Mgt Audit	Management audit
ISO	ISO family of standards
CoQ	Cost of Quality
6S DMAIC	Six Sigma Design-Measure-Analyze-Improve-Control
6S DFSS	Six Sigma Design for Six Sigma
SCM	Supply Chain Management
QFD	Quality Function Deployment
BSC	Balanced Score Card

Each of the above process improvement approaches guides the implementer into higher levels of organizational and performance maturity. The tools recommended at higher maturity levels require data-based and quantitative performance measures for effective improvement.

Most benchmarking is done by more mature organizations. Not many ad hoc or CMMI* Level 1 and Level 2 companies are prepared to perform a Best Practice assessment. This book provides a tool for assessing whether what one is doing as a process is a Best Practice and how that practice can be continuously improved.

A process is made up of linked activities with the purpose of producing a program or service for a customer (user) within or outside your organization. Generally, processes involve combinations of people, machines, tools, techniques, materials, and improvements in a defined series of steps or actions. Processes rarely operate in isolation and must be considered in relation to other processes that impact them. In some situations, processes

* Capability Maturity Model Integration (CMMI) is a process level improvement training and appraisal program. CMMI defines the maturity levels for processes. Administered by the CMMI Institute, a subsidiary of ISACA, it was developed at Carnegie Mellon University (CMU).

might require adherence to a specific sequence of steps, with documentation (sometimes formal) of procedures and requirements, including well-defined measurement and control steps.*

Not every process needs to be developed into a Best Practice. Only a small number of critical processes contribute to the realization of a strategic plan. Most case studies and success stories published in journals or corporate newsletters are focused on recognition and project close out reports. A Best Practice requires a detailed analysis and documentation of critical information as described in this book (Chapters 5 and 6).

2.12 Benefits of the BEST-Tool

The BEST-tool provides a *structure* for an organization to assess its Best Practices to achieve excellent and sustainable results.

In our work over the past 40 years, the authors have made the following *observations*:

- Effectively documenting and measuring the outcomes of a Best Practice provide a confirmation that the organization does have an excellent approach and corresponding excellent results.
- Just calling a process a Best Practice does not make it one. Clear evidence of how the process is designed, how the process performs, and the effectiveness of the results must be provided.
- A Best Practice does not have to be perfect. The process has to deliver excellent results. It must provide enough information for benchmarking partners to assess their process against to complete a gap analysis.
- Sharing Best Practices allows the benchmarker to learn from other organizations.
- An excellent organization is an organization that produces excellent and sustainable results, but it also produces some true Best Practices.

When using a new method or approach, it is useful to ask the question, "*What is the added value of the use of Best Practices?*" The following are a few of the advantages:

* Baldrige Performance Excellence Program, Criteria for Performance Excellence, 2013–2014, p. 48, National Institute of Standards and Technology (NIST), United States Department of Commerce, January 2013.

- It provides better access to the improvement potential. It is a source of inspiration to find opportunities for improvement.
- It requires the process owner to keep learning. Processes are continuously under better control for achieving more sustainable results.
- It avoids reinventing the wheel. Benchmarkers learn from groups that have already proven how the method leads to excellent results.
- It helps define key performance indicators: "If they can do it, then we can do it too!"
- Larger organizations can easily compare performance across different entities (production centers, service centers, divisions, departments, etc.) and define common targets.
- A systematic application of the methodology of Best Practices facilitates growth towards an excellent organization.
- The use of Best Practices contributes to better achievement of the strategy of the organization.

Given the level of detail provided in the criteria and characteristics of the BEST-tool, the reader will perhaps find additional applications for the assessment beyond benchmarking. The BEST-tool for assessing and writing a Best Practice is described in Chapters 3 and 4. The structure for a Best Practice is synonymous with the development of a World Class process. The BEST-tool is also a good approach for designing a new process or for planning an extensive process redesign.

2.13 Use of Case Studies for Demonstrating the BEST-Tool

The authors realize the examples used in this book are taken from case studies written without access to the BEST-tool and that there was no intention on the part of the case study authors to be all inclusive in their documentation. This book and BEST-tool are offered to help those writing a full Best Practice to be inclusive in the information they provide to others. The high level of detail provided in the BEST-tool is also available to those who are looking to learn from a Best Practice. All the criteria and characteristics of a Best Practice are available for them to use to improve their own systematic performance.

The text for most of the case studies is not included in this book because to do so would make the volume enormous. Information for accessing the case studies is provided for each example.

2.14 Why We Use Older Case Studies

Advantages

- We can demonstrate our tool BEST Quick Scan and the detailed BEST-tool on real so-called Best Practices, even older ones.
- The application of the tool is independent of the number of years since the case study was written. The criteria of the BEST-tool do not include the characteristic of "age."
- The authors expect that our BEST-method (and our book) will still be useful and valuable 10 years from now, although the case studies from 2019 will then be "10 years old."
- This text assesses descriptions of a Best Practice. It is not an assessment of a benchmark. In the latter case, recent material needs to be used. Techniques are not always time independent.

Disadvantages

- Where a Best Practice depends upon technology for excellent results, it is possible that the concepts shared in the case study are no longer valid. The authors have attempted to filter out case studies where the process is not appropriate for our current readers.

Organizations implementing an excellence model (e.g. Malcolm Baldrige Award or EFQM-model) will apply one or even several ideas listed above. The authors note that leaders of most organizations talk about improving and learning, but rarely does the improvement happen in a structured and systematic manner. *Structured* means that the results are achieved step by step. Excellent results are achieved by proceeding methodically, i.e. the results are caused by a series of enabling activities. *Systematic* means that all departments, services, and teams use Best Practices to make improvements and progress. Systematic means also that the improving and learning process is part of everyday practice. A Best Practice allows executives to see how others put improvements into practice.

The references in the market today are old. Bob Camp did not recommend a format for writing or assessing the value of a Best Practice. His case studies are simply descriptions of processes without a consistent framework. This book takes Camp's work to a more defined level.

2.15 Conclusion

Using the BEST-method is beneficial for the following reasons:

- Effectively documenting and measuring the outcomes of a process provides a confirmation that you have an excellent approach and corresponding excellent results.
- Sharing Best Practices allows the researcher to learn from other organizations that have excellent methods and corresponding results.
- It helps the organization avoid the blinders of only focusing internally for process improvement. If only comparing results internally, you would think the process cannot get better or it is difficult to see improvement opportunities.
- It is also a confirmation for the employees that they have worked well in achieving a Best Practice. This is motivating. They get appreciation from their management as well as third parties for their outstanding performance.

The objective of applying the BEST-method isn't to prove that you have a Best Practice but to support you in your journey to excellence. The BEST-method guides you to make improvements to critical processes. We think that this is the most valuable point of our approach. The BEST-tool does not make judgments; it allows you to assess processes and results on your journey to excellence. This is done in a structured and pragmatic way using the BEST-tool.

Consider the perspective of a Chief Executive Officer in a competitive industry: assume you're a CEO. There are two possibilities: either there are one or more Best Practices in your organization or there are none. In the former case the CEO makes use of the BEST-methodology to check whether there are truly Best Practices in his organization. He will discover quickly whether his managers are right to say that the organization has some Best Practices, or he will find out which opportunities for improvement the organization has. In the latter situation (no Best Practices present), he must ask himself if he can live with that situation. This means that the organization aims for mediocrity. Can shareholders (private company) or the government (public sector) accept an attitude of mediocrity? In the first instance, the shareholders miss income and in the second, it can be questioned whether public funds are being well spent.

A CEO could expect that his organization develops at least one new Best Practice every year. If not, he can ask himself, "Why not?" Is it due to a lack of priority, resources, training, etc.? In each case, it is a management controllable act. Therefore, it is up to the CEO to make the necessary decisions and to set up an action plan so that the organization moves forward in its journey to excellence.

Chapter 3

The BEST-Tool: Checklist of Criteria for the Assessment of a Best Practice

This chapter describes the BEST-method and details of the BEST-tool and closes with some experiences, tips, and tricks used by the authors to maximize the effectiveness of the BEST-tool.

BEST is an acronym for: "a **B**etter way to **E**xcellent results and **S**uccess through the application of an appropriate **T**ool." This method consists in the **assessment** of 1) the **approaches** used in the Best Practice, 2) the achieved **results**, and 3) the **process** of the Best Practice. The assessment is supported by the BEST-tool, which consists of checklists of criteria and characteristics of Best Practice activities.

There are two types of the BEST-tool: a detailed one, which is called the **BEST-tool**, and a shorter version, which is called the **BEST Quick Scan**.

Sections 3.1–3.4 describe the components of the BEST-tool. The tool consists of four *components*: Enabler, Results, Process, and Format. Each component contains several *criteria*. Finally, each criterion consists of one or more *characteristics*.

3.1 Assessment of the Approaches Used in a Best Practice

3.1.1 Enabler

The enabler is the method, approach, or process used by the company to achieve the results they are documenting as a Best Practice. Whether a formal model such as the Malcolm Baldrige Performance Excellence Model, the European Foundation for Quality Management Model, a Quality Management System, Hoshin Kanri,* or another structured organizational design process, an enabler has the same basic format for the management of the chosen model. This format can be separated into four phases which reflect the phases of the Plan-Do-Check-Act (PDCA)-cycle. Each of these phases contains several criteria.

The PDCA-cycle is used to organize the sequence of the Enabler component. This model encourages observation and planning to identify the requirements of a process, develop effective actions, pilot the solution, measure the results, and then document the changes and new process to hold the gains. This tool is a good beginning approach for improvement in an organization, regardless of operating maturity. A complete listing of the criteria and characteristics of a Best Practice using the PDCA-approach is presented in Figures 3.3 and 3.4. These Excel tables can also be downloaded from our website www.comatech.be.

More mature organizations may wish to use other improvement methods, as mentioned in Chapter 1. The steps are basically the same. The criteria and characteristics will need to be associated with the sequence of steps required of whichever approach is chosen by the organization.

3.1.2 Plan

The Plan phase consists of 8 criteria and 16 characteristics which should be present in a Best Practice document. Figure 3.3 BEST-tool (*complete* and *detailed* checklist) gives the complete listing of criteria and characteristics for the Plan phase of the Enabler (PDCA). The following discussion provides an explanation of the value of including these criteria and characteristics into a Best Practice document.

The eight criteria for the Plan stage are:

1. Description
2. Stakeholders
3. Responsibilities
4. Key performance indicators (KPIs) and performance indicators (PIs)
5. Deployment and segmentation
6. Prevention
7. Benchmarking
8. Data

* https://en.wikipedia.org/wiki/Hoshin_Kanri accessed 12/28/2019.

Let us discuss criterion by criterion. The first criterion consists of four characteristics.

1. **Description**
   - The approach is repeatable and based on reliable data and information.
   - The core process is identified and described.
   - The methods are documented.
   - The process reflects common sense and is well thought out (logical sequence, clearly linked to organizational strategy, interactions with other processes and sub-processes).

The approach is repeatable and based on reliable data and information.

This seems obvious; however, the authors have unfortunately seen that information can be manipulated to support the allegation of a Best Practice.

BOX 3.1 Manipulation of Information

Scenario: A newly appointed general manager reports that he has excelled in his new assignment. Productivity and profit increased more than 3% annually over the last two years. He can also prove an increase of customer satisfaction over the last two years. His conclusion: the company is flourishing thanks to his policies and decisions.

Interpretation of the scenario: the manager's allegation seems logical and the first tendency is to believe his report. The general manager has been in position for only three years. When the data are plotted over the last 10 years, it becomes apparent that the increase in productivity and customer satisfaction started more than 7 years ago. If the reader had this data before reading the manager's report, he would not have believed the general manager. The reader would recognize the general manager as a manipulator with only one goal: to improve his personal image.

The core process is identified and described.

Not everything done in an organization is of equal importance. A small number of core processes contribute to the realization of the strategic and business plans. A Best Practice is always based upon one of the core processes.

The methods are documented.

People familiar with ISO* and Kaizen, know that only documented methods lead to repeatable processes and reliable products and services. Documentation of the method is not enough. The documents need to be regularly updated. A systematic revision of the documents is proof that people learn. Only when every activity within the process is documented, can we ensure that the supplied products and services are reliable. When the processes are systematically reviewed and revised, the processes then become simple, straightforward, more transparent, and robust.

The process reflects common sense and is well thought out (logical sequence, clearly linked to organizational strategy, interactions with other processes and sub-processes).

Processes rarely work in a vacuum. The outputs of a previous process become inputs to a subsequent process. Core processes must support the overarching goals of the organization and align with the strategic plan. Measures must be in place that clearly reflect the appropriate outcomes of the system of processes identified in the Best Practice.

2. **Stakeholders**
   - The process is tailored to the needs, requirements, and expectations of interested parties (stakeholders).
   - The indicators and targets are set and the relationship with the core process is clearly defined.

The process is tailored to the needs, requirements, and expectations of interested parties (stakeholders).

Every key process has at least one stakeholder. The number of stakeholders depends on the complexity of the function and the Best Practice described. Each stakeholder has specific needs, requirements, and expectations. The organization has a method to determine these needs, requirements, and expectations.

---

* ISO is a label for the International Standardization Organization. ISO standards have much in common with the principles of better regulation: consistent, transparent, and targeted. Developed through the consensus of globally established experts and regulators, governments count on ISO standards to help develop better regulations. ISO standards provide a strong basis that can be applied in the development of national and international regulation. Not only do ISO standards help save time, they are essential tools for reducing barriers to international trade. ISO has developed over 23,157 International Standards. Source : ISO.org.

Table 3.1 Stakeholders of a hotel

List of stakeholders and their expectations:
• Business customers: late check-in, Wi-Fi, available seminar facilities, complaint resolution • Tourists: tourism information, complaint resolution • Shareholders: profitable growth, room occupancy • Hotel school: apprenticeships • City: employment, sponsoring local initiatives • Society: energy saving, CO_2 reduction • Employees: stable employment, training, motivation • Suppliers: on-time payment, new business

The concept of stakeholders is illustrated with a service example in Table 3.1, i.e. a hotel in a city. This city is visited by business travelers and tourists.

This list is certainly not complete but illustrates how many stakeholders an organization can have and the variety of expectations to be addressed.

The indicators and targets are set and the relationship with the core processes is clearly defined.

For each stakeholder expectation, the hotel in example 3.2 will have at least one key performance indicator (KPI), or measure of performance. Each of these KPIs must be tracked and reported in the Best Practice.

Table 3.2 illustrates that not only does the contractor have expectations for the current contract, but he also has expectations for future work.

The expectations, needs, and requirements for every stakeholder are translated into one or more KPIs.

Table 3.2 List of expectations of a contractor at an industrial plant

Current contractor expectations of industrial plant management
• Clear contract • Work specifications • Payment on time • Safe environment
Future expectations of the contractor
• New contracts • Repeat business • Expansion of existing business lines • Development of new opportunities

3. **Responsibilities**
   - The responsibilities and accountabilities are clearly defined.
   - Each process has a process owner.
   - The process description considers the skills and experiences required by the persons responsible for carrying out the process and approaches.

The responsibilities and accountabilities are clearly defined

Accountability is an outcome of the assignment of responsibility. All too often, an organization designates responsibility for a process without holding the designee accountable for the results of their actions. Two definitions of Accountability are:

1. The obligation of an individual or organization to account for its activities, accept responsibility for them, and to disclose the results in a transparent manner. It also includes the responsibility for money or other entrusted property.*
2. Taking the personal responsibility to do what you say you'll do within the timeframe you've agreed to do it.†

Each process has a process owner

From these two definitions it is expected that the process described in the Best Practice mentions the title of the person accountable for the management of the process and the corresponding results. As illustrated in Chapter 6, many case studies of Best Practices do not mention a name or function.

Benefits of applying the concept of accountability:

- Someone (e.g. a backup) is always responsible for taking initiative, making decisions, and monitoring a process and KPI, even when the primary accountable person is absent (sickness, holiday, business trip, etc.).
- The process is audited and revised regularly. These updates are identified through a higher process document revision number.
- The KPI shows a gradual improvement of achieved results. As management of the process becomes increasingly better, so will results improve.

* http://www.businessdictionary.com accessed 12/23/2017.

† Greg Bustin, http://www.bustin.com/tough-love-accountability-workshop accessed 12/23/2017.

The process description describes the skills and experience required by the persons responsible for carrying out the process and approaches.

Training is provided so that the individual performs the process in a way that delivers reliable products and services. It is the responsibility of the process owner to check whether all operators receive appropriate training.

BOX 3.2 New Hire Training

A company is active in a cyclic business. It recruits temporary workers a few months before a high workload cycle starts. The production manager explains the methods and activities briefly. After a few hours, the new hire can become productive in his new assignment.

Although new employee training is a very common practice, this training does not always assure that the new operator can do the job without producing defective products. Defective products reduce the reliability of the process. In Chapter 6 examples will illustrate that very few organizations pay attention to the effectiveness of new employee training.

4. **KPIs and PIs**
   - Each process contains one or more KPI and one or more PI.

Besides a full description of the process, the assessor expects to see which KPIs are used and how these are managed. These KPIs must be completely described (see later in this chapter under "Format") leading to the achievement of the planned results. We expect in all cases that the results are aligned to the strategy of the organization.

If it is difficult to demonstrate an alignment between the results and the organization's strategy, ask: "To what extent is it worthwhile to describe this Best Practice?" Only important subjects and processes are worth the effort to develop and bring to a higher (process) maturity level.

It is easier to determine which type of indicator needs to be managed once the process is described. KPIs can be classified into four groups: input, process, output, and outcome indicators.

The example in Figure 3.1 explains the difference between these four types of indicators. We use a well-known process, i.e. cooking.

A practical example of indicators from industry is illustrated in Box 3.3. In an industrial plant, safety is an important issue. Many different indicators can be used based on the situation.

Figure 3.1 Types of indicators for the cooking process.

BOX 3.3 Safety Indicators in a Chemical Plant

INPUT INDICATORS

- Number of people attending safety training (PI)
- Number of hours of safety training provided (PI)
- Number of safety incidents (PI)
- Planning of safety audits (PI)
- Budget for safety training (PI)
- Number of trainers (PI)

THROUGHPUT OR PROCESS INDICATORS

- Number of work sessions/workshops on safety provided to the team (PI)
- Number of suggestions implemented (PI)
- Number of safety audits (PI)
- Revision of Standard Operating Procedures (SOPs) and work instructions (PI)
- Number of audits performed by process owner (PI)

OUTPUT OR LEADING INDICATORS

- Number of safety improvement suggestions introduced by operators recognized (PI)
- Number of suggestions successfully implemented (PI)
- Frequency rate of accidents (KPI)
- Absenteeism due to safety accidents (KPI)

- Number of corrective actions taken and implemented (PI)
- Number of people recognized for their efforts and results (PI)
- Number of revisions of safety processes (PI)
- Decrease of operating costs because of safety improvements (KPI)

EFFECT, OUTCOME, OR LAGGING INDICATORS

- Severity index of accidents (no loss of production) (KPI)
- Lower insurance rates due to a high safety level (KPI)
- Plant is the sector benchmark (KPI)
- No damage to the surrounding community (KPI)

Legend: PI, Performance Indicator; KPI, Key Performance Indicator

The number of sample indicators in Box 3.3 may be overwhelming for those new to quality improvement. The list separates measures between input and process indicators, on the one hand, and output and outcome indicators, on the other. Box 3.3 also illustrates that some indicators are PIs and others KPIs. The generic PI gives a result that does not necessarily contribute to the achievement of the strategy (e.g. the number of incidents). The KPI level of measurement contributes to the achievement of the business plan and/or strategic plan of the organization (e.g. decrease operating costs).

Indicators are often developed without understanding the difference between output and outcome indicators. *Output* indicators measure whether the product or service delivered by the process meets the criteria for which it is designed. An *outcome* or impact indicator describes whether the product or service meets the needs of the customer for whom it is intended. For a process to be a Best Practice, both output and outcome indicators must be monitored and validated.

If the Best Practice doesn't mention output and outcome indicators, we cannot verify its status as a Best Practice. The first question the owner of the Best Practice should ask is: "How does this process contribute to the achievement of the business and strategic plan of the organization?" The answer to this question suggests the type of results (and KPI) to be measured.

As illustrated in Chapter 6 (BEST Quick Scan), not all the investigated case studies mention the indicators tracked to document the performance of the process, nor do they differentiate between performance indicators at the process level and KPIs at the results level. It is difficult to speak of a Best Practice when there is no validation of the accuracy of the results this process will deliver.

5. **Deployment and Segmentation**
   - The description of the process and approaches considers the specificities of all segments of the organization (division, department, work unit) and the variety of products and services.

To have a complete picture of the organization, you need to check how well all work units have performed. There could be significant variation in performance between work units. This drill down to individual segments or work units is what the tool calls *deployment* of the results.

BOX 3.4 Deployment of the Results

For an organization, the overall budget can be in balance, but some departments have a budget in the positive and other departments in the negative. Showing the result for individual departments will reveal which departments perform well and which need improvement.

It is not enough to give an overall view of the results. The results can be aggregated across the whole organization, or they can be *segmented* according to individual work units. Let us illustrate this with an example from the automotive industry: segmentation of customers.

BOX 3.5 Car Dealer, Segmentation According to the Customer Type

A car dealer has different segments of customers for the same car model. The expectations of younger customers may not be the same as retired customers. Therefore, it would be better to show purchasing results and feature preferences for each of these segments separately.

The same is true for other types of customers: civil servants, operators, professionals (doctors, pharmacists, public notaries, architects, etc.), teachers, and retired persons. All these groups have different needs, expectations, and requirements – even if they buy the same product, e.g. food from a supermarket.

6. **Prevention**
   - Prevention is built into the process.
   - The core process description considers the specific circumstances of the organization and prevention is integrated into the daily work.

Prevention is built into the process

All quality and safety professionals are familiar with the concept of prevention. This means that preventive measures are developed and incorporated into the process flow. Therefore, the number of safety incidents and non-conformities is kept to a minimum.

The core process description considers the specific circumstances of the organization and prevention is integrated into the daily work

Prevention can be integrated into a process in several ways: systematic training and retraining of individuals, systematic revision of SOPs and work instructions, application of poka-yoke,* audit and revision of the process, application of Total Productive Maintenance (TPM),† application of Lean Six Sigma (LSS),‡ or other strategic organizational approaches.

It is remarkable that in most Best Practice case studies the authors examined in preparing this text, only a few documented the concept of prevention (see Chapter 6).

7. **Benchmarking**
   - The process description considers similar benchmarks and Best-in-Class examples.

The reason for including this characteristic is to avoid arrogance. When results and approaches are compared with the Best-in-Class, it becomes clear where and what kind of improvements need to be executed. Failing to compare our own results and approaches with others may cause us to think

---

* Westcott, Russell T. and Duffy, Grace L. *The Certified Quality Improvement Associate Handbook*, 3rd ed., ASQ Quality Press, Milwaukee, WI, (2015), pp. 154, 155.

† Manos, Anthony, and Vincent, Chad, Editors, *The Lean Handbook*, ASQ Quality Press, Milwaukee, WI, (2012), pp. 116–123.

‡ Arthur, Jay, *Lean Six Sigma Demystified*, McGraw Hill, New York, (2011).

our processes work very well, when there are improvements that can be realized.

BOX 3.6 What We Can Learn from Others

Assume a civil servant is responsible for the economic development of his country. One benchmark is the experience of Singapore. This city-state realized an uninterrupted economic growth of more than 4% per annum for more than 40 years. If the civil servant takes the factors of economic growth in Singapore as a benchmark, he will discover which factors are the foundation for their success. Then he can compare these factors to those being employed by his own country. From this analysis he then establishes an improvement action plan to correct the gaps in his country's economic activities.*

There is a caution to be noted in benchmarking. Do not try to make an exact copy of the benchmark. The situation and circumstances of the company documenting their Best-in-Class processes are different from yours. Take the concepts and apply them to the characteristics and requirements of your own organization.

The example in Box 3.6 is helpful for another reason. Occasionally in the West comments may be made that Singapore is not a good example because their experiences cannot be translated in our culture's economic situation. When considering benchmarking, it is more important to take the attitude of: 1) "if they can, why can't we?" without prejudice and 2) only when the situation is different (and better) can we learn from others. Learning happens when we have an open mind. We must be eager to learn and prepared to act if we are to change our usual way of doing things.

US President Woodrow Wilson (1856–1924) stated: "*As a nation, we can never learn either from our own weaknesses or our own virtues by comparing ourselves with ourselves.*" Change the word "nation" to "organization" in this sentence and the message becomes crystal clear.†

---

* Ghesquiere, Henri, *Singapore's Success, Engineering Economic Growth*, Thomson Learning, Mason, OH, (2007).

† Ghesquiere, Henri, *Singapore's Success, Engineering Economic Growth*, Thomson Learning, Mason, OH, (2007) Chapter 6. Singapore: Past, Future and What Other Countries Might Learn.

8. **Data**
   - The measurement methods are described clearly and unambiguously, including securing the relevance, integrity, and reliability of the measurement results.
   - The data are presented at the proper level of segmentation to effectively reflect performance and results at different levels of the organization.

The measurement methods are described clearly and unambiguously, including securing the relevance, integrity, and reliability of the measurement results

In this criterion, we emphasize all aspects of the *measuring method*. We need to have a detailed and precise measuring method. This could be an international standard such as ISO* or ASTM,† but it can also be an internally developed measurement method. There are some important points to consider:

- Sampling: the sampling method is done in a professional way. Consider an existing sampling method such as an ISO standard or other proven method. Sometimes the sample the organization takes for their measurement is too small or not representative of the population (lot). A good sample is taken in an approved manner and is representative of the whole lot.

---

* ISO creates documents that provide requirements, specifications, guidelines, or characteristics that can be used consistently to ensure that materials, products, processes, and services are fit for their purpose. https://www.iso.org/standards.html.

† ASTM is an international standards and testing organization with headquarters in West Conshohocken, Pennsylvania, and offices in Belgium, Canada, China, Mexico, and Washington, D.C. It was founded in 1898 by a group of Pennsylvania Railroad engineers and scientists, led by chemist Charles Benjamin Dudley, to address the frequent rail breaks in the fast-growing railroad industry. Originally called the American Society for Testing and Materials, it changed its name to ASTM International in 2001. The association has more than 30,000 members, classified as users, producers, consumers, and general interest. The latter are usually academics and consultants. ASTM develops and publishes technical standards that are arrived at through consensus and used on a voluntary basis for a wide variety of products, materials, systems, and services. To date, some 12,000 ASTM standards are used around the world with 143 technical standard writing committees. The standards are developed in accordance with the guiding principles of the World Trade Organization which include "coherence, consensus, development dimensions, effectiveness, impartiality, openness, relevance, and transparency." ASTM internal standards fall into six categories: test method, specification, classification, practice, guide, and terminology standards. Each year ASTM International publishes the Annual Book of ASTM Standards. http://www.craftechind.com/what-is-astm-international/.

- The parameters are clearly defined for the measuring method.
- The precision of the method is known. This is included in the measuring procedure and checked on a regular basis.
- Calibration methods of the measuring instruments are available and applied.
- Precision and accuracy are known and there is a method to check it.

BOX 3.7 Sampling Method

Only five customers are interviewed in a customer satisfaction survey.

When you have thousands of customers and prospects, too small a sample can lead to incorrect conclusions. The small sample of this example is not representative.

BOX 3.8 Measuring Method, Cycle Time

A retail bank offers mortgages to their customers. Management decides to use cycle time for mortgage approval as one way to measure the performance of the bank. Target: the total cycle time should be less than eight days.

In the example given in Box 3.8, cycle time initially looks to be clearly defined. However, a second look raises some questions. To be more precise in measuring, consider the following questions:

- Is cycle time expressed in working days, calendar days, or bank working days?
- At which point in the process does the cycle start: when the customer initially applies for the mortgage or when the first offer is made by the bank?
- Likewise, what is the endpoint of the cycle?

It was originally assumed that the process was described in enough detail to be consistently measured. This is often not the case.

BOX 3.9 Precision

Many chemical and microbiological measurements are done in a medical lab daily. It is important that all measurement instruments are *calibrated* on a regular basis. This ongoing calibration routine allows the laboratory manager to assure measurement results are precise and reliable.

In the situation described in Box 3.9, calibration is part of the measurement method. The gap between the measured value and the true value is zero when equipment is correctly calibrated.

BOX 3.10 Accuracy

Measurement of workers' skills, customer satisfaction, etc. demonstrates a (natural) variation in results. This variation can be expressed as standard deviation.

The better the process is under control, the lower the variation (standard deviation) will be. This *minimal* standard deviation will be present when the process is under control. Statistical Process Control (SPC)* charts are used to minimize variation and maintain processes within control limits. In many situations, process performance is not statistically monitored or put under control (see examples in Chapter 6).

The data are presented at the proper level of segmentation to effectively reflect performance and results at different levels of the organization

Segmentation and deployment were already mentioned in the fifth criterion "Deployment and Segmentation." Here we present the data at the different levels of the organization and we analyze the performance for this segmentation.

3.1.3 Do

The Do phase consists of five criteria and seven characteristics. This phase is generally the best developed in most organizations.

* Statistical process control, https://en.wikipedia.org/wiki/Statistical_Process_Control accessed 12/28/2019.

The five criteria for the Do phase are:

1. Implementation
2. Deployment
3. Cause-effect
4. Accountability
5. SMART*

1. **Implementation**
   - The daily activities are in conformance with the process descriptions and documented methods.
   - The implementation of the core process is integrated into daily work.

The daily activities are in conformance with the process descriptions and documented methods.

This criterion verifies that tasks are performed as described in the documented process. Very often no process description is available (see examples in Chapter 6). When there is no formal description of the process, everyone in the process tries "to work at their best" in the way they understand "how to do the work." Consequently, there is great variation of outcome from the process. This is the opposite of a Best Practice. A reliable process consists of activities that are *standardized* and *documented.* What is described and documented is also executed and vice versa.

The implementation of the core process is integrated into daily work.

It is not enough to have a process which is nicely described if it is not put into practice. What is *done* in *daily life* is exactly the same as what is documented.

2. **Deployment**
   - The approach is used by all appropriate work units.

It is not enough that one service or department applies what is described in the process. All work units (teams, services, departments, plants, business units, etc.) must apply the requirements of the process in the same way.

---

* SMART is an acronym, giving criteria to guide in the setting of objectives. Each corporate, department, and section objective should be: Specific – target a specific area for achievement or improvement; Measurable – quantify or at least suggest an indicator of progress; Assignable – specify who will do it; Realistic – state what results can realistically be achieved, given available resources.; Time-related – specify when the result(s) can be achieved.

Deployment of the Best Practices approach must be organized not only horizontally across functions, but also vertically from top management to the front lines of the organization.

3. **Cause-effect**
   - The use of the process leads to concrete and measurable results.

Results caused by unstable or undocumented approaches are not reliable. Therefore, applied methods must be improved in such a way that results can be predicted over time. Reliable and robust approaches lead to reliable results.

Many people have difficulty understanding the cause-effect relationship or in explaining it to collaborators. Process owners are responsible for the effective use of cause and effect analysis and to explain it to operators.

BOX 3.11 Profit

A general manager claims responsibility for the increase of profit because of his management actions.

If the general manager does not explain why this increase is due specifically to his management actions, his statement is "management by fiction." The manager must clearly describe the series of efforts and investments he pursued over the last five years, showing proof of increase of productivity and quality, and a decrease in scrap and defects. Only with clear cause and effect attribution can he claim that his management actions lead to the increase in profit.

The example in Box 3.11 shows a common pitfall. If the Best Practice describes the exceptional results as an accomplishment of a single person (e.g. the general manager), double-check the context of the situation. It could be that the Best Practice is more a public relations paper than a true Best Practice.

4. **Accountability**
   - All employees and managers clearly exhibit how they are responsible and accountable for their assigned tasks.

The Accountability characteristic as part of the Responsibilities criteria in the Plan phase describes the way the company is organized, i.e. the description of the applied method. Accountability in the Do phase addresses the implementation of methods.

A Culture of Accountability is the manner through which people develop successful solutions daily. It is the approach necessary to find answers, overcome obstacles, and deliver results. People in a Culture of Accountability follow through to make sure they do what they say they will do, commit themselves to getting to the truth, and feel free to say what needs to be said.*

The process owner has the necessary authority to achieve planned objectives and is held accountable for overall performance and results. Therefore, when the process owner notices issues reflected in a KPI, he finds solutions and implements improvements. He doesn't wait until problems occur; he addresses the issue proactively. The process owner takes the initiative not only to put improvements in place, but also to audit the process regularly.

5. **SMART**
   - KPIs and PIs are used systematically.
   - SMART decisions are made, and action plans are developed.

KPIs and PIs are used systematically.

Indicators are used systematically. The word "systematic" means on a regular basis, e.g. weekly or monthly.

Each indicator has his target. These targets are formulated using the SMART criteria, i.e. Specific, Measurable, Actionable, Realistic, and Time-bound. Some additional useful criteria for targets are: Accountable, Ambitious, and Relevant.

The target is set to be ambitious, but realistic. All too often we see that people put their targets too low, so that they easily achieve the target. This is a reflection of a defensive thinking style. The achieved results are mediocre and don't belong to a Best Practice.

SMART decisions are made, and action plans are developed.

KPIs should be reviewed and discussed, SMART decisions made, and actions assigned for prevention or improvement on a consistent cycle. Benchmarking using a Best Practice requires clear, measurable action that can be translated into the situation of the user.

---

* Connors, Roger and Smith, Tom, *How Did That Happen? Holding People Accountable for Results the Positive, Principled Way*, Publisher Portfolio, 2009. Penguin Group (USA) Inc. New York.

If the criteria of the Do phase are well described, the original organization as well as a benchmarking partner may expect to achieve effective results. If *excellent* results are desired, the two next phases, Check and Act must be actively applied.

3.1.4 Check

The Check phase consists of four criteria and 13 characteristics. The role of the process owner is very important in this phase. Without the participation of the process owner, it is very difficult to achieve excellent results.

The four criteria for the Check phase are:

1. Integration
2. Monitoring
3. Audit
4. Adjustment and learning

1. **Integration**
   - Plans, processes, results, analysis, learning, and actions are harmonized across process and work units to support organization-wide goals.

There are two types of activities: one related with the process of the Best Practice and one with the "normal daily" activities. When the Best Practice is viewed as separate from daily work, collaborators experience the activities of the Best Practice as a burden and an extra workload. When the process is integrated consistently into daily activities, there is no differentiation between a Best Practice and "what we do every day."

Processes must be integrated to be truly effective. Much is written about the danger of conducting activities in silos. For excellent results, processes must be developed to work with related processes. KPIs must reflect the reality of the interdependence of processes to meet desired outcomes.

Management does not always appreciate the benefit of process integration. When researching a Best Practice, be alert when a manager says there is no time, headcount, or budget to spend on theoretical concepts such as learning and process management. This reactive type of management indicates the process owner does not understand the value of the broader picture of the organization and how processes must work together. The reactive manager rarely engages in prioritization or strategic problem solving. The manager and his organization are always busy with short-term firefighting, rather than effective, strategically beneficial activities.

2. **Monitoring**
   - The performance of each core process is regularly measured and monitored.
   - The results obtained related to a core process are regularly discussed with all relevant stakeholders.
   - The method to determine the target value of the KPI (target) is validated and opportunities for improvement are recorded.
   - Relevance, integrity, completeness, and reliability of the results achieved are checked.

The performance of each core process is regularly measured and monitored.

The performance of the process is monitored in two ways: 1) through a weekly or monthly meeting where the KPIs are reviewed by the management team and 2) improving the process by eliminating non-value-added activities.

The obtained results related to a core process are regularly discussed with all relevant stakeholders.

All aspects of results management are addressed in the KPI review meeting. *All those directly concerned* participate in the discussion and decide which actions to take to reach expected results.

The method to determine the target value of the KPI (target) is validated and opportunities for improvement are recorded.

The process owner has a method to determine targets. The concerned stakeholder validates the targets of the KPIs. As said earlier, the agreed targets are ambitious, but nevertheless realistic. The process owner with all people concerned, including the relevant stakeholders, examines and reports the areas for improvement.

Relevance, integrity, completeness, and reliability of the results achieved are checked.

The process management team consistently monitors the relevance, integrity, completeness, and reliability of the achieved results. Notice that the process owner has to examine four subjects systematically:

1. Are the data and results *relevant* for our Best Practice? Do these data contribute directly and positively to the realization of the strategic goals?
2. Does the data have *integrity*? Can we trust the results presented?
3. Are the data and results *complete*? Think about the deployment and segmentation of the results.
4. Are the data *reliable?* You can only make correct decisions based upon correct (reliable) data.

From our experience we see that many people don't ask themselves these kinds of questions.

In a May 2019 APQC* survey, 91% of respondents reported supporting or managing process improvement efforts, with 62.5% establishing a process performance dashboard and 46.4% utilizing auditing to gather information for improvement opportunities.[†] This confirms our finding that many so-called Best Practices are not truly a Best Practice because they miss, among others, characteristics, a performance dashboard and a systematic audit of the process.

3. **Audit**
   - Each core process owner audits his or her process regularly.
   - The process owner examines what can be done to bring the core process to a higher maturity level (to determine improvement opportunities).

Each core process owner audits his or her process regularly.

Regular audits are an excellent way to manage the processes and KPIs better. Regularly means that processes are audited at least once a year. The audits not only confirm what is performing effectively, but also where new opportunities for improvement exist.

The process owner examines what can be done to bring the core process to a higher maturity level (to determine improvement opportunities).

Using audits to improve processes helps the organization grow to higher levels of performance maturity.

---

* APQC is the world's foremost authority in benchmarking, best practices, process and performance improvement, and knowledge management. APQC membership includes access to the ever-growing Resource Library, with more than 5000 research-based best practices, benchmarks and metrics, case studies, and other valuable APQC content.Source : apqc.org.

† Lyke-Ho-Gland, Holly and Morgan, Lochlyn, *Putting Process Frameworks into Action*, APQC Survey Summary Report Announcement materials. May 2019, APQC, slide 11.

4. **Adjustment and Learning**
   - Deviations from the desired and/or planned results serve as input for the improvement and revision of the core process and/or approaches.
   - Identification of problems related to the sufficient availability and appropriate resources such as budget, machinery, equipment, provisions, tools, and Information Technology (software, hardware, networking, security, etc.).
   - Identification of an adequate number of employees and/or of shortcomings of skills and experiences of employees in the process and/or approaches.
   - Comparison of the results obtained with the benchmark and Best-in-Class.
   - Prioritization of opportunities for improvement.
   - Encouragement of breakthrough change to the approach applied through innovation.

The first three characteristics of this criterion are concerned with solving problems in a pragmatic way. The Check phase is a time for verifying the stability of the process through problem-solving techniques.*

Deviations from the desired and/or planned results serve as input for the improvement and revision of the core process and/or approaches.

People familiar with Kaizen know that there is always a better way to do things. Even small improvement activities need to be done on a regular basis (daily, weekly). When an improvement is executed, you need to revise the standards, SOP, work instructions, etc. You increase the revision number. This higher revision number is also a visualization of the learning process.

Identification of problems related to the sufficient availability and appropriate resources such as budget, machinery, equipment, provisions, tools, and Information Technology (software, hardware, networking, security, etc.).

Shortage of resources needs to be addressed. It is the responsibility of the process owner to maintain stability of the process. The process owner shall take the necessary actions and decisions when there are not enough available resources.

---

* Westcott, Russell T. and Duffy, Grace L. *The Certified Quality Improvement Associate Handbook*, 3rd ed., Quality Press, Milwaukee, WI, (2015) p. 131.

Identification of an adequate number of employees and/or of shortcomings of skills and experiences of employees in the process and/or approaches.

The process owner needs not only adequate technical resources but also collaborators. He won't be able to achieve excellent results if there are not enough collaborators to perform the tasks and/or if there is a lack of collaborator skills. It is the responsibility of the process owner to verify that every collaborator knows the work instructions very well and applies these in detail in daily life. He also has to verify that all collaborators doing the same job are doing the task in an identical way. There is only one best way to perform the task.

Comparison of the results obtained with the benchmark and Best-in-Class.

Results are not only compared with an internal target, but also with other Best-in-Class examples. Getting feedback from third parties is the best way to stay informed of excellent approaches or results.

Prioritization of opportunities for improvement

Prioritizing opportunities for improvement is a constant challenge. The list of opportunities will generally be much greater than can be addressed in a reasonable amount of time. The process owner must constantly balance resources and time to prioritize the improvement opportunities.

Encouragement of breakthrough change to the approach applied through innovation.

Continuous improvement can be done by application of techniques like Kaizen,[*] Statistical Process Control,[†] and LSS.[‡] Besides continuous improvement, *breakthrough improvements* are also possible. Breakthrough becomes necessary when the strategic plan requires productivity increases of 10% or more. In that situation there are two options: 1) reengineer the whole process[§] or 2) automate the process. The second option may require significant investment.

* Duffy, Grace L. *Modular Kaizen, Continuous and Breakthrough Improvement*, Quality Press, Milwaukee, WI, (2014) pp. 15–25.

† Burke, Sarah E. and Silvestrini, Rachel T. *The Certified Quality Engineer Handbook*, 4th ed., Quality Press, Milwaukee, WI, (2017).

‡ Kubiak, T. M. and Benbow, Donald W. *The Certified Six Sigma Black Belt Handbook*, 3rd ed., Quality Press, Milwaukee, WI, (2016).

§ Ibid, p. 19.

The Check phase encompasses techniques for stabilizing processes and for finding areas for improvement. To complete the development of a Best-in-Class process, we must put these techniques into practice, i.e. to Act. The last step in the PDCA-cycle is the opportunity to prepare a new Plan, i.e. document gains realized and cycle back to step 1 in the PDCA-cycle.

3.1.5 Act

The Act phase consists of five criteria and eight characteristics.

The five criteria for the Check phase are:

1. Improvement
2. Process
3. Resources
4. Knowledge and experience
5. Benchmarks

1. **Improvement**
   - The output of the measurement and learning is analyzed and used to identify additional improvements – to prioritize, to plan, and to implement these opportunities for further improvement.

The Check phase introduces ideas and areas for improvement. The Act phase closes the feedback loop. After analyzing results of the Plan, Do, and Check phases, the Act phase is to plan and implement improvements prioritized through the Adjustment and Learning characteristics of the Check phase. Those with the greatest leverage or return get priority in the new Plan phase.

Normally you'll have a long list of possible improvement activities. You have to prioritize the improvement opportunities. By applying the Pareto principle,* you take the 20% improvement opportunities which will deliver 80% of the planned results.

2. **Process**
   - The process, methods, and approaches are revised and improved in response to the findings gained in the Check phase.

* https://en.wikipedia.org/wiki/Pareto_principle accessed 12/28/2019.

The key words here are *revised* and *improved*. Verify revision numbers of procedures, instructions, processes, and KPIs currently followed. SOPs, instructions, and measurements should be reviewed at least annually. Most organizations do not have a scheduled cycle to revise and improve these materials. This is the responsibility of the process owner.

It is not enough, however, to revise and improve the process and documentation; it is necessary to train the people who are working with the process on these changes. Alerting the workforce of changes is often forgotten, only to have confusion and a loss of improvement when people slide back to the old way of doing things.

3. **Resources**
   - The amount and nature of the resources that were adjusted because of the findings in the Check phase are documented.
   - The number of employees assigned to the process is adjusted considering the opportunities of improvement and the outcome of the process, methods, and approaches.

The amount and nature of the resources that were adjusted because of the findings in the Check phase are documented.

The process owner makes a detailed analysis of the resources required. A plan is developed to overcome resource barriers (budget, equipment, etc.). In case of a complex process, it might be necessary to rebalance workload across portions of the activity. Fortunately, as productivity increases, resources (people, equipment, ...) can be returned to other parts of the business.

The number of employees assigned to the process is adjusted considering the opportunities of improvement and the outcome of the process, methods, and approaches.

The process owner takes the necessary initiatives to ensure that there are enough collaborators to perform the activities in his area. Having the adequate number of collaborators is not enough; he also needs to verify to what extent the skills of the collaborators correspond to the needs.

4. **Knowledge and Experience**
   - New training and/or refresher training is given to meet the findings gained in the Check phase.

- Refinements and innovations are shared with other relevant work units and processes.
- The knowledge and experience of those involved in the process are documented and validated as Best-in-Class or Benchmark level.

New training and/or refresher training is given to meet the findings gained in the Check phase.

The findings of the Check phase lead to a training program of specific topics for the collaborators.

Refinements and innovations are shared with other relevant work units and processes.

Individuals and teams have an opportunity to share their ideas, results achieved, and experiences with other teams.

The knowledge and experience of those involved in the process are documented and validated as Best-in-Class or Benchmark level.

Key words here are *knowledge* and *experience*. How are these two concepts put into practice? Is there *systematic progress* in the development of process knowledge, procedures, and activities? When this systematic progress is successful, organizational knowledge approaches the status of wisdom. Only a few organizations can demonstrate this level of progress.

Not every professional can demonstrate that he or she has learned more than they knew last year or has made progress in their professional situation. This progress can be achieved through on-the-job-training, formal training, video sessions such as webinars or open training, etc. The following non-exclusive set of questions may suggest how knowledge and experience can be developed.

- How many days of training per year has the participant attended?
- Are individuals and teams better in finding solutions for the problems encountered in their daily work each year?
- Is there an increase in the number of suggestions to improve team productivity and quality, and to decrease costs and cycle times?
- Do workers make suggestions to integrate preventative measures into the process?

Positive answers to questions such as these are a measure of the development of personal knowledge and experience.

5. **Benchmark**
   – The organization can be set as a model for other organizations.

We can learn from others. The reverse is also true. Others can learn from us. This criterion explores to what extent your organization can be used as a benchmark for others. If other organizations are referring to your organization as well organized, with processes producing excellent results, you can indeed conclude that you are a benchmark in your sector.

This section has described in detail what makes an improvement model (PDCA) an excellent enabler for developing a Best Practice. An enabler without results provides no tangible target. The next section describes the requirements for the achievement of *excellent results.*

3.2 Assessment of the Achieved *Results*

3.2.1 Results

This section consists of 7 criteria and 20 characteristics. The criteria and related characteristics are listed in Figure 3.4. The reader will note that just as processes are interdependent, so are the criteria for the enabler and the results. The enabler describes the activity. The results describe the characteristic outcomes of the activity.

The seven criteria for the results are:

1. Scope and relevance
2. Integrity of data
3. Segmentation
4. Trends
5. Targets
6. Comparisons with targets and benchmarks
7. Cause-effect

We have to avoid a classic pitfall: some people have the tendency again to describe approaches here, such as methods, procedures and instructions, i.e. enabling elements. Don't do that. What you have to describe in this criterion for results are data and results.

1. **Scope and Relevance**
   – The results are aligned with the expectations and needs of the relevant stakeholders.

- The results are aligned with policy and strategy of the organization.
- The most important key results are identified and prioritized.
- The relationship between the results is understood.

The results are aligned with the expectations and needs of the relevant stakeholders.

It is not enough to have a general alignment with shareholders' needs and expectations. All the stakeholders' needs and expectations must be met, including customers, employees, suppliers, contractors, partners, society, sponsors, etc. Here you have to give the *results* as aligned with those needs and expectations.

The results are aligned with policy and strategy of the organization.

It has been stated previously that a Best Practice describes the essential and important activities of the organization. Therefore, an alignment must exist between the Best Practice and the achievement of the Business and/or Strategic Plan of the organization. Here the *results* are shown.

The most important key results are identified and prioritized.

There may be different types of *results* depending on the process under study. It is necessary to define which results are important and which results have the highest priority for sustainability and improvement.

When monitoring a process, there can be input, process, output, and outcome indicators. Each of these indicators measures a result. Considering all these different measures, one Best Practice can have many results. The Best Practice must describe which of these results are most critical to process excellence and what relationship exists between those results. For example, see Enabler criterion number 3: KPIs and PIs, Figure 3.1.

The relationship between the results is understood.

If you present the KPIs in a process way, such as Figure 3.1, you can see immediately the relationships between results. Of course, you may also explain the relationship between results with words.

2. **Integrity of data**
   - Results are timely.
   - Results are reliable and accurate.

Results are timely.

Not only the level of the target, e.g. a 10% increase of productivity or a 20% decrease of the cycle time for delivering the permit, but also when these results are achieved, i.e. the deadline, is important. You can't move fast and forward if you have to wait weeks before you get the results.

Results are reliable and accurate.

Process assessment must stop if there is a problem with the integrity of the data. It is not useful to make an assessment based upon unreliable results.

BOX 3.12 Unreliable Results

An internal safety audit is conducted in a large industrial plant. The audit findings are clear: there is a series of unacceptable non-conformities. The supervisor of the audited cell hears this negative report and demands the auditor to describe his findings less negatively. The division head, who is not happy with the report either, changes some wording and deletes the most negative examples to make the message sound more acceptable. The report goes to a higher level. The department manager is also not happy with the report. He further "polishes" the text and then passes it to the general manager. The general manager, overall, is satisfied with the "sanitized" audit report because he feared negative findings and the report he receives puts his mind at rest. The final decision is that no major steps for corrective action need to be taken.

This example, based upon the actual experience of one of the authors, illustrates how company culture can lead to unreliable results and incorrect decisions. It is clear from this example that if there is incorrect information included in a process description or supporting reports, it is not worthwhile to investigate additional aspects of a Best Practice. On-site interviews often uncover incidents where the documentation of a process is inconsistent with actual performance.

BOX 3.13 Missing Data in Customer Complaint Treatment

All customer complaints are logged into a software application in chronological order. Occasionally customers have submitted a complaint that was confusing or seemed odd to the person entering the data. The data entry clerk would not enter these confusing complaints.

Filtering complaints before capture is a common occurrence. Terms such as "real" complaints and "unaccepted" complaints are used. When complaints are screened before entry into the complaint handling system, the data base does not reflect the totality of customer concerns.

There is a risk in filtering complaints before including them in the data base. If the goal is to reduce the number of complaints and the manager sees an increase, he or she is tempted to omit "the least important" complaints. When the data is corrupted by inappropriate filtering, it is impossible to make correct decisions based upon the existing data and results.

3. **Segmentation**
   - Results are segmented in a suitable manner
     - by region, country
     - by department, business line, division, unit
     - by product and service type

Segmentation or stratification of information may make it easier to focus on the correct action. Combining too much data smooths out performance highs or lows that would ordinarily prompt questions.

A real Best Practice always shows the results by its segmentation.

Sometimes the graphs created to present data analysis are too complicated. Try to limit the number of lines in a graph to three or four. It is easier and faster to assess five simple graphs than a single graph with too many lines.

4. **Trends**
   - Trends are positive for five years or more.
   - Results are sustainable and show good performance.

Trends are positive for five years or more.

A reliable Best Practice should demonstrate a positive trend of improving results for more than 5 years, and preferably, 10 years. It is not possible to draw a conclusion from a set of results for three years. We know that many people think that a progress in results for three years will last for more years. In our experience this is not true. Reason: there are so many changes in the context of the organization, that these can have a negative effect on the results. Therefore, we prefer a 10-year positive trend. Then you can more safely say that you have a true positive trend.

Results are sustainable and show good performance.

A positive trend should be sustained for more than five years. Positive results for a significant period increase the probability that these results are not an accident but are sustainable.

When illustrating the trend of positive results, it is not enough to simply show a line graph of the trending period. It is more useful as a benchmark if the backup data showing the performance measures of the last 5 or 10 years are provided in an accompanying table. If the actual data is competitively sensitive, percentages may be better than raw figures.

5. **Targets**
   - Targets for core results are set.
   - Targets are suitable.
   - Targets are achieved.

Targets for core results are set.

The expectation for claiming a Best Practice is to have ambitious performance targets. It is sometimes difficult, however, to tell whether the results achieved are ambitious. When the Best Practice describes the method of setting objectives and targets, it is easier for the benchmarking partner to ascertain whether the presented results are indeed excellent. Exceptional improvements vary across industries. Providing some baseline of performance expectation helps the reader of the Best Practice truly appreciate the results obtained.

Targets are suitable.

This seems logical, but it isn't always the case. Box 3.14 provides an example of target setting, based upon a real production situation.

BOX 3.14 Increase in Productivity

A production manager sets an annual target for a 3% productivity increase. When asked why he targets only a 3% increase, he answers "because we always set a 3% target. This satisfies our general manager." Based upon the production reports of the last year, it would be realistic to set a 7% productivity increase instead of 3%. However, the production manager refused to accept this "too ambitious target." When he is asked to explain his motivation for a non-ambitious target (3%), his explanation is simple: "because I will get my bonus at the end of the year when I achieve my planned objective of 3%. If I plan 7% and maybe only achieve 5%, I will not get my bonus."

This example makes two important points:

1) Company culture plays an important role in setting targets (i.e. the production manager feels punished when he "only" achieves a 5% productivity increase instead of the planned 7%. On the other hand, he feels rewarded if he achieves the 3% goal and gets his bonus.
2) The *method* for setting objectives and targets is important. Evidence of what prompts the creation of the target must be in the description of the Best Practice.

Targets are achieved.

Setting ambitious targets means also that you'll only achieve these targets in 70% or 80% of the cases. If you achieve 100% of all your targets, then you have to investigate whether these targets were "ambitious."

The authors have observed that occasionally targets are not set for the coming year but established at the end of the period. A target that is set to correspond with the performance already attained is a form of manipulation. The target should always be set at the beginning of the performance period to reflect the desired performance, not the performance that can easily or has already been attained.

6. **Comparisons with targets and benchmarks**
   - Comparisons for core results are made.
   - Comparisons are suitable.
   - Comparisons are favorable.

Why do we need to compare ourselves with a Benchmark or other Best Practice? This avoids complacency and allows you to learn from a good example. This can inspire you to make further improvements in your Best Practice.

Comparisons for core results are made.

It is obvious that you not only compare your Best Practice with others, but also that your achieved results are equal or better than the Benchmark.

Setting targets as a comparison for benchmarking is important. Criterion 6 (Comparisons with targets and benchmarks) takes criterion 5 (Targets) to the next level. Not only are targets set at the beginning of the performance cycle, but they are also compared with the results achieved. The additional characteristic in criterion 6 is that the comparison of target and achieved performance is favorable. Not only is the process following requirements, but the process meets or exceeds the targets set at the beginning of the performance period (for more information on PI and KPI, refer to the Plan phase in the Enabler section).

Comparisons are suitable.

By comparing your Best Practice with a Benchmark, you must pay attention to the fact that it is logical to make that comparison with that specific external organization.

Comparisons are favorable.

You compare your achieved results with the Best-in-Class or Benchmark. If you can say that in most cases, e.g. 75%, your achieved results are better than the Benchmark, you have an excellent result.

Once results have been achieved and compared with a benchmark, the owner of the KPI should ask: "What have I learned? What action do I need to take to adjust the process or improve it further?"

7. **Cause-effect**
   - The results are clearly achieved through the chosen approach (cause-effect).
   - The relation between results achieved and the approach taken (the enabler) are understood.
   - Based on the evidence presented, confidence should be high that the positive performance will continue, i.e. the results are sustainable.

The results are clearly achieved through the chosen approach (cause-effect).

The cause-effect criterion is the opposite of achieving results by accident. The owner of the Best Practice must explain how the methods and approaches are used and how they lead to excellent results.

The relation between results achieved and the approach taken (the enabler) are understood.

The better the owner understands the relationship between the achieved results and the approach taken, the easier it becomes to undertake further corrective actions, i.e. improvement initiatives and preventative measures.

Based on the evidence presented, confidence should be high that the positive performance will continue, i.e. the results are sustainable.

When the relationship is understood and corrective actions are taken in a structured and systematic way, you'll discover that the results become predictable and sustainable.

3.2.2 Test of Results Criteria on a Real-Life Example

The following Figure 3.2 gives a presentation of results of a real-life example of Primary and Secondary Syphilis treatment in different hospitals. Let us apply the seven criteria of the Results part of the BEST-tool on this example.

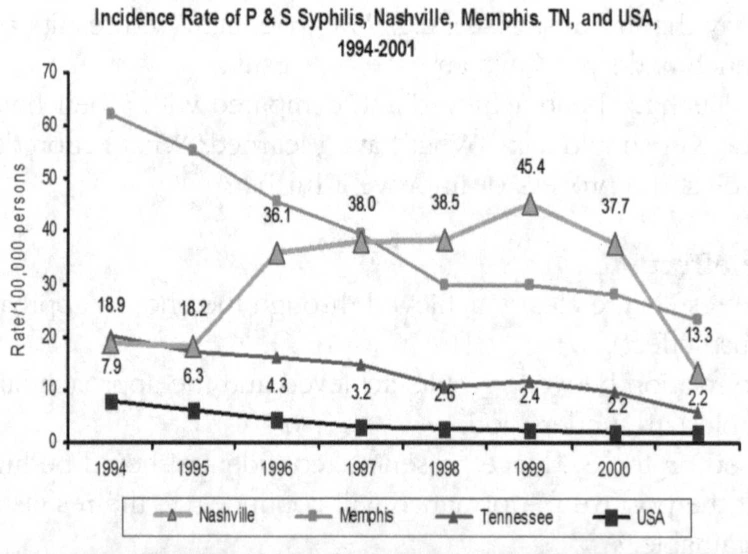

Figure 3.2 Incidence rate of P&S Syphilis at Nashville, Memphis, Tennessee, and the USA (period 1994–2001).* P&S: Primary and Secondary Syphilis.

* Bialek, Ron, Duffy, Grace L. and Moran, John W. *The Public Health Quality Improvement Handbook*, Quality Press, Milwaukee, WI, (2009), Bailey, Stephanie, M.D., MSHSA, Chapter 12: *Already Doing It and Not Knowing It.*

The following text analyzes the material available in the syphilis case study with the list of results criteria described above.

1. **Scope and relevance**
   Not available
   There is an introduction of the reason for choosing the project, although with not enough detail in this case study to validate the scope and relevance. The credentials of the author imply that the scope and relevance are closely aligned with the public health charter and are appropriate.
2. **Integrity of data**
   Not available
   It is reasonable to assume the data is correct based on the professional credentials of the health sector author.
3. **Segmentation**
   Yes, we see here the segmented results for Nashville, Memphis, Tennessee, and the USA.
4. **Trends**
   The results for Nashville show a positive trend of reduced incidence for only the last three years. On the contrary, the results for Memphis and Tennessee show a positive trend of reduced incidence for eight years.
5. **Targets**
   Not available
   It is difficult to say whether these results are ambitious and excellent. We can assume that targets are implicitly present in comparison with the state and US results.
6. **Comparison with targets and benchmarking**
   Caution must be taken when assuming excellent performance. A benchmark should always be the Best-in-Class, never the average. Therefore, it is not known whether the US result is a benchmark. A true benchmark city in the USA would be one that is larger than 200,000 inhabitants which is ranked as number one in the reduction of cases of primary and secondary syphilis.
7. **Cause and effect**
   Not available
   Although this level of information is not present in the limited six-page case study, the relationship is probably evident in more detailed project reports.

3.2.3 Conclusion

When this graph is first studied, it appears most impressive. Comparing the information with that required by the BEST-tool reveals that complete data is not available for four of the seven criteria. This observation is not to say that the project was not extremely successful. The case study was not written to provide all the information to be used as a Best Practice by benchmarking partners. Only when all the seven criteria for "results" are described in a positive way, is there enough information for a benchmarking partner to improve their own similar process and be assured of achieving *excellent results.*

Even when all seven criteria for results are described, it cannot be definitively concluded that this is an example of a Best Practice. It is too early in the improvement cycle to establish sustainability. A full Best Practice case study will apply the checklists of enabler (PDCA), results, process, and format. This case study, however, has a good foundation for being expanded into a true Best Practice document.

The next section describes the assessment criteria for documenting a Best Practice **process**.

3.3 Assessment of the Management of the Best Practice *Process*

3.3.1 Definition of a Process

An activity or group of activities that takes an input, adds value to it, and provides an output to an internal or external customer; a planned and repetitive sequence of steps by which a defined product or service is delivered.*

The process that is described for a Best Practice is often illustrated through a ***flowchart***. Formatting the flowchart into four columns (Who, Where, When, How) provides a complete and transparent process description (see example of Blood Draw Process in Chapter 7).

A process description provides evidence that the company is well organized, activities are standardized, and results are reliable and repeatable. In only a few case studies analyzed in the research for this book have the authors seen a process description that provided evidence of reliability and

* Westcott, Russell T. and Duffy, Grace L. *The Certified Quality Improvement Associate Handbook*, 3rd ed., Quality Press, Milwaukee, WI, (2015) p. 238.

Table 3.3 Assessment of the *management of the process* of a best practice

	Subject	*NOK*	*OK*	*Comment*
1	Owner of key process			
2	Integrity			
3	Risk management			
4	Relation with strategic plan			
5	Adding value			
6	Systematic simplification			
7	KPI			
8	Audit			
9	Maturity level of process			

Legend: KPI = key performance indicator; NOK = not complete; OK = complete

repeatability. Remember that for a **Best Practice, all four components must be linked together: 1) Enabler (PDCA), 2) Results, 3) Process description and 4) Format of the Best Practice, i.e. the detailed documentation of the Best Practice.**

The following is a closer look at the characteristics of the **management of a process**. This segment is comprised of nine criteria. Table 3.3 shows a complete listing of the criteria for the management of a process.

1. **Owner of key process**

The key process owner is usually a member of executive management. When executive management is assigned responsibility, the message to the organization is that this is a critical process. W. Edwards Deming is often alleged to have said that 85% of organizational problems are management controllable, while only 15% are worker controllable.* Process management is a typical function for an executive manager, not a line manager. A process description is nothing more than a description of how work is done. As described through the concept of Kaizen, there is only *one best way* to do

* Westcott, Russell T. and Duffy, Grace L. *The Certified Quality Improvement Associate Handbook*, 3rd ed., Quality Press, Milwaukee, WI, (2015) p. 13.

things; we need to arrange the process and activities in such a way that this "best way of doing things" is achieved in a repeatable way.

2. **Integrity**

Integrity is a difficult criterion to describe, since it is an intangible concept. The comparison between integrity and the lack of it, however, is recognizable. Lack of integrity presents itself in a business in many ways: fraud, corruption, bribery, misappropriation of funds, laundered money, tax evasion, etc. The temptation to manipulate processes for organizational or personal gain is real. The pressure to maintain the appearance of a Best Practice can prompt inappropriate behavior in activities such as purchasing, military equipment sales, financial (banks, trading firms) or global transactions such as oil, and agricultural crops.

Reliable process management is dependent upon the integrity with which the organization functions. The way we organize and monitor activities allows or prevents inappropriate behavior. Building transparency into critical processes is a way to encourage integrity in the workplace.

BOX 3.15 Purchasing Department

The management of activities for sending Requests for Pricing is separated from the management of activities for ordering the materials from the supplier. Having two different managers involved with the purchasing process reduces the possibility of inappropriate behavior.

BOX 3.16 Bank

To discourage fraud in a bank, high ranking officers are required to take all their holidays. The concern is that someone who comes into the office on a holiday might be hiding transactions from all but a small number of accomplices. A manager who is always in the office may be a signal of inappropriate behavior: to keep illicit transactions fully under control. Another signal is staying late in the office when everyone else has returned home. Managers are rotated out of position every two years to minimize improper use of their authority.

These two examples illustrate the importance of integrity and transparency.

3. **Risk management**

Does the organization assess risks to business on an annual basis and take the necessary preventive actions? Are these preventive activities integrated into the process description?

The risks to a business can be diverse: environmental, safety, currency exchange, political risks (export to certain developing countries), food safety, health risks, labor accidents, etc. The business maturity of a company performing processes at Best-in-Class level will be aware of their risks and be actively managing to reduce their exposures.

4. **Relation with strategic plan**

A company should only invest the extra time, and resources in developing a Best Practice where it expects to gain the highest return. The highest return means there is a positive contribution to the achievement of organizational strategic objectives. The alignment of the process with the strategy of the organization should be clearly documented.

5. **Adding value**

Each project consists of a sum of value adding and non-value adding activities. Masaaki Imai uses the Japanese word "*muda*" to identify non-value adding activities as waste.* A process is managed in a professional way when there is an approach used to systematically decrease the amount of *muda*. Imai taught us that there is much more *muda* than real added value in a process. Therefore, there is always an opportunity for improvement. People familiar with LSS know that the improvement process is endless and results not only in increased productivity, but also customer and employee satisfaction, and the satisfaction of partners and society.

---

* Imai, Masaaki, *Gemba Kaizen, A Commonsense, Low-Cost Approach to Management*, McGraw Hill, New York, (1997).

BOX 3.17 EXAMPLE OF APPLICATION OF REDUCTION OF *MUDA*

An Ontario District Health Unit realized their patients were wasting time getting from the lobby to their scheduled medical appointment. A recent office re-arrangement had moved several medical suites. The receptionist had not been informed of these changes. Patients were confused, often returning to the lobby in frustration. A process improvement team recognized the time being wasted and the bottleneck in the lobby caused by patients trying to find the correct treatment area. An updated map of the facility, with treatment areas highlighted, was created for the receptionist and distributed to all employees. New signage was placed in the lobby providing directions to major areas of the building. These new tools got patients where they needed to go quickly and reduced the bottleneck from the lobby.

6. **Systematic simplification**

If waste is removed from the process on a *systematic* basis, the process becomes simple and transparent.

Once the process is flowcharted and understood, inefficiencies and conflicts in the process become more obvious. Misinterpretations of wording and instructions can be corrected to further simplify the process. Effectively managing the process leads to reduced waste. Eventually the process becomes transparent*.

7. **KPI**

Every key process has at least one KPI. The importance of KPIs is described in criteria in earlier sections of this chapter.

8. **Audit**

A key process is audited at least annually either by the owner of the process or by a third party. It is difficult to recognize gaps in performance

* Van Nuland, Yves and Duffy, Grace L. *Professional Process Management*, The Quality Management Forum, ASQ Quality Management Division, Milwaukee, WI (2019) vol 45 number 4 pp. 1–11.

in activities that are seen every day. Someone not directly involved with the daily tasks can more easily see imperfections. A scheduled program of process audits allows the organization to make gradual and continuous improvement. Integrating continuous improvement into daily activities is the most effective way to sustain performance.

9. **Maturity level of process**

The concept of maturity levels for process management is explained in Chapter 2. There is a logical sequence of actions that allow an organization to increase their level of operating maturity over time.

Thus far, Chapter 3 has described the first three components of a Best Practice: enabler (PDCA), results, and process management. The fourth and last assessment component is the *description of the format.*

3.4 Assessment of the *Format* of a Best Practice

The last point in the complete assessment of a Best Practice is how the Best Practice is described and documented. There are 13 criteria for the format that can be examined. The objective is not to create a lengthy document, but a document that is precise and explains all the characteristics described in the BEST-tool.

The details of how to write a Best Practice are shared in Chapter 4. Table 3.4 introduces the table of criteria for the *assessment* of the *format* of a Best Practice.

3.5 Use of the *BEST-Tool* (Complete and Detailed Checklist)

Chapter 2 explained the content of the BEST-method and introduced the requirements of a true Best Practice. The criteria are separated into components of: Enabler, Results, Process, and Format. All four components are brought together in a comprehensive Excel checklist. This set of Excel worksheets provides not only an overview of the complete assessment, but also a way to focus on the areas of strength and improvement. Excel spreadsheets containing these checklists are available free to the reader on the author

Table 3.4 Assessment of the description of the *format* of a best practice

	Subject	*NOK*	*OK*	*Comments*
1	Title			
2	Subject			
3	Author (name, title, company, contact)			
4	Context (sector, country restrictions)			
5	Description of the method and results			
6	Measurement method			
7	Process description and maturity			
8	KPIs and results			
9	Distribution of the results			
10	Cause and effect			
11	Measurement: RADAR*, PDCA, or other			
12	Limiting conditions			
13	Date and Revision Level			

Legend: KPI = key performance indicator; NOK = not complete; OK = complete; PDCA = Plan-Do-Check-Act

* The RADAR logic provides a structured approach to question the performance of an organization. It also supports the scoring mechanism behind the EFQM Excellence Award. Source : efqm.org.

website. Refer to information in the Introduction to this text for links to the downloadable materials.

The Excel table represented in Figure 3.3 consists of four sections, including:

Enabler: 22 criteria and 44 characteristics
Results: 7 criteria and 20 characteristics
Process: 9 criteria
Format: 13 criteria

Is such a detailed framework necessary to assess a Best Practice? Remember: we use the full BEST-tool only for those processes which are key for success and contribute in a positive way to the achievement of the strategy of the organization. It is only through comprehensive analysis and improvement can we establish and manage excellent processes (enablers) (Figure 3.4).

		Criteria and characteristics	0%	25%	50%	75%	100%	Not described	Comments
1	Plan	**Description**							
		· The approach is repeatable and based on reliable data and information							
		· The core process are identified and described							
		· The methods are documented							
		· The process is the reflection of common sense and is well thought out (logical sequence, clearly linked to organizational strategy, interactions with other processes and sub-processes)							
2		**Stakeholders**							
		• The process is tailored to the needs, requirements and expectations of interested parties (stakeholders)							
		• The indicators and targets are set and the relationship with the core process is clearly defined							
3		**Responsibilities**							
		• The responsibilities and accountabilities are clearly defined							
		• Each process has a process owner							
		• The process description takes into account the skills and experiences required by the persons responsible for carrying out the process and approaches							
4		**KPI's and PI's**							
		• Each process contains one or more KPI's (Key Performance Indicator) and one or more PI's (Performance Indicator)							
5		**Deployment and Segmentation**							
		• The description of the process and approaches considers the specificities of all segments of the organization (division, department, work unit) and the variety of products and services							
6		**Prevention**							
		• Prevention is built into the process							
		• The core process description takes into account the specific circumstances of the organization and prevention is integrated into the daily work							
7		**Benchmarking**							
		• The process description takes into account similar benchmarks and best-in-class examples							
8		**Data**							
		• The measurement methods are described clearly and unambiguously, including securing the relevance, integrity and reliability of the measurement results							
		• The data are presented at the proper level of segmentation to effectively reflect performance and results at different levels of the organization.							

		Criteria and characteristics	0%	25%	50%	75%	100%	Not described	Comments
1	DO	**Implementation**							
		• The daily activities are in conformance with the process descriptions and documented methods							
		• The implementation of the core process is integrated into the t daily work							
2		**Deployment**							
		• The approach is used by all appropriate work units							
3		**Cause-effect**							
		• The use of the key process leads to concrete and measurable results							
4		**Accountability**							
		• All employees and managers clearly exhibit how they are responsible and accountable for their assigned tasks							
5		**SMART**							
		• KPI's and PI's are used systematically							
		• SMART decisions are taken and action plans are developed							

Figure 3.3 Criteria for the evaluation of the *approaches (enablers)* of a Best Practice process. Use of BEST-tool (complete and detailed checklist).

		Criteria and characteristics	0%	25%	50%	75%	100%	Not described	Comments
Check	1	**Integration** • Plans, process, results, analysis, learning and actions are harmonized across processes and work units to support organization-wide goals							
	2	**Monitoring** • The performance of each core process is regularly measured and monitored							
		• The obtained results related to a core process are regularly discussed with all relevant stakeholders							
		• The method to determine the target value of the KPI (target) is validated and opportunities for improvement are recorded							
		• Relevance, integrity, completeness and reliability of the results achieved are checked							
	3	**Audit** • Each process owner audits his or her core process regularly							
		• The process owner examines what can be done to bring the core process to a higher maturity level (to determine improvement opportunities)							
	4	**Adjustment and Learning** • Deviations from the desired and/or planned results serve as input for the improvement and revision of the core process and/or approaches							
		• Identification of problems related to the sufficient availability and appropriate resources such as budget, machinery, equipment, provisions, tools, and Information Technology (software, hardware, networking, security, etc.)							
		• Identification of an adequate number of employees and/or of shortcomings of skills and experiences of employees in the process and/or approaches							
		• Comparison of the results obtained with the benchmark and Best-in-Class							
		• Prioritization of opportunities for improvement							
		• Encouragement of breakthrough change to the approach applied through innovation							

		Criteria and characteristics	0%	25%	50%	75%	100%	Not described	Comments
Act	1	**Improvement** • The output of the measurement and learning is analyzed and used to identify additional improvements; to prioritize, to plan and to implement these further opportunities for improvement							
	2	**Process** • The process, methods and approaches are revised and improved in response to the findings gained in the Check phase							
	3	**Resources** • The amount and nature of the resources that were adjusted because of the findings in the Check phase are documented							
		• The number of employees assigned to the process is adjusted considering the opportunities of improvement and the outcome of the process, methods and approaches							
	4	**Knowledge and Experience** • New training and/or refresher training is given to meet the findings gained in the Check phase							
		• Sharing of refinements and innovations with other relevant work units and processes							
		• The Knowledge and experience of those involved in the process are documented and validated as Best-in-Class or Benchmark level							
	5	**Benchmark** • The organization can be set as a model for other organizations							

Figure 3.3 (Continued) Criteria for the evaluation of the *approaches (enablers)* of a Best Practice process. Use of BEST-tool (complete and detailed checklist).

KPI	Key Performance Indicator (this has a direct relationship with the strategy of the organization).
PI	Performance Indicator (several performance indicators contribute to the validity of a KPI).
SMART	This is an acronym and stands for **S**pecific, **M**easurable, **A**ssignable (Accountable), **R**elevant and **T**imely executed

x	For each of these 7 criteria you can make an **estimation** of the score

Scores

0	No evidence or anecdotal
25%	Some evidence
50%	Evidence described
75%	Significant evidence described
100%	Can be considered as benchmark and a world-class approach

Figure 3.3 (Continued) Criteria for the evaluation of the *approaches (enablers)* of a Best Practice process. Use of BEST-tool (complete and detailed checklist).

	Criteria and characteristics	0%	25%	50%	75%	100%	Not described	Comments
1	**Scope and Relevance** • The results are aligned with the expectations • The results are aligned with policy and strategy • The most important key results are identified • The relation between the results is understood							
2	**Integrity of data** • Results are timely • Results are reliable and accurate							
3	**Segmentation** • Results are segmented in a suitable manner o By region, country o By department, business line, division, unit o By product and service type							
4	**Trends** • Trends are positive for 5 years or more • Results are sustainable and show good							
5	**Targets** • Targets for core results are set • Targets are suitable • Targets are achieved							
6	**Comparisons with targets and benchmarks** • Comparisons for core results are made • Comparisons are suitable • Comparisons are favorable							
7	**Cause-effect** • The results are clearly achieved through the • The relations between results achieved and * Based on the evidence presented, it is assured							

x	For each of these 7 criteria you can make an **estimation** of the score

Scores

0	No evidence or anecdotal
25%	Some evidence
50%	Evidence described
75%	Significant evidence described
100%	Can be considered as benchmark and a world-class approach

Figure 3.4 Criteria for the evaluation of the *results* of a Best Practice process (complete and detailed checklist).

The first step for assessing a case study as a Best Practice is to read the document. Once the document has been read through completely, use the sequence of Excel tables, row by row, and characteristic by characteristic to assess whether the information required to follow a Best Practice is available within the document. Score each characteristic as indicated by the columns from 0% to 100% or Not Described. Add comments as appropriate to help remember any details useful for implementing the Best Practice characteristic.

Chapter 5 presents examples of how the BEST-tool is applied in the complete and detailed format.

3.6 Use of the *BEST Quick Scan* Tool

The first part of Chapter 3 describes the *complete and detailed BEST-tool checklist*. The detailed checklist consists of 22 criteria and 44 characteristics for the *enabler* component and 7 criteria and 20 characteristics for the *results* component. Finally, you have 9 criteria for the *management of the process* component and 13 criteria for the *format of the process* component.

However, there are many case studies or project reports that are too short to apply this detailed checklist. The case study was probably not intended to present a full Best Practice, but only share information for recognition or other reporting purposes. For these documents, the authors have developed a shorter checklist, i.e. BEST Quick Scan. This abbreviated tool considers only the 7 criteria for the Results and 22 criteria for the Enabler. Process and Format criteria are considered in the same way as the detailed BEST-tool checklist. Figure 3.5 illustrates the BEST Quick Scan criteria.

When analyzing a true Best Practice which has been described in detail, the BEST-tool (detailed checklist) is the appropriate choice. When researching a shorter document, it is more effective to use the BEST Quick Scan. This easier and faster tool provides a high-level assessment to decide whether there is enough data to warrant contacting the document author for further information.

The authors learned after applications of assessment of numerous examples of so-called Best Practices, to first apply the BEST Quick Scan tool because you can have an initial overview of the extent of Best Practice in less than 20 minutes. From this assessment you can decide to continue and apply the complete and detailed BEST-tool. We have seen that more than 90% of the co-called Best Practices on the Internet can be better assessed

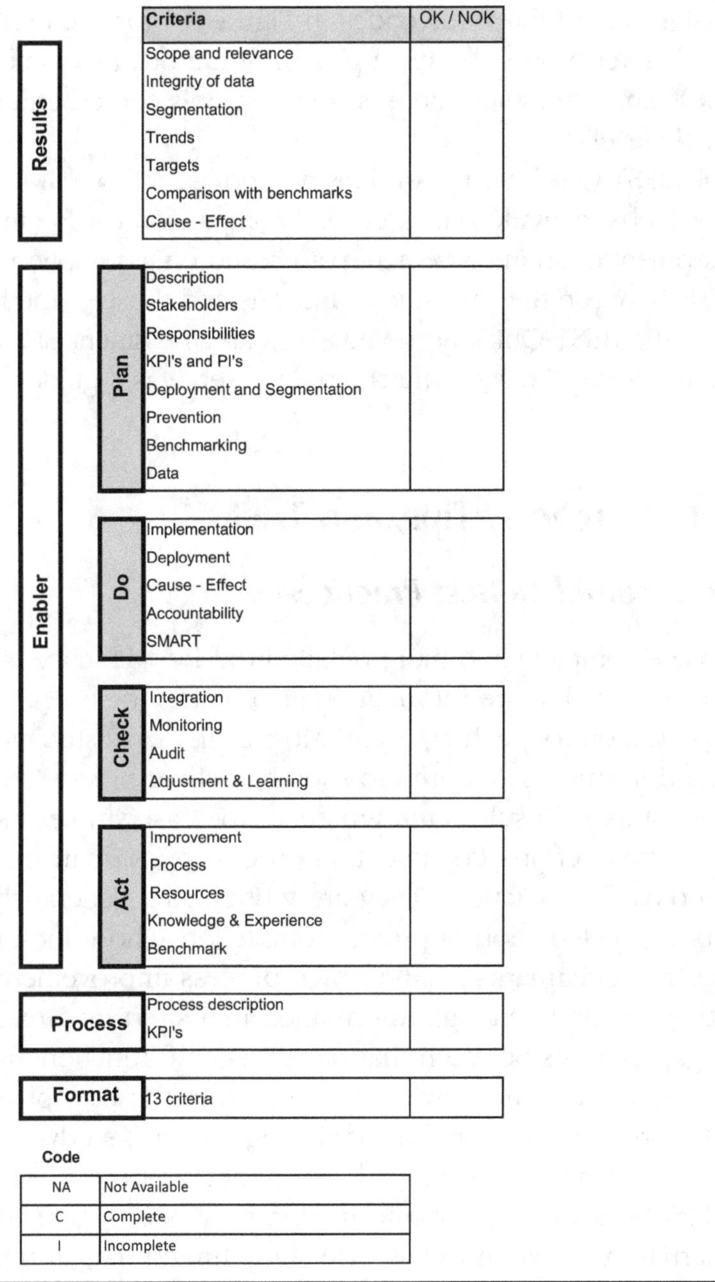

Figure 3.5 BEST Quick Scan (checklist).

with the BEST Quick Scan. Reason: these are not Best Practices at all. Realize that we can only draw conclusions based upon the text available on the Internet. We cannot assume more than is presented in the materials posted. Perhaps in the real context of that organization it could be a real Best Practice.

Assign one of the three codes in Figure 3.5 for each criterion listed in the table. Chapter 6 provides examples of numerous assessments using the BEST Quick Scan. Assessment here is done on only the criteria level, not the characteristic level.

The BEST Quick Scan tool does not require a score. If researching the case study as a benchmark, only a general comparison can be made, prompting the development of an improvement plan based on assumptions made in a gap analysis between the case study functions and those of the benchmarking company. If the BEST Quick Scan is used as an assessment of a case study being written as a Best Practice, the criteria will serve as a guide to improve the text.

3.7 Experiences, Tips, and Tricks

3.7.1 Incomplete Best Practices

The more complete and more detailed the Best Practice is, the better it can be assessed. More information also makes it easier to comment upon the application for each criterion. Most of the case studies of Best Practices analyzed in this book were too short to deliver precise comments. This is not meant as an insult to the writers of the case studies used. It is simply to say that most reports documenting process performance are not written to be used as Best Practices. They are written as a general sharing of process results or a celebration of project completion. Those looking to use case studies as benchmarks for their own process improvement should be aware that there is rarely enough information in a short document to perform a valid gap analysis between that organizational function and their own.

As mentioned earlier, when the criteria in the Plan phase are weak, it is not worthwhile to continue analyzing the case study. In Chapters 5 and 6, the authors chose to apply all components of the BEST-tool or the BEST Quick Scan, knowing that information was missing. Our premise was that the partial information in the case study hinted that stronger data existed within the organization. Several of the examples in Chapters 5 and 6 suggest that an on-site visit would uncover the missing information.

From our experience the criteria in the Enabler and Results components, often weakly or not developed, are described in Table 3.5.

It is possible that the information has been developed, but not included in the documented case study. Often, an on-site visit or a scripted interview will uncover the required information.

Table 3.5 Criteria in the Enabler and Results components often weakly described

Plan	Description, stakeholders, responsibilities, KPIs, segmentation, prevention, benchmarking, and data
Do	Cause and effect, accountability, SMART measures
Check	Audit, adjustment, and learning
Act	Processes, resources, knowledge and experience, benchmark
Results	Scope and relevance, integrity of data, trends, targets, comparisons, cause and effect

Legend: KPI = key performance indicator

3.7.2 Complete Best Practices

A *complete* Best Practice consists of the four following components:

1. Description of the enabler (this text uses the PDCA sequence)
2. Description of the results
3. Description of the process
4. Format of the Best Practice

It is unrealistic to expect to achieve 100% in each characteristic in the checklist. A perfect organization does not exist. Be satisfied if the case study complies with approximately 75–80% of all the characteristics of the BEST-tool. An 80% score is reflective of a true Best Practice. Any process assessed at an 80% level is something to be proud of.

3.7.3 Scores

Scores in the BEST-tool suggest to what extent a criterion or characteristic has been developed or where improvements are necessary.

The tool gives *rough estimates* such as 0%, 25%, 50%, 75%, and 100% of whether the characteristic is completely described. It is not necessary to be exacting on these estimates. It is more the first impression of how completely the characteristic is described that is important. The authors recommend the assessor spend no more than one minute per criterion in scoring it. Ten seconds would be even better.

The objective is not to achieve a 100% rating in each characteristic. Case studies published by recipients of the US Malcolm Baldrige Award or the European Foundation for Quality Model Excellence Award reflect scores in a range of 60–70%. A score of 100% should only be given if the criterion or characteristic is fully developed. Do not spend significant energy and time in the scoring process.

We urge the reader *not* to use the BEST-tool for publicly scoring a Best Practice written by another. The objective of the BEST-method is to help the reader understand the requirements for developing and implementing a true Best Practice. The criteria and characteristics are guides to develop the approach (enabler), measures (results), process, and format to implement and document a Best Practice of their own.

3.7.4 Realistic Tool

The authors realize that the rigors of the BEST-tool may appear overwhelming. The objective is *not* to find weaknesses or to make judgments about whether a case study is a Best Practice. The real objective of the book is to discover where improvements are feasible (compared with the ideal situation) and how to document a Best Practice so it can be used by others for their improvement efforts.

An unexpected advantage of the BEST-tool is the recognition that a professional tool is needed to measure the degree of excellence of a Best Practice. Most of the case studies researched as a Best Practice are not complete enough to achieve an excellent rating. Comparison with the characteristics of a Best Practice is intended to highlight opportunities for improvement.

Chapter 4

Writing a Best Practice

There are four reasons to write a detailed Best Practice:

1. Systematic documentation of a true Best Practice is the foundation for benchmarking and sharing excellence with third parties.
2. While describing the specifics of the Best Practice, you will be referring to the BEST-tool. The criteria in the BEST-tool will highlight further opportunities for improvement beyond the excellence currently being documented.
3. The Best Practice, when documented in this systematic way, can be used for training purposes. New hires learn the process more quickly and effectively.
4. Visibility of the Best Practice develops pride in their work for all involved in the process. They are recognized for building an excellent approach and obtaining excellent results.

4.1 What Is a Best Practice?

So as not to focus too narrowly, we identify a few precise definitions that serve as the basis for what a Best Practice is. Though the term Best Practice can be applied to topics relating to products or procedures, we are focused on Best Practice as it relates to *processes*, which encompasses a broader view of systems within an organization.

The authors make no judgments in this book. Therefore, we don't like to use the word "good," because this is a judgment. We offer the reader a tool to assess his process, which, if it scores highly from the assessment, is called a Best Practice. The process owner will discover the *degree of excellence* of his process through sustainable results. It is up to the process owner to judge whether these results are good enough to be shared as a Best Practice.

There is a second reason why we don't like the term "Good Practice." There is a risk that people become complacent in using this term. They stop improving their process. Is top management of an organization really satisfied with mediocre results? It is important that there be a difference between mediocre processes and a process under improvement on the journey toward excellence.

In our opinion, the following few definitions in management literature convey most precisely the purpose and characteristics of a true Best Practice:

Best Practices are "those practices that have been shown to produce superior results; selected by a systematic process; and assessed as exemplary, well or successfully demonstrated."*

A best practice is a technique or methodology that, through experience and research, has proven to reliably lead to a desired result.†

Best practices are often exemplary behaviors modeled into processes. Conceptually, best practices are ethical, legal, fair, replicable, and applicable to anyone within an organization … therefore they are "Good Practices." But they are not only "Good Practices." They are "Best Practices," because their implementation aims at improving an organization's performance through additional accountability, compliance, transparency, and risk control.‡

Those methods or techniques that have consistently shown results superior to those achieved with other means in a given situation and that could be adapted for other situations *can be considered as Best Practice*. This must be shown to work effectively and produce successful outcomes by the evidence provided by subjective and objective data sources.§

Best Practice definitions often focus on the ability of a method or process to consistently show superior results. We believe Best Practice is about using approaches that not only deliver superior results but also consider sustainability and ongoing development of the approach.

---

* Dani, S., Harding, J. A., Case, K., Young, R. I. M., Cochrane, S., Gao, J. and Baxter, D. A methodology for best practice knowledge management. *Proceedings of the Institution of Mechanical Engineers, Part B: Journal of Engineering Manufacture*, 2006, 220 (10), 1717–1728. doi:10.1243/09544054JEM651 (original quotes taken from APQC, specific document unknown).

† https://searchsoftwarequality.techtarget.com/definition/best-practice accessed 23 April 2020

‡ https://www.answers.com/Q/what_are_best_practices accessed 23 April 2020.

§ Dani, S., Harding, J. A., Case, K., Young, R. I. M., Cochrane, S., Gao, J. and Baxter, D. A methodology for best practice knowledge management. *Proceedings of the Institution of Mechanical Engineers, Part B: Journal of Engineering Manufacture*, 2006, 220 (10), 1717–1728. doi:10.1243/09544054JEM651. (original quotes taken from APQC, specific document unknown).

According to Hackett Benchmarking,* a Best Practice must:

1) Place the company in a top percentile ranking within its industry.
2) Leverage and take advantage of technology.
3) Improve quality and speed, and also lower costs.
4) Give management more control and influence.
5) And finally, it has to be working; i.e. it is planned and implemented.

The Hackett Best Practices are based on unparalleled database of more than 13,000 empirical studies from 3,500 participating organizations around the globe. Best Practices are defined as:

- Aligns with strategy.
- Reduces costs.
- Improves productivity.
- Promotes timely execution.
- Enables better decision making.
- Leverages/exploits existing/emerging technologies.
- Ensures acceptable levels of control and risk management.
- Optimizes the skills and capabilities of the organization.†

To clarify our target for these Best Practices, we are not referring to the use of Standard Operating Procedures (SOPs) which serve to provide a very specific written procedure used to perform a job function, whether that is assembly of a product or a machine or an administrative procedure. These functions might collectively be part of a larger system within the company and therefore part of a process, but they are not targets for our pursuit of Best Practices in the scope of this book.

4.2 A High-Level Sequence for Developing and Writing a Best Practice

Writing the Best Practice case study is the terminating activity of a cycle of process improvement. It is not the end of continuous improvement. A Best Practice shares the excellence achieved by the organization based on using

* https://exinfm.com/board/define_best_practices.htm accessed 23 April 2020
† Defining Best Practices. https://www.thehackettgroup.com/best-practices/ accessed 23 April 2020

the BEST-method or other improvement approach. The suggested sequence of events to achieve a Best Practice process performance level is:

1. Assess the current process using the BEST Quick Scan tool to identify major opportunities for improvement (see examples of Quick Scan use in Chapter 6).
2. Use a preferred improvement model, such as the Plan-Do-Check-Act to close the identified gaps in performance.
3. Employ the detailed BEST-tool criteria to fine-tune the process as described in Chapters 5 and 7.
4. Iterative cycles of assessment and improvement will guide the organization to at least Level 4 process maturity.
5. Sustainability measures and trending should be available for at least 5 years to qualify as a Best Practice.
6. Maintain documentation and control measures to show the effects of either continuous or breakthrough improvement achieved during the Best Practice journey.

Many organizations are already on the Best Practice journey and will enter the above sequence of events mid-stream. This was the situation in the case study described in Chapter 7 Orange County Health Department. One of the authors assisted the client in improvements to an existing process using the PDCA-cycle without the benefit of the BEST-method. A BEST-method Quick Scan 12 years after the project was completed indicated that the process qualified as a Best Practice and highlighted gaps in the documentation that needed to be addressed before the process could be properly documented. Chapter 7 describes the final iterations of improvement and sustainability measures.

4.3 Documenting a Best Practice Case Study

According to the Total Quality Management (TQM)* philosophy a process is only reliable and repeatable if it is well described and standardized. A Best Practice is completely described through the 13 elements listed in Table 4.1.

* Wescott, R. T. and Duffy, G. L. *The Certified Quality Improvement Associate Handbook*, 3rd ed., Quality Press, Milwaukee, WI, (2015), p. 91.

Table 4.1 Best Practice – Standardized Presentation of a Best Practice

1. Title
2. Subject
3. Author (name, title, company, contact)
4. Context (sector, country restrictions)
5. Description of the method and results
6. Measurement method
7. Process description and maturity
8. KPIs (key performance indicator) and results
9. Distribution of the results
10. Cause and effect
11. Assessment of enabler and results
12. Conditions
13. Date and revision level

Use the following descriptions as a guide for documenting the recommended components of a Best Practice.

4.3.1 Title

Brief and precise description of what the Best Practice is about.

Good example: "Energy consumption in a paper mill of company ABC."

Bad example: "Energy consumption in a factory." This is too general.

4.3.2 Subject

Description (maximum 15 lines) of the subject of the Best Practice. What are the requirements, and which are the most important ones? This section also explains the scope of the process and any limiting conditions.

After reading this short text, the reader should have enough information to decide whether this example might be useful and worth reading.

4.3.3 Author

Provide practical information about the author:

- First and last name
- Function

- Company and address
- Contact information for the author (telephone, phone, and e-mail)

It is helpful to put the name and other information about the process owner into the Best Practice document. This is useful for contacting the author of the Best Practice.

4.3.4 Context

An organization or company does not exist on an island, but is embedded within a specific sector, region, or country. There are also special situations in a country that have an impact on the Best Practice. The reader must understand the local circumstances before deciding whether to take ideas from the Best Practice (Table 4.2).

For Belgians, this data may be obvious, but for foreign visitors, this may not be so. When comparing a Best-in-Class case study, you should always consider the context and understand how the company achieved the results based on their own operating conditions.

It is risky to blindly copy a Best Practice. Consider your own context. It is frequently necessary to translate the Best Practice into your own work situation.

Be aware that in addition to country- and sector-specific constraints, company culture plays an important role.

Table 4.2 Contextual conditions in Belgium

• High productivity
• High quality of education system
• Strong unions
• High energy costs
• Slow delivery of licenses
• High taxes and social contributions
• Extensive social system, including various systems of leave
• Multilingualism
• Many universities of high quality
• Outstanding and affordable health care system
• Strong networking between leaders and managers
• For some sectors Belgium is a world leader, e.g. pharmaceuticals

BOX 4.1 Example of Company Culture and Leadership

People in a defensive organization will not gain much from the application of the BEST- method in assessing their best practice. They have difficulties in accepting the messages from the BEST-assessment. They don't like to hear that a number of things can be done differently. The probability that they will realize a Best Practice in the short or long term is low.

On the other hand, people working in an organization where constructive thinking styles are very well developed will be more ready to accept the findings (criteria and characteristics) from the BEST-method. They are open to discover areas for improvement. They also make action plans to improve the process. The probability of achieving a real Best Practice is high in this case.

Company culture is strongly dependent on the thinking styles and behaviors of the leaders.

4.3.5 Description of the Method and Results

The method is described in detail. A detailed description doesn't mean that you need to provide a lot of organizational details (history, list of products and services, description of the installations, equipment and buildings, etc.). Try to answer the questions:

- What contributes directly to the achievement of the objectives of the Best Practice?
- Which factors have an influence on the results?
- How is this process aligned with the Business and Strategic Plan?

The text needs to be precise and balanced.

The owner of the Best Practice can use the BEST-tool (detailed checklist) as a *guideline* to describe his Best Practice. By doing so he avoids missing important characteristics.

BOX 4.2 Impact of Company Culture on Customer Complaint Process

An industrial company where a Best Practice is developed has a *constructive organizational culture*, i.e. the *constructive thinking styles* are dominant. This culture is characterized by values such as integrity, team spirit, trust, empathy, respect, self-actualization, entrepreneurial spirit, open-mindedness, prevention, and pro-activity.

An organization structured in a hierarchical way with more developed *defensive thinking styles* might face difficulties in translating the BEST-method into their culture. The following values are most prevalent in a defensive thinking organization: conformist, distrust, individualism, reactivity (fire fighting), criticism, avoidance, skepticism, gossip, power, and dependence.

When the Best Practice describes a process where frequent human interactions are involved, the company culture can have a tremendous impact on the way the process is managed. In a defensive culture the customer complaint treatment will be handled in an ad hoc way. While in a constructive culture a totally different approach is followed. They ask questions like "How can we avoid a similar complaint in the future and how do we build prevention into the process?" People living in a defensive company culture will not grasp the importance of such questions and will not investigate longer-term solutions.

Defensive cultures have difficulty understanding the role leaders play in support of a proactive customer complaint process.

If the Best Practice is well written, the reader should be able to make a translation to his own situation based on this documentation. After investigating numerous Best Practices, the authors see that often the descriptions are far too vague and therefore not useful (in the sense of the definition of Best Practice described in Chapter 1).

Besides the description of the method used, the Best Practice also shows the results achieved. These are the outputs and outcomes of the method used. A clear *cause and effect* relationship must exist between actions (enablers) and results. However, in many cases, it is difficult to put this relationship into words. To be useful to others, the method and ensuing results must be described at the level where the reader can see why decisions were made for specific actions (e.g. per segment, by region, by country, by type of customer, by product type, etc.).

4.3.6 Measurement Method

Effective decisions can only be made based on correct principles, criteria, methods, and results. This implies that the results are described in detail:

- Precision of the measurement method. What is the measurement error?
- Significant results. Are the results appropriate and reliable?
- Representative results. To what extent do the results of the sample reflect the results of the population?
- Random sample. Is the sample taken *at random* and does it reflect the composition of the population?
- Calibration method. Which calibration method was used? What standards were employed?
- Reproducible results. Are consistent results achieved if there are multiple users?

If a standardized method is used, such as ISO* or ASTM,† you need mention only the title of the referenced method.

4.3.7 Process Description

In many cases it is useful to develop the description by creating a flowchart of the process. This allows the reader to see immediately if the method is simple and robust, if the methods are foolproof and where problems might arise.

4.3.8 Maturity of the Process

The owner of a process documented as a Best Practice should audit the process on a regular basis. Best Practices are those that are assessed at the highest levels of organizational maturity. Figure 4.1 is a duplicate of an example of maturity levels covered in Chapter 2.

A Best Practice is assessed at least at a maturity Level 4. As stated before, the authors find that often executives think they have a Best Practice, although they have only achieved a maturity Level 2 or 3. It is not enough to have good plans (e.g. a description of a procedure in accordance with ISO 9001 is considered a maturity Level 3), you must demonstrate that the procedures not only give the desired and planned results, but these procedures are systematically revised and improved. For example, any error in a product or service is an occasion for a revision of the process, procedure, and/or instruction (Level 4).

---

* International Organization for Standardization, https://www.iso.org/home.html accessed 23 April 2020

† ASTM International offers global access to fully transparent standards development. https://www.astm.org/BOOKSTORE/BOS/index.html accessed 23 April 2020

Levels	Description
0	**Non-existent** Within the organization there are no or very little management measures. Control awareness is rather low and only few actions are taken to achieve an adequate system of organizational management (internal control system).
1	**Ad-hoc basis** Only ad-hoc management measures are in place within the organization. The awareness of the need for appropriate management (internal control) is growing, but there is still no structured or standardized approach present. The system of organizational management (internal control) is more focused on people than on systems.
2	**Structured start** A structured impetus is given to the development of management measures. The management tools are therefore being developed but are not yet applied (Plan)
3	**Defined** (= level 2 + ...) Control measures are provided. These are standardized, documented, communicated and implemented (Do).
4	**Management system** (= level 3 + ...) The control measures are internally assessed and adjusted (Check & Act). There is a "living" adequate and effective system of organizational management.
5	**Optimized** (= level 4 + ...) The control measures are continuously optimized through benchmarking and obtaining quality certificates or external evaluations (PDCA).

Figure 4.1 Example of maturity levels of a process.*

In many cases, the *overall cycle time*, i.e. the time between the first step in the process until the last step in the process, is a very good measure of the efficiency of a process. After all, the total cycle time includes not only the steps with added value (for customers and end-users), but also all the steps which do not have an *added value* for the customer. The shorter the process, the more robust the process and the more reliable the results.

A process description which looks complicated is an indication that the process is probably not audited and improved often. Excellent processes are simple, transparent, short, and robust.

Pitfall: don't describe the process only in major blocks. This type of "high level" description may hide underlying complexity of activities and decisions. Provide enough detail of the process to show where enabling and control measures provide data for continuous improvement.

* Interne Audit Vlaamse Administratie, Annual report 2008, p. 63.

4.3.9 Key Performance Indicators (KPI) and Results

Once the measurement and calibration methods and process description reflecting the corresponding maturity level are provided, it is time to identify indicators and corresponding expected results.

The following are the required components of a Best Practice indicator:

- KPI title (KPI: Key Performance Indicator)
- Name and function of the KPI owner. This is a simple illustration to identify the accountability of the leader
- Objective, scope, and target of the indicator
- Relationship of the KPI to the strategy of the organization (alignment)
- Current results (in table and/or graph) reflected through the indicator for a period of 5 years or longer
- Segmentation of the results over the different departments and work units
- Interpretation and discussion of the results plus decisions and next action plan

4.3.10 Distribution of the Results

It may be useful to point out the standard deviation of the measurement parameter used. If the variation of the measurement is low, there is no reason to do so. However, in cases where the standard deviation is high, it is worthwhile to explain why the variation is so high and whether the distribution is normal or not. Often processes working with humans rather than machines have wider variation, such as healthcare or customer service activities.

Accurately reporting the variation in measurements and results is a good indicator that the company documenting their Best Practice is at the level of maturity where processes and systems are so well defined that the data can be gathered and analyzed reliably.

4.3.11 Cause and Effect

As mentioned above, the description of cause and effect between enabler and result is important. It is imperative to show that the results planned are caused by the chosen approach and not achieved through ad hoc interventions.

If the Best Practice is documented using the criteria and characteristics mentioned thus far in this book, the reader of the Best Practice can see the consistency of the approach, the logic between approach and results, and the relationship of measurements, results, and strategy.

4.3.12 Assessment of Enabler and Results

As you assign a maturity level to a process, you can also attribute a degree of excellence for the methods (enablers) used and results achieved. Chapter 3 describes the use of the BEST-tool for assessment of enabler and results. The strengths and areas for improvement in your Best Practice are immediately apparent.

4.3.13 Limiting Conditions

Limiting conditions and preconditions are mostly *internal factors* such as staff education, level of technological expertise, and organizational design (e.g. centralized, decentralized, hierarchical, matrix structure, etc.). Limiting conditions influence the approach and implementation of a Best Practice, just as the context in which the business functions influences the method used and the results obtained.

Context conditions are usually *external factors* (taxes, licenses, climate conditions, industrial standards, etc.). Therefore, a Best Practice should mention both context and limiting conditions.

4.3.14 Date and Revision Number

Finally, specify the date and revision number of the Best Practice document. It is recommended that Best Practice documents reflect revision numbers, so you can immediately observe whether the owner of the Best Practice is applying continuous improvement. A small revision number indicates a slow evolution of the Best Practice method over time. If the Best Practice has not been updated to reflect improvements, it is questionable whether this description is truly a Best Practice.

4.4 How Many Best Practices?

Normally we should expect approximately one Best Practice update per year from a Level 4 (Management System) or Level 5 (Optimized Organization). After all, the Best Practice supports the achievement of the strategy of the organization. Systematic improvement of core processes is an indicator of long-term sustainability. It is *not* recommended that the organization dedicate the resources required to update all core process descriptions each year. This level of activity might prove disruptive to normal business operations.

Look for those processes which contribute the most to strategic growth. Over time, most organizations refine their Best Practices to those few, core processes that define their industry or product leadership. They focus on these core processes as critical to strategic growth and success.

The sequence for developing and writing a Best Practice described in this chapter should be a planned, iterative activity.

USE OF THE BEST-TOOL

Chapter 5

Use of the Detailed BEST-Tool: Three Case Studies

The authors hope you are benefiting from our book, *Validating a Best Practice: A Tool for Improvement and Benchmarking*. The website www.comatech.be offers you free downloads of the BEST-method assessment, i.e. the Quick Scan and the detailed BEST-tool (Excel spreadsheets).

In addition to providing you with the tools you need to achieve and maintain a Best Practice process, the authors also encourage you to share your Best Practice with us. There is an upload feature on this website to send your process description. We are gathering Best Practice examples for the next update to our book and will gladly consider yours for inclusion. When you upload your Best Practice, please include contact information so we can get back with you for further discussion. Thank you for your commitment to Best Practice!

This chapter provides three practical examples of how the full BEST-methodology can be applied:

a. Case study 1: Organizational culture change at Lion Nathan (Australia)
b. Case study 2: Corporate Social Responsibility (CSR) at Loblaw (Canada)
c. Case study 3: Dream Hotel

In this chapter we exhibit the full BEST-tool in *detailed* Best Practice assessments. The detailed BEST-assessment includes all the aspects comprising the BEST-tool, i.e. the following four building blocks:

1. Enabler: 22 criteria and 44 characteristics
2. Results: 7 criteria and 20 characteristics

3. Process: 9 criteria
4. Format: 13 criteria

The case studies have been chosen because the information shared by the writers of the case study is comprehensive enough to show the full strength of the BEST-tool. The authors of this text have no connection with the corporations represented by the first two case studies. The third case study is a didactic example originating from our imagination and creativity.

5.1 Case Study 1 Organizational Culture Change at Lion Nathan (Australia)

Source of the case study: *In Great Company, Unlocking the Secrets of Cultural Transformation*
Authors: Quentin Jones, Dexter Dunphy, Rosalie Fishman, Margherita Larné, and Corinne Canter
A Human Synergistics Publication (2011) ISBN 0-9775753-0-6.

The main subject of this case study, selected from *In Great Company*, is how a company can change its organizational culture and what this change delivers to the company, employees, and customers. Because of this specific focus, little information is given for the other organizational stakeholders.

This case study is not an example of the management of an operational process, but rather an illustration of the management of a process of transformation in the organizational culture of a company.

5.1.1 Who is Lion Nathan?

Lion Nathan is an Australia-based beverages company, with operations primarily in Australia and New Zealand. Lion Nathan's core purpose is "To make our world a more sociable place" and its vision is "To be the leading alcoholic beverage company in Australia and New Zealand." It brews and distributes around 9 million hectoliters of beer annually.

In addition to its beer and wine businesses, Lion Nathan is involved in several related businesses in Australia and New Zealand. These include the distribution of licensed wine and spirits brands, the production and distribution of Ready-to-Drink beverages (RTD), liquor retailing, and malt extraction for home brewing and the food industry.

5.1.2 Organization of Lion Nathan

Two thousand eight hundred people in Australia, New Zealand, the USA, and the UK and an annual revenue of A$1.8 billion.

5.1.3 History

Lion Nathan started their cultural transformation process in 1998 after suffering heavy financial losses in previous years. The authors of this text first assessed a 2006 case study of the Lion Nathan cultural transformation. That case study was already at a level of excellence to warrant inclusion as a Best Practice for the purposes of the BEST-tool. Upon communicating with Human Synergistics, it was discovered that Lion Nathan has continued its improvement journey with even more strength reflected in a 2011 case study, also published by Human Synergistics. This chapter recognizes the performance results of both the 2006 initial improvements and the 2011 continuous improvement results.

5.1.4 Three Pillars of Cultural Transformation Strategy

- Creating a sense of purpose, vision, and values. The values of Lion Nathan are
  - Act with integrity
  - Face reality
  - Passion for the business
  - Achieving together
  - Being sociable
- Developing leadership capability
- Reinforcing the desired behaviors through people management processes and systems.

5.1.5 Leadership Drives Cultural Transformation

In Lion Nathan's view the primary determinant of the culture of a team is the leadership style of its leaders. Lion Nathan developed and delivered its own leadership development program based upon four levers:

- A motivating sense of purpose
- Talent management

- Future focus
- Creating a high-performance culture, using the *Organizational Culture Inventory*® (OCI®) template*

5.1.6 Human Synergistics Measurement Instruments

Organizational culture† is defined as "The behavioral norms and expectation, shaped in part by shared values and beliefs, that guide organizational members in how they should approach their work and interact with one another." The Organizational Culture Inventory® (OCI®)‡ was used to quantify these "behavioral norms and expectations."

Styles toward the top of the circumplex (12 styles in a circle) reflect behavioral expectations directed toward higher-order needs for growth and satisfaction (also called Constructive styles). Those toward the bottom of the circumplex illustrated in Figure 5.1 reflect behavioral expectations that focus on meeting lower-order needs for security (also called Defensive styles).

5.1.7 Organizational Culture Inventory® (OCI®)

Styles located on the right side of the circumplex (1 o'clock to 6 o'clock) reflect expected *behaviors directed to interactions with people.* Styles located on the left side (7 o'clock to 12 o'clock) reflect expectations regarding *task-related behaviors* (Figure 5.1).

The circumplex can further be divided into three parts:§

- Constructive Cultures (11 o'clock to 2 o'clock)

  Constructive cultures in which members are encouraged to interact with others and approach tasks in ways that will help them to meet their higher-order satisfaction needs (including Achievement (style 11

* *Organizational Culture Inventory*® is a registered trademark of Human Synergistics International. OCI® Circumplex from Robert A. Cooke and J. Clayton Lafferty, *Organizational Culture Inventory*®, Human Synergistics International. Copyright © 1987–2015. All Rights Reserved. Used by permission. www.humansynergistics.com.

† Cooke, R. A. and Szumal, J. L. *Measuring Normative Beliefs and Shared Behavioral Expectations in Organizations: The Reliability and Validity of the Organizational Culture Inventory*®, Psychological Reports, 72, (1993) pp. 1299–1330.

‡ Cooke, R. A. and Lafferty, J. C. *Organizational Culture Inventory*® *(OCI*®*),* Human Synergistics Plymouth, MI, (1987).

§ OCI® style names and descriptions are from Robert A. Cooke, Ph.D. and J. Clayton Lafferty, Ph.D., Organizational Culture Inventory®, Human Synergistics International, Plymouth, MI. Copyright © 1987–2020. All Rights Reserved. Used by permission.

Organizational Culture Inventory
N=1192

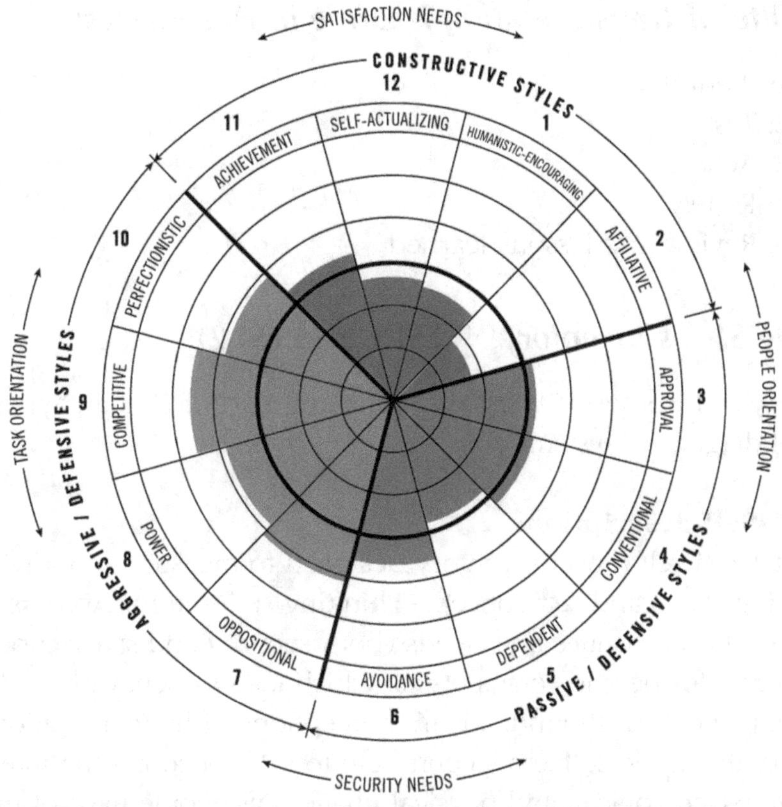

Figure 5.1 ***Organizational Culture Inventory*® (OCI®) of Lion Nathan represented in a circumplex (situation 1998). Lion Nathan – Actual Culture 1998.**

o'clock), Self-Actualizing (style 12 o'clock), Humanistic-Encouraging (style 1 o'clock), and Affiliative (style 2 o'clock) cultural norms).

- Passive/Defensive Cultures (3 o'clock to 6 o'clock)

  Passive/Defensive Cultures in which members believe they must interact with people in defensive ways that will not threaten their own security (includes Approval (style 3 o'clock), Conventional (style 4 o'clock), Dependent (style 5 o'clock), and Avoidance (style 6 o'clock) cultural norms).

- Aggressive/Defensive Cultures (7 o'clock to 10 o'clock)

  Aggressive/Defensive Cultures in which members are expected to approach tasks in forceful ways to protect their status and security (includes Oppositional (style 7 o'clock), Power (style 8 o'clock),

Competitive (style 9 o'clock), and Perfectionistic (style 10 o'clock) cultural norms).

5.1.8 Cultural Transformation is Done in Five Phases:*

Phase 1: Pre-test
Phase 2: Test
Phase 3: Action
Phase 4: Re-test
Phase 5: Review and lessons learned

5.1.9 Life Styles Inventory™ (LSI 1 and LSI 2)†

The Life Styles Inventory ™ (LSI) is an integral part of Human Synergistics' multi-level diagnostic system‡.

- **LSI 1 Self-description**
  LSI 1 is a self-report inventory designed to measure an individual's thinking styles and self-concept. Thinking styles are viewed as a combination of values and needs (both security and satisfaction) and concerns (for people versus tasks), which lead to behaviors and have consequences for the individual's perceptions of his/her relations to the environment. These factors contribute to self-concept – the intellectual, social, psychological, and physical image that people have of themselves. Thinking styles thus have consequences for job performance, the quality of interpersonal styles, leadership effectiveness, and the individual's ability to cope with stress.
- **LSI 2 Description by Others**
  The LSI 2 questionnaire is completed by other people who know the focal individual well. The descriptions provided by others are combined and profiled on a circumplex (LSI 2 average) which can be compared

---

* Jones, Quentin, Dunphy, Dexter, Fishman, Rosalie, Larné, Margherita, and Canter, Corinne, *In Great Company: Unlocking the Secrets of Cultural Transformation*, A Human Synergistics Publication, (2006). Human Synergistics Australia (Sydney) and Human Synergistics New Zealand (Wellington).

† Lafferty, J. C. Lifestyles Inventory™ (LSI), Human Synergistics International Plymouth, MI, (1987). The Life Styles Inventory™: A Brief Introduction, Part I—Data, Words, Causes, and Effects https://www.humansynergistics.com/resources/content/2016/12/07/the-life-styles-inventory-a-brief-introduction-part-i-data-words-causes-and-effects accessed April 23, 2020.

‡ www.humansynergistics.com.

to the individual's self-report profile (LSI 1). Given that the responses of others are based on their observations, the LSI 2 tends to focus more heavily on behavioral styles than thinking styles. The two profiles are often inconsistent.

The LSI is critical for organizational change given that cultural transformation generally requires personal development on the part of members at all levels of the organization. The LSI 1 instrument measures leaders' styles. Their *leadership styles* can have a tremendous impact on the company culture and even the achievement of results (business results, motivation of employees, customer satisfaction, and even society results).

Readers who are interested in more details about the Human Synergistic methodology can consult the book *In Great Company* or the Human Synergistics website.

5.1.10 Assessment of Case Study: Lion Nathan

This section applies the full BEST-tool assessment to the Lion Nathan case study. The main measurement instruments used in this case study are OCI® and LSI. Several other key performance indicators are employed in the results section.

The OCI® and LSI profiles are similar, i.e.:

- The leadership style of the CEO at the time was predominately Defensive as was the culture of the organization. On both profiles, the extensions along the Defensive styles (3 o'clock to 10 o'clock) were stronger than those along the Constructive styles (11 o'clock to 2 o'clock).
- On both profiles, the extensions on the styles to the left (task orientation) were stronger than those on the styles to the right (people orientation). This indicates that the CEO exhibited an orientation toward tasks rather than people and that behavioral norms similarly emphasized tasks over people (Figure 5.2).

Top management wants to develop a Constructive organizational culture; i.e. the surface of the styles 11 o'clock to 2 o'clock are much larger than the Defensive styles. See Figure 5.3.

Once the desired situation (i.e. target) is clearly defined, the transformation process can start.

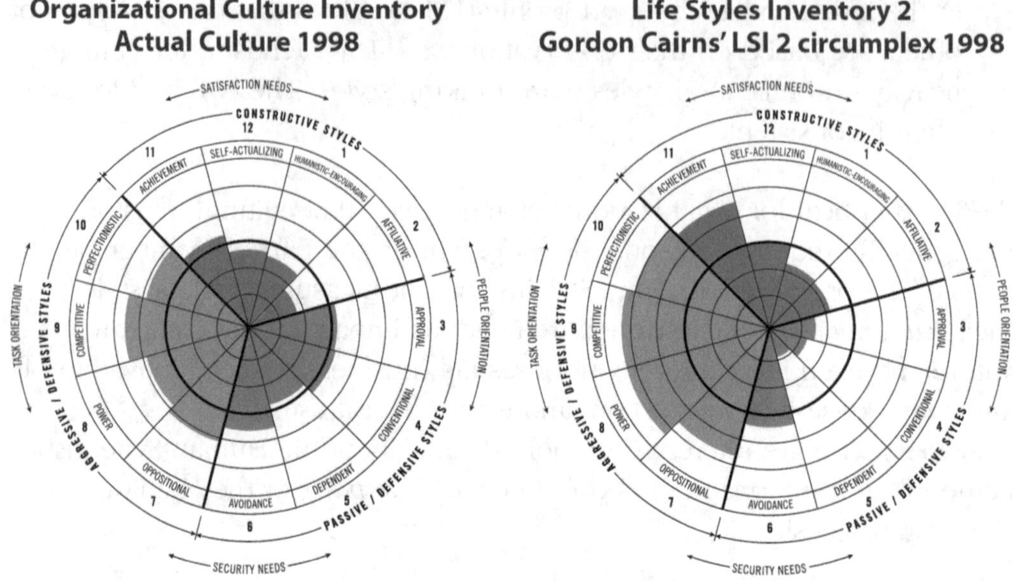

Figure 5.2 Comparison of the Lion Nathan company's culture (measured by the OCI®) at the start of the transformation process and the CEO's leadership styles (measured by the LSI 2).

Lion Nathan organized LSI workshops for the leaders. These workshops guided the leaders to personal action plans for change.

The research Lion Nathan conducted on change and its participation in a series of change workshops in 1997, combined with a collaborative approach to problem solving, provided some key insights which led the company to develop its cultural transformation strategy around three pillars:

- Create a sense of purpose, vision, and values.
- Develop leadership capability (developing competencies of leaders).
- Reinforce the desired behaviors through people management processes and systems.

One hundred and fifty of Lion Nathan's top leaders came together in 2004 to test the values (act with integrity, passion, achieving together, and being sociable) and core purpose ("To make our world a more sociable place"). Their levels of commitment were very high (>94%).

Every two years, Lion Nathan rolls out a leadership development program. The emphasis was on self-coaching: giving leaders the tools to be able to develop themselves and continue building their own capacity. At their most recent leadership conference, one of the themes was about building trust and the impact that trust can have on relationships.

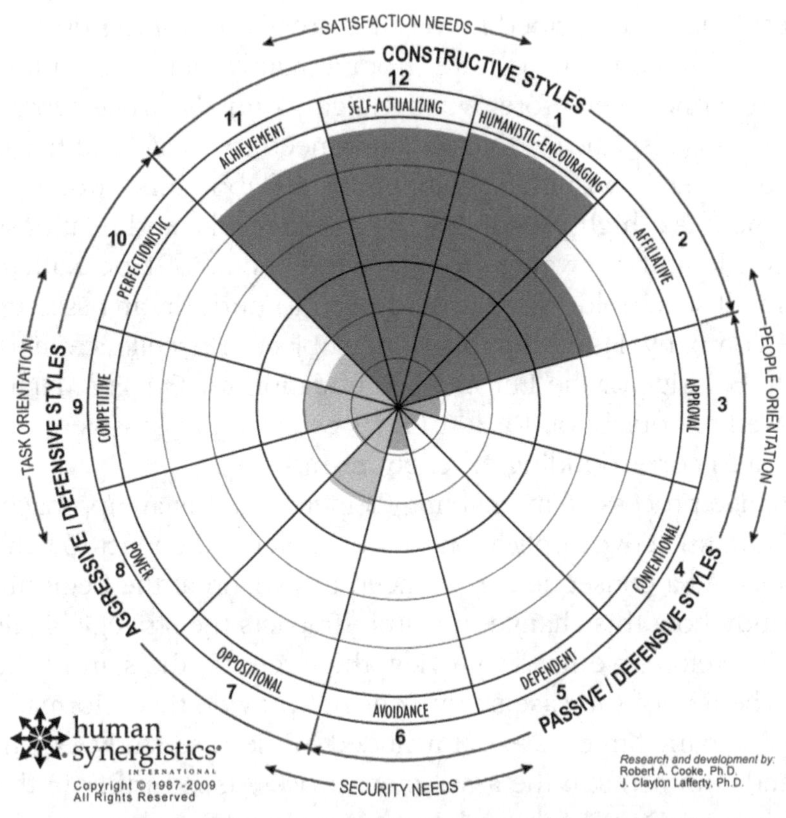

Figure 5.3 ***Organizational Culture Inventory*® (OCI®). Ideal culture 1998. N = 108. Research and development by Robert Cooke, PhD and J. Clayton Lafferty, PhD. Copyright © 1973 by Human Synergistics International; all rights reserved.**

Leadership drives cultural transformation through:

- A motivating sense of purpose
- Talent management
- Future focus
- Creating a high-performance culture, using OCI® as a template

5.1.11 Important Preliminary Remarks

The Lion Nathan Best Practice case study is about change in company culture (transition from a Defensive culture to a Constructive one) and the change in thinking styles of Lion Nathan leaders from Defensive thinking styles toward Constructive ones. Therefore, the authors focus the BEST-assessment on this process of cultural change.

The Best Practice described here is the process of a progressive and systematic change in company culture (from a mainly Defensive culture toward a Constructive one). Therefore, we investigate *only the process leading to this change*. This also means that we don't need to consider other stakeholders (customers, consumers, community, collaborators, suppliers, etc.). However, there is a high probability that these results and relationships are also excellent. If we wanted to assess the impact of Lion Nathan's processes with all stakeholders, we would need to perform an assessment of the whole company. However, this is the subject of excellence models such as Malcolm Baldrige or the European Foundation for Quality Management (EFQM). We limit our book to Best Practices, i.e. the assessment of one process leading to corresponding excellent results.

This change process is an enabling element; i.e. it is an approach or method. From an active application of an enabler, we expect to achieve better results. As a consequence, we need to explain at the beginning of the case study how this change in culture impacts the strategic goals of the company. Therefore, we need to review the targets at the start of the change program. The text of the case study does not provide this information. That the initial company targets are not included in the case study explains our findings and comments in the assessment process (see further in the assessment tables: Plan, Do, Check, and Act).

There is not only a direct relationship and impact of an enabler on the results, but it can also be seen how the approaches are improved based on feedback and learning from the results achieved (see Figure 5.4). This case study explains these improvements well.

The BEST-tool consists of four building blocks:

1 Enabler
2 Results
3 Management of process
4 Process format

5.1.12 Building Block: Enabler

This building block consists of 22 criteria and 44 characteristics.

The BEST-assessment of the enabler is accomplished in four steps: Plan, Do, Check, and Act.

The highest score can be assigned to the Lion Nathan case study for nearly all characteristics.

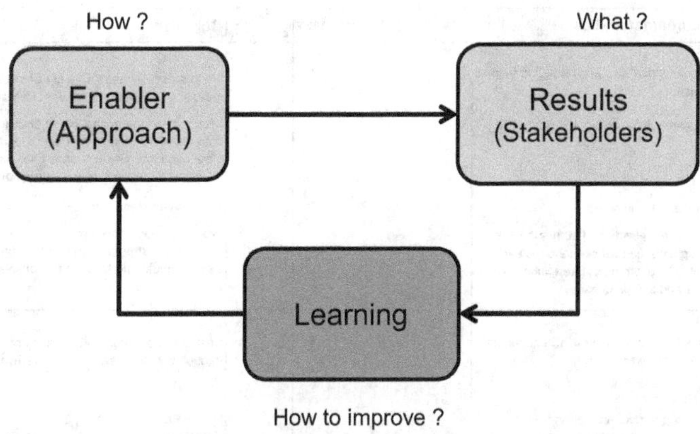

Figure 5.4 Relationship between enabler, results, and learning.

5.1.12.1 *Analysis of the* Plan *Step of the BEST-Method*

The main subject of the Lion Nathan case study is the organization's cultural transformation. This is illustrated through numerous results driven by the OCI®s and LSI 1s. These can be considered as process results. Normally we also expect to see output and outcome (impact) results. However, the accompanying business and customer results are only briefly described.

A discussion of criterion per criterion follows (see Figure 5.5).

5.1.12.1.1 Strategy (Description)

In 1996 Lion Nathan's top management decided to develop a brand strategy, reinforce the sales and marketing function, and to change and develop the organizational culture. The results of the latter (OCI® and LSI) are clearly described in the case study. The results of the other strategic goals are not. The processes reflect common sense and are well thought out (clearly linked to organizational strategy).

Relative to the third bullet under "description," we cannot determine whether this 1996 strategy is a complete Lion Nathan strategy because we don't see goals for shareholders, customers, or consumers. It is also not clear whether the strategy of Lion Nathan changed from 1996 until 2011.

5.1.12.1.2 Stakeholders

The text of the case study mentions the following stakeholders: consumers, customers, investors, suppliers, partners, and community.

The main stakeholders in this case study are shareholders, employees, and customers. Only some results for these three stakeholders are included in the case study.

		Criteria and characteristics	0%	25%	50%	75%	100%	Not described	Comments
1	Plan	**Description**							
		· The approach is repeatable and based on reliable data and information					x		The two approaches OCI and LSI are standardized measurement instruments from Human Synergistics
		· The core process are identified and described					x		On one hand the impact of the change in thinking styles and behavior of the leaders on the company culture and on the other hand the business processes leading to business results and customer satisfaction results are described.
		· The methods are documented					?	x	Implcitely present
		· The process is the reflection of common sense and is well thought out (logical sequence, clearly linked to organizational strategy, interactions with other processes and sub-processes)					x		Well explained in the text Lion Nathan strategy : brand development, development of sales & marketing function and change in organizational culture
2		**Stakeholders**							
		• The process is tailored to the needs, requirements and expectations of interested parties (stakeholders)					x		Customer's requirements, needs and expectations are met through customer satisfaction surveys.
		• The indicators and targets are set and the relationship with the core process is clearly defined					x		Main KPI's : OCI, LSI 1, LSI 2, Complementary KPI's : Employee satisfaction, Role clarity, Customer Service, Sense of purpose, High Performance Culture, Talent Management Business KPI's : Revenue, EBITDA and Net Profit After Taxes
3		**Responsibilities**							
		• The responsibilities and accountabilities are clearly defined					x		All leaders apply the LSI 1 - LSI 2 approach extensively Top management is accountable for the OCI indicator People and Culture Director, is accountable for the Meta-Capability Model
		• Each process has a process owner					?		No evidence of process owner for the other key processes
		• The process description takes into account the skills and experiences required by the persons responsible for carrying out the process and approaches					x		Competency Assessment and Development : Competencies x Results framework Meta-Capabily Model
4		**KPI's and PI's**							
		• Each process contains one or more KPI's (Key Performance Indicator) and one or more PI's (Performance Indicator)					x		Two type of indicators: 1) Change of leadership styles and company culture (LSI and OCI) 2) Business indicators (revenue, EBITDA, Net Profit After Taxes) and indicators for customers
5		**Deployment and Segmentation**							The top down **deployment** of the OCI and LSI instruments is not explicitly explained in the text. However, as the instruments OCI and LSI are widely used (600 individuals received individual feedback through LSI 1 and LSI 2, including Board Members), we can expect the deployment is done for all aspects of cultural change and leadership thinking style. There is no evidence of the **segmentation** of the approaches for the different types of activities (e.g. the segments such as beer, wine, Ready-to-Drink beverages, liquor retailing, and malt extraction for home brewing and the food industry).
		• The description of the process and approaches considers the specificities of all segments of the organization (division, department, work unit) and the variety of products and services					?	x	
6		**Prevention**							This is not described in the text. However, a Constructive culture implies that preventive and proactive thinking and acting are present, Prevention is indirectly present to the systematic use of problem solving methodology.
		• Prevention is built into the process					x	x	
		• The core process description takes into account the specific circumstances of the organization and prevention is integrated into the daily work					?		
7		**Benchmarking**							
		• The process description takes into account similar benchmarks and best-in-class examples					x		The concentric circles on the circumplex are percentiles from the large data base of Human Synergistics. The results on the LSI and OCI cirumplex lie on the higher percentiles.
8		**Data**							
		• The measurement methods are described clearly and unambiguously, including securing the relevance, integrity and reliability of the measurement results					x		The relevance, integrity and reliability are part of the method of Human Synergistics
		• The data are presented at the proper level of segmentation to effectively reflect performance and results at different levels of the organization.					?	x	Segmentation is not described in the text. There is a high probability that segmentation is done, because the Constructive thinking styles in the company are well developed (see results from OCI and LSI)

Figure 5.5 Enabler assessment Plan for case study Lion Nathan.

It would be helpful to check these data in more detail on-site to verify how segmentation and deployment of the approaches are done.

5.1.12.1.3 Competency Assessment and Development

Lion Nathan has developed nine competencies which are used in the process of assessing individuals and designing development plans. These competencies were developed in conjunction with the leadership team to ensure a high degree of ownership and are grouped according to the C x R framework (product of Competencies and Results). For example:

Competency

- Developing solutions
- Personal awareness
- Coaching and developing others

Results

- Achieving results
- Functional excellence

In 2006, as part of their evolving approach, Lion Nathan changed the framework to Behaviors × Results, which served to reinforce the underlying principle.

5.1.12.1.4 Type of Indicators

Lion Nathan makes use of two types of indicators to monitor the processes:

1) Change of leadership styles and company culture (LSI 1 and OCI®)
2) Business indicators (revenue, EBITDA*, Net Profit after Taxes) and customer results

However, there is no evidence in the text whether these indicators are deployed throughout the whole organization. This is probably the case since otherwise it would be nearly impossible to achieve a strong Constructive company culture in 2003 and beyond.

* EBITDA, Earnings Before Interest Taxes Depreciation and Amortization. Income before interest and taxes and depreciation and amortization have been subtracted. This is an indicator of a company's profitability that is watched by investors. Source: https://www.definitions.net/definition/EBITDA accessed April 23, 2020.

5.1.12.1.5 Deployment and Segmentation

The text of the case study does not give details about deployment (are the methods and KPIs applied to the lowest levels at all work units?) and segmentation (are results achieved in all work units of Australia and New Zealand and applicable to all products and services?) of the methods applied. This would be a major point to check during a site visit.

Probably the deployment and segmentation are done, because creating a global Constructive company culture is not possible if not everyone in every team is participating in applying the same methods. Nevertheless, there is no written evidence of it.

It is a pity that we do not have OCI® and LSI examples for the different regions (New Zealand and Australia), nor the different business units like breweries and wineries. This would prove how well the culture change has taken place across the whole company.

5.1.12.2 Analysis of the Do *Step of the BEST-Method*

5.1.12.2.1 Implementation

There is no description of how the Human Synergistics method is applied in the daily work of the different departments and business units. We assume that Lion Nathan followed the methodology and general instructions of Human Synergistics which is described in Chapter 2 of the book *In Great Company.*

5.1.12.2.2 Cause and Effect

Many Best Practices have difficulty proving how results are caused by the approach applied. In the Lion Nathan case study, clear evidence of cause-effect is described: the personal thinking styles of the leaders have a tremendous impact on the company culture. This is nicely demonstrated in this case study.

The case study demonstrates not only a positive change in culture (from Defensive to Constructive) but also a positive trend in business results (Figure 5.6).

An overview of the assessment of the DO phase is illustrated in Figure 5.7.

5.1.12.3 Analysis of the Check *Step of the BEST-Method*

All criteria, except for audit, are well developed (Figure 5.8).

5.1.12.3.1 Adjustment and Learning

In the fifth phase of the case study, Review, they explain "lessons learned." This is exceptional because, from our experience, most of the case studies

Figure 6. Outcomes associated with Life Styles Inventory

Factor	Constructive	Passive / Defensive	Aggressive / Defensive
Managerial Effectiveness	++	0	
Quality of Interpersonal Relations	++	+	–
Job Satisfaction	++	--	
Psychological/Physiological Health	++	-	--
Problem-Solving Effectiveness	+	-	
Interest in Self-Improvement	++	+	--
Organisational Level	+	--	
Salary	0	--	+

+ Indicates positive significant relationship; 0 Indicates non-significant relationship; - Indicates negative significant relationship

Figure 5.6 Outcomes associated with Life Styles Inventory™.

neglect to mention what they have learned. As a consequence of considering lessons learned, Lion Nathan benefits from the results and makes decisions for improvements in activities for the next steps of the project.

Over the years, Lion Nathan has reflected on each stage of its on-going transformation, and identified a number of insights and key learnings:

		Criteria and characteristics	0%	25%	50%	75%	100%	Not described	Comments
1	DO	**Implementation** • The daily activities are in conformance with the process descriptions and documented methods					x	x	Process : change in company culture; cycle bi-annual. The whole process took 11 years and consisted of 5 OCI cycles There is no description how the method is applied in daily life in the different departments and business units. We assume that Lion Nathan followed the general instructions of the methodology of Human Synergistics which is described in chapter 2 of the book
		• The implementation of the core process is integrated into the daily work					?	x	There is no evidence of implementation of other core processes
		Deployment • The approach is used by all appropriate work units					x	x	A large change in culture is only possible if (nearly) everybody participates in the transformation process.
2		**Cause-effect** • The use of the key process leads to concrete and measurable results					x		There is clear evidence of a cause-effect: the personal thinking styles of the leaders have a tremendous impact on the company culture. This is nicely demonstrated in the case study. Getting leaders to facilitate workshops is really leading by example. It enables the leaders to internalize what they have learned.
3		**Accountability** • All employees and managers clearly exhibit how they are responsible and accountable for their assigned tasks					x		Constructive styles mean that everyone feels and behaves accountable. Through an extensive use of feedback mechanisms everyone feels and behaves responsible and accountable.
4		**SMART** • KPI's and PI's are used systematically					x		Clear evidence of a systematic use of the KPI's OCI and LSI and Revenue, EBITDA, Net Profit After Taxes and customer surveys.
		• SMART decisions are taken and action plans are developed					?	x	The text doesn't give details about the other KPI's.

Figure 5.7 Enabler assessment Do for case study Lion Nathan.

		Criteria and characteristics	0%	25%	50%	75%	100%	Not described	Comments
1	Check	**Integration**							
		• Plans, process, results, analysis, learning and actions are harmonized across the process and work units to support organization-wide goals					x		Yes, explained in general, not in detail for the cultural change.
		Monitoring							
		• The performance of each core process is regularly measured and monitored					x		OCI is measured bi-annually from 1998 till 2009. Since then also LSI is systematically used.
		• The obtained results related to a core process are regularly discussed with all relevant stakeholders			x				Text gives evidence of discussion of the results with employees. There is no evidence that this is also the case with customers.
		• The method to determine the target value of the KPI (target) is validated and opportunities for improvement are recorded					x		The active development of constructive style is validated by the CEO and his team.
		• Relevance, integrity, completeness and reliability of the results achieved are checked					?	x	This is part of the Human Synergistics method, but not explicitely described in the text. There is no evidence for integrity, completeness and reliablity of the results for the business KPI's.
2		**Audit**							
		• Each process owner audits his or her core process regularly	x						There is no evidence
		• The process owner examines what can be done to bring the core process to a higher maturity level (to determineimprovement opportunities)	x						There is no evidence
3		**Adjustment and Learning**							
		• Deviations from the desired and/or planned results serve as input for the improvement and revision of the core process and/or approaches					x	x	Problem solving is used systematically. However there are no concrete examples of it given in the text.
		• Identification of problems related to the sufficient availability and appropriate resources such as budget, machinery, equipment, provisions, tools, and Information Technology (software, hardware, networking, security, etc.)					x	x	Yes, explained in general, not in detail
		• Identification of an adequate number of employees and/or of shortcomings of skills and experiences of employees in the process and/or approaches					x	x	Yes, explained in general, not in detail
		• Comparison of the results obtained with the benchmark and Best-in-Class					x		The results are compared with the data of the database of Human Synergistics products, i,e. the 10%, 25%, 50%, 75%, 90% and 99% percentiles which are described as concentric circles in the OCI and LSI circumplex.
		• Prioritization of opportunities for improvement					?	x	The cases study concentrates on the priorities in changing the company culture. There is little evidence how priorities are set for the business activities and results.
		• Encouragement of breakthrough change to the approach applied through innovation	x						There is no evidence

Figure 5.8 Enabler assessment Check for Lion Nathan case study.

- CEO and leadership team must be involved and committed
- Leaders are the key
- Understand the current culture and the link to performance
- Articulate a clear plan
- Be consistent and focused in efforts over a long period (it's a marathon, not a sprint)
- Behavior change takes time and commitment
- Congruence of behavior. Don't say it if you're not prepared to do it!

Important aspects of the company's transformation

- A set of assumptions that adopting a methodical, collaborative, and inclusive approach to problem solving was necessary to deliver the required insights and actions.
- The journey of transformation was to define its core purpose and values as a company.
- One of the best ways to motivate people to deliver great results is to inspire them to a cause, a sense of purpose – to help them see the significance of their work within the bigger picture. Core purpose, vision, and values are about direction and reason for being.
- Individual change is a prerequisite of cultural transformation. Things don't transform, people do.
- A great culture is achieved when high levels of emotional connection (engagement) between an individual, their role, their leader, and the organization are developed.
- Set clear expectations, make sure the right people are in the right roles, communicate the vision, and integrate values into your people management systems. The secret ingredients are consistency and sustainability.
- Demonstrate a commitment to its espoused values and beliefs.
- Formula for success = behavior × results.

All these aspects have been treated by Lion Nathan and have contributed to the success of the organizational culture change.

5.1.12.4 Analysis of the Act *Step of the BEST-Method*

Information and evidence are missing in the Resources and Knowledge and Experience criteria (Figure 5.9).

In this case study the enabler is well developed, and much evidence is given. Let us now assess the *results* of the case study.

5.1.13 Building Block: Results

This building block consists of 7 criteria and 20 characteristics.

The Lion Nathan case study shows three types of indicators:

1) Change of leadership styles and company culture (LSI 1 and OCI®)
2) Business indicators (revenue, EBITDA, Net Profit After Taxes) and results for customers

		Criteria and characteristics	0%	25%	50%	75%	100%	Not described	Comments
1	Act	**Improvement**							
		• The output of the measurement and learning is analyzed and used to identify additional improvements; to prioritize, to plan and to implement these further opportunities for improvement					x		This is clearly done
2		**Process** • The process, methods and approaches are revised and improved in response to the findings gained in the Check phase					x		E.g. Competencies x Results framework is changed in 2006 to Behaviors x Results framework.
3		**Resources** • The amount and nature of the resources that were adjusted because of the findings in the Check phase are documented					?	x	There is no evidence found in the text.
		• The number of employees assigned to the process is adjusted considering the opportunities of improvement and the outcome of the process, methods and approaches					x	x	Not documented. This is probably done, however this has to be checked on-site.
4		**Knowledge and Experience**							
		• New training and/or refresher training is given to meet the findings gained in the Check phase					?	x	Not documented. This is probably done, however this has to be checked on-site.
		• Sharing of refinements and innovations with other relevant work units and processes	x					x	There is no evidence found in the text.
		• The Knowledge and experience of those involved in the process are documented and validated as Best-in-Class or Benchmark level					?	x	The OCI and LSI instruments allow the comparison of the company and leadership styles with the database of Human Synergistics. However the text doesn't give details about it.
5		**Benchmark** • The organization can be set as a model for other organizations					x		Nathan Lion is a nice example of change from a Defensive Culture to a Constructive company culture.

Figure 5.9 Enabler assessment Act for case study Lion Nathan.

3) Customer satisfaction surveys (five surveys from 2001 to 2004), i.e. perception of customers

These results are excellent, according to the results assessment table (Figure 5.10).

If we look at the table of the assessment of the results, we see some shortcomings.

5.1.13.1 Scope and Relevance

Results of OCI® and LSI are clearly present and show a positive trend (Figure 5.11).

As we mentioned earlier, there is not enough information on what impact the planned change in company culture has on the results of the different stakeholders. The 2011 update indicates that Constructive cultures produce higher levels of employee commitment and greater levels of cooperation

	Criteria and characteristics	0%	25%	50%	75%	100%	Not described	Comments
1	**Scope and Relevance**							
	• The results are aligned with the expectations and needs of the relevant stakeholders					?		The text is mainly a description of the cultural transformation. The shareholder results shown are EBITDA and NPAT (period 1998-2005) and ROCE (period 2000-2008) and share price (period 1999-2008). Perception results of customers are done through customer satisfaction surveys period 2001-2004). Results for the different stakeholders are probably available on site, but is not described in the text
	• The results are aligned with policy and strategy of the organization					?	x	This is probably done, but is not described in the text
	• The most important key results are identified and prioritized				x			Clearly done for OCI and LSI results Less evidence for the other results
	• The relation between the results is understood					x		Clearly done for OCI and LSI results Evidence of performance results and outcome results for the shareholders, less evidence for the other stakeholders' results
2	**Integrity of data**							
	• Results are timely					x		
	• Results are reliable and accurate					x		
3	**Segmentation**							
	• Results are segmented in a suitable							
	o By region, country,					?		This isn't explicitly explained in the text. However, as the instruments OCI and LSI are widely used, we can expect that the deployment is done.
	o By department, business line, division, unit					?		
	o By product and service type							
4	**Trends**							
	• Trends are positive for 5 years or more					x		OCI and LSI results are positive for more than 10 years
	• Results are sustainable and show good performance					x		The OCI and LSI results over this long time period are remarkably positive and sustainable
5	**Targets**							
	• Targets for core results are set					x		Targets for OCI and LSI are set, however a precise measure was not agreed to upfront
	• Targets are suitable					?		Targets for customer satisfaction surveys are not given
	• Targets are achieved					x		OCI and LSI results are achieved. No information available on targets for all other stakeholder"s needs and expectations.
6	**Comparisons with targets and benchmarks**							
	• Comparisons for core results are made			x				Comparison is made with the standardized OCI and LSI measurement instruments. No information available in the text for the other stakeholders results.
	• Comparisons are suitable			x				
	• Comparisons are favorable			x				
7	**Cause-effect**							
	• The results are clearly achieved through the chosen approach (cause - effect)					x		Clear cause-effect relationship: constructive thinking styles of leaders create a Constructive company culture. There is a relationship of the approaches used by the leaders (e.g. exemplary behavior of leaders) and the results achieved. The behaviors of leaders are now Constructive, these belong to the company culture. Leaders of Lion Nathan created a robust company culture that produces sustainable and excellent results.
	• The relations between results achieved and the approaches are understood					x		
	* Based on the evidence presented, it is assured that the positive performance will continue in the future, i.e. the results are sustainable					x		

Figure 5.10 ***Results*** **assessment for case study Lion Nathan.**

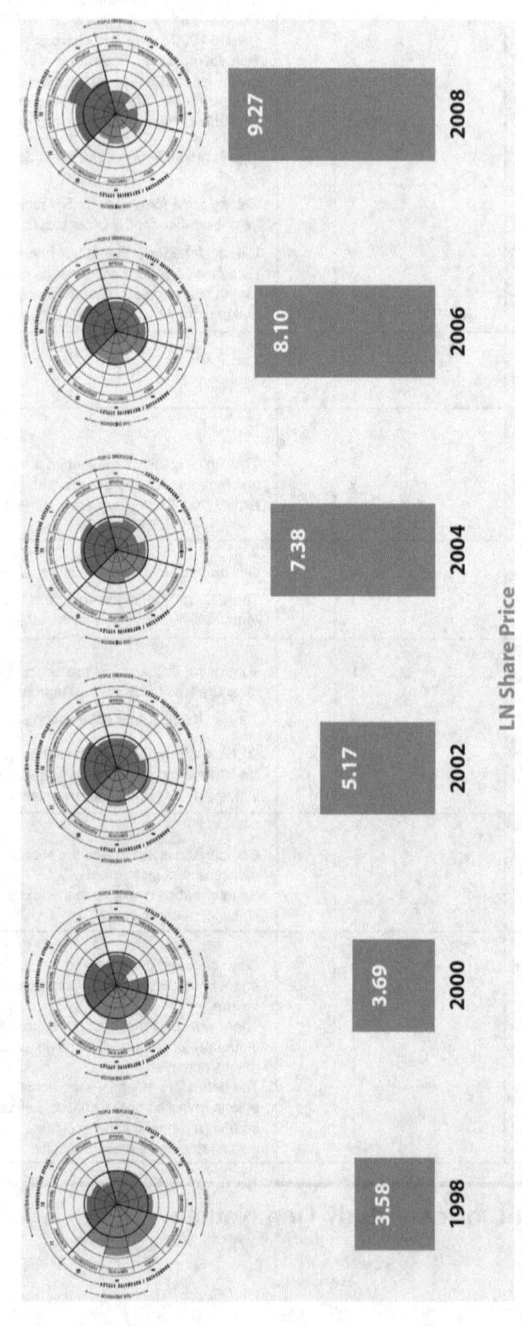

Figure 5.11 Evolution of the organizational culture from 1998 to 2008. (a) Relationship between Constructive Culture and Share Price. (b) Relationship between Constructive Culture and Return on Capital. Research and development by Robert Cooke, PhD and J. Clayton Lafferty, PhD. Copyright © 1973 by Human Synergistics International; All rights reserved. Quentin Jones, Dexter Dunphy, Rosalie Fishman, Margherita Larné and Corinne Canter, *In Great Company, Unlocking the Secrets of Cultural Transformation*, A Human Synergistics Publication (2006).

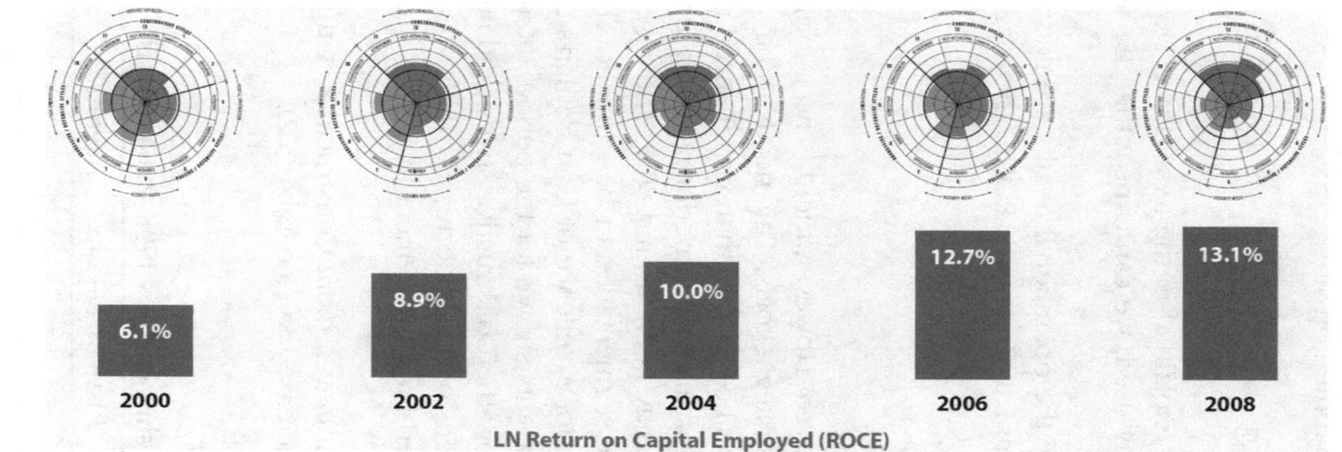

Figure 5.11 (Continued) Evolution of the organizational culture from 1998 to 2008. (a) Relationship between Constructive Culture and Share Price. (b) Relationship between Constructive Culture and Return on Capital. Research and development by Robert Cooke, PhD and J. Clayton Lafferty, PhD. Copyright © 1973 by Human Synergistics International; All rights reserved. Quentin Jones, Dexter Dunphy, Rosalie Fishman, Margherita Larné and Corinne Canter, *In Great Company, Unlocking the Secrets of Cultural Transformation*, A Human Synergistics Publication (2006).

across groups in the organization, and have an increased capacity to adapt to the changing marketplace through innovation and productivity. However, no data are shown for the last 10 years. More detailed information is probably present but needs to be verified on-site.

5.1.13.2 Segmentation

Segmentation is not explicitly explained in the text. However, as the instruments OCI® and LSI are widely used, we can expect that the deployment for OCI® and LSI is done.

There is a good probability the operational results are good to excellent as the results for Return on Capital Employed (ROCE) increase year after year.

5.1.13.3 Targets

OCI® and LSI results are achieved. However, there is no information available on targets for the other strategic goals. This needs to be verified on-site.

Over the course of 5 years since Lion Nathan commenced using the customer satisfaction survey, the organization's performance in terms of customer satisfaction has consistently been around 80%. The case study does not mention the target nor the segmentation or benchmark. Therefore, it is difficult to determine the level of excellence of Lion Nathan's customer satisfaction results. There are no results shown for the period 2004–2008.

Table 5.1 illustrates well how the Constructive styles gradually increased over the years, while the Defensive styles decreased. This was also the objective specifically addressed for improvement by Lion Nathan top management.

As the company culture shifts to a more Constructive culture (see Figure 5.5), the operational results increase too (see Table 5.2).

Table 5.1 Lion Nathan shift in styles 1998–2004 (percentile score)

Year	*Constructive*	*Passive/Defensive*	*Aggressive/Defensive*
1998	40	55	75
2002	55	40	55
2004	60	35	45

Table 5.2 Evolution of share price (A$), Net Profit after Taxes (million A$) (NPAT) and Return on Capital Employed (ROCE) (%)

Year	*Share price*	*NPAT*	*ROCE*
1998	3.58		
2000	3.69	120	6.1
2002	5.17	160	8.9
2004	7.38	220	10.0
2006	8.10		12.7
2008	9.27		13.1

5.1.13.4 Comparison with Benchmarks

The text doesn't give information about this comparison. Is a ROCE of 13.1% for the brewery sector exceptional? How have these results evolved between 2008 and 2011? This could be the proof of sustainability of results.

5.1.14 Building Block: Management of Process

This building block consists of nine criteria.

The Lion Nathan case study describes the project of cultural change. The cultural change project is a bi-annual cycle and has been repeated several times. This is different from a normal business process, which is part of daily management. It is not clear why aspects such as risk management, relationship with a strategic plan, systematic simplification of the process, and audit are not applied. We would expect that a major change program, i.e. cultural change, would be driven by strategic motives.

Table 5.3 gives a quick overview of the assessment results of the *management of process* of change management at Lion Nathan. Four management activities are not described and need to be verified on-site.

We can also review the *maturity of the process.* The process being assessed for maturity is the process of change in organizational culture (Figure 5.12).

We assign Lion Nathan a score of 4 for the process of cultural change. This is a good, working level for a successful organization.

Finally, we can assess the last item in the BEST-tool, i.e. *process format.*

Table 5.3 Assessment of the *management of the process* of Lion Nathan Best Practice

	Subject	*NOK*	*OK*	*Comment*
1	Owner of key process		x	Top managers are responsible for the application of OCI and LSI.
2	Integrity		x	Constructive styles imply also integrity.
3	Risk management	x		Not described in the text.
4	Relation with strategic plan	x		Not described in the text.
5	Adding value		x	Cultural change has a positive impact on business results and customer results.
6	Systematic simplification	x		Simplification of processes and procedures is not described in the text.
7	KPI		x	Mainly OCI and LSI for this case study.
8	Audit	x		Not described in the text.
9	Maturity level of process		x	

5.1.15 Building Block: Process Format

This building block consists of 13 criteria.

Here we assess to what extent the process is *described* fully. Figure 5.13 shows very strong assessment results. All 13 characteristics are considered as OK.

5.1.16 Summary of the Assessment of the Lion Nathan Case Study and Conclusion

The Lion Nathan case study can be considered as a Best Practice. The clear majority of characteristics of the BEST-tool receive high scores for the enabler (Plan, Do, Check, and Act) and results segments. Also, the format of the process gets a high score.

It would be helpful to visit the company to confirm the findings observed in this assessment. Some complementary checks could be conducted, like

Levels	Description	Assessment	Comments
0	**Non-existent** Within the organization there are no or very little management measures. Control awareness is rather low and only few actions are taken to achieve an adequate system of organizational management (internal control system).		
1	**Ad-hoc basis** Only ad-hoc management measures are in place within the organization. The awareness of the need for appropriate management (internal control) is growing, but there is still no structured or standardized approach present. The system of organizational management (internal control) is more focused on people than on systems.		
2	**Structured start** A structured impetus is given to the development of management measures. The management tools are therefore being developed but are not yet applied (Plan)		
3	**Defined** (= level 2 + ...) Control measures are provided. These are standardized, documented, communicated and implemented (Do).		
4	**Management system** (= level 3 + ...) The control measures are internally assessed and adjusted (Check & Act). There is a "living" adequate and effective system of organizational management.		The process of change of company culture is not only under control, but also gradually improved each time they measured the company culture (bi-annually)
5	**Optimized** (= level 4 + ...) The control measures are continuously optimized through benchmarking and obtaining quality certificates or external evaluations (PDCA).		

Figure 5.12 Assessment of the *maturity of the management of the process* of Lion Nathan Best Practice.

segmentation of the processes and results, the deployment of the constructive company culture to the lowest levels, satisfaction and motivation of employees and customers, and the alignment of objectives with the strategy of the company. It would also be valuable to verify KPIs, in particular, business results, employee results, and customer results.

5.2 Case Study 2: Corporate Social Responsibility at Loblaw

Source of the case study: www.loblaw.ca

Loblaw has a long track record pertaining to CSR. Loblaw has published a detailed annual CSR report since 2007.

	Subject	NOK	OK	Comments
1	Title		x	
2	Subject		x	
3	Author (name, title, company, contact)		x	
4	Context (sector, country restrictions)		x	
5	Description of the method and results		x	This is mainly the method of Human Synergistics.
6	Measurement method		x	Typical measurement system of Human Synergistics.
7	Process description and maturity		x	
8	KPIs (Key Performance Indicator) and results		x	Mainly OCI and LSI
9	Distribution of the results		?	Deployment of the results over the departments/services is not described in the text. This is probably present. This has to be verified on-site.
10	Cause and effect		x	Very nicely demonstrated by change in leadership styles that creates a Constructive company culture.
11	Measurement: RADAR, PDCA, or other		x	OCI and LSI measurements are used.
12	Limiting conditions		x	Before beginning to use the OCI and LSI methods, it is necessary to hold workshops where the methodology and instruments are fully explained.
13	Date and Revision Level		x	The measurement of OCI is done bi-annually.

Figure 5.13 Assessment of the description of the *format* of a Best Practice for Lion Nathan's Change of company culture.

5.2.1 Who is Loblaw?

Loblaw Companies Ltd is Canada's largest food distributor and a leading provider of grocery, general merchandise, drugstore, and financial products and services. Loblaw provides products and services that meet the everyday household needs of Canadian consumers. Besides the classical brand names, it offers the customers their private-label *President's Choice* and *no name* brands. Loblaw has approximately 192,000 employees.

This section describes the strategic approaches used by Loblaw. Then we make an assessment of the CSR approaches used and the corresponding results. We employ the detailed BEST-tool in this chapter to show the strength of the tool for robust process improvement.

5.2.2 Loblaw Companies CSR Vision

Strong commitment to CSR which is defined by the way people of Loblaw do business and the role they aim to play in society.

5.2.3 Loblaw Purpose

Loblaw's purpose – Live Life Well – supports the needs and well-being of Canadians.

Vision and purpose are the basis for the development of CSR approaches at Loblaw.

5.2.4 Core Values of Loblaw

Care, Ownership, Respect, and Excellence.

5.2.5 The Way of Doing business

People of Loblaw consider a strong commitment toward CSR and delivering products and services as opportunities to help Canadians.

Priorities for Loblaw are sourcing with integrity and caring for the environment. This is fully in line with the Loblaw values of care and respect.

5.2.6 Loblaw CSR Pillars

The starting point is the company purpose, i.e. Live Life Well. Loblaw applies a responsible sourcing policy, protects the environment and all people are committed toward the application of the corporate social responsibility principles.

Leaders and collaborators of Loblaw prioritize their work based on the urgency of an issue, its importance to Canadian citizens and customers, its relevance to the business and the potential for Loblaw to take a leadership position.

1. **Sourcing: Source with Integrity**

   Customers want the products they buy to be safe and responsibly sourced. This means a meticulous application of the Loblaw values throughout the supply chain, a promotion of safe and sustainable products, and the support of Canadian suppliers.
2. **Environment: Respect the Environment**

   Commitment to the reduction of the impact on the environment. Loblaw has a considerable influence on the reduction or better management of waste, energy consumption, transportation, refrigerants, and packaging, due to the national scale (Canada) and range of operations.

3. **Community: Make a Positive Difference**
   Loblaw contributes to the well-being of Canadians through the products and services offered. Their efforts center on the promotion of health and wellness. Loblaw delivers this to communities throughout the country.

For each of these three pillars there are several objectives, KPIs, action plans, and corresponding targets. E.g. for the Environment pillar:

- Moving forward on reducing the carbon footprint
- Improving energy efficiency and cutting carbon emissions
- Converting the fleet to electric
- Converting refrigerants and reducing leak intensity
- Reducing and diverting waste
- Plastic bag reduction
- Food donations

For each of the two other pillars (sourcing and community) there are also several objectives with KPIs, action plans, and targets.

The Loblaw website explains the relationship between these three pillars and the impact on society through a comprehensive illustration.

5.2.7 CSR Annual Reports

Loblaw has already published 11 annual CSR reports* (also available on the Loblaw website). We can speak of a "tradition of CSR at Loblaw." Very few companies can claim this extensive experience with CSR.

Each annual CSR report (from 2007 until 2017) contains a foreword from the chairman and CEO of Loblaw. This executive visibility is like the traditional financial annual report.

The annual CSR report already gives detailed information. Extra information is also available on the website on a variety of subjects such as Carbon Reduction Strategy, Corporate Donations Policy, Local Store Donations, Environmental Commitment, Customer Service Accessibility, Bisphenol-A

* https://www.loblaw.ca/en/responsibility.html accessed April 23, 2020 Previous CSR reports (2007-2017) are available at: https://www.loblaw.ca/en/responsibility/reports.html accessed April 23, 2020 CSR report 2017 is available in pdf-format: https://www.loblaw.ca/content/dam/lclcorp/pdfs/pdfjs/web/viewer.html?file=LoblawCSR2017_FINAL.pdf

(BPA) Statement, Animal Welfare Principles, Animal Welfare Video, Food Waste Video, and Visit W. Garfield Weston Foundation.

5.2.8 Long-Term Targets and Stakeholder Engagement

5.2.8.1 Long-Term Targets

Thanks to the application of CSR principles Loblaw started to learn what matters most to customers, colleagues, and external stakeholders (e.g. suppliers). Loblaw also takes into consideration the long-term challenges facing the company, their communities, and the country. Those issues where Loblaw can have the greatest impact are chosen as objectives. Loblaw is a leader in Canada's food sector. It works with vendors, customers, and other partners to drive for positive change.

Loblaw has existed for almost a century and therefore understands the value of long-term commitment. Many of the issues addressed are complex. This means that achieving certain goals will take time. The CSR reports provide annual updates of the progress and results already achieved.

5.2.8.2 Stakeholder Engagement

The CSR activities must be relevant to business, customers, colleagues, and partners, and to society at large. To understand societal and stakeholder priorities and concerns, Loblaw uses a variety of surveys and engagement processes to proactively reach out to experts. Experts from Loblaw collaborate with people of like-minded organizations to develop solutions to complex issues.

5.2.9 What Customers Tell Loblaw

Consumers continue to see local sourcing, healthier food choices, and safe working conditions as top CSR priorities for grocery retailers (observation from 2017). These expectations were recognized and put in the new Loblaw CSR action plans. Regular customers and those who only occasionally shop at Loblaw recognize Loblaw as the CSR leader among Canadian retailers.

5.2.10 Insights from Valued Stakeholders

Biannually a panel of stakeholders assesses the quality and value of the CSR reports. This assessment includes surveys and interviews with senior representatives from key vendors, academic institutions, and non-governmental organizations (NGOs), as well as CSR, sustainability research, and advisory firms. Ad-hoc conversations are also routinely conducted with major ethical fund managers.

Historically, stakeholders told Loblaw that their size and scale provide a unique opportunity to lead their sector in sustainable practices. In recent years, they've encouraged Loblaw to play a stronger role in two categories:

(1) Helping Canadians embrace preventive health and wellness, including healthier eating
(2) Establishing a strong carbon and climate-change strategy

We discuss one objective here (CO_2 reduction) from the Environment pillar of the Loblaw CSR strategy. The Loblaw report explains at a high level how they treat the subject, including a description of the transformation of the focus areas into targets, action plans, and KPIs (see Table 5.4).

5.2.11 Moving Forward in Reduction of the Carbon Footprint

Canada was one of the 195 countries to sign the Paris Agreement on Climate Change in 2015. As part of its commitment, Canada set a target to reduce national carbon emissions by 30% by 2030. Loblaw is one of the country's largest carbon emitters through the operation of the retail stores. In reducing the CO_2 emissions Loblaw will contribute toward Canada's national goals. Loblaw also wants to lead by example and to demonstrate, through actions and results achieved, that these goals can be achieved without sacrificing economic growth. Consequently, Loblaw established ambitious targets for reducing the carbon footprint 20% by 2020 and 30% by 2030, based on 2011 baseline results, as outlined in Loblaw's Carbon Reduction Strategy.

By 2017, Loblaw reduced the carbon emissions by 21.9% against the baseline 2011 and is making good progress toward their 30% carbon reduction goal by 2030 (Table 5.5). In order to reach the 30% goal, it developed a comprehensive science-based carbon reduction plan in collaboration with climate experts and other partners. The strategy targets greenhouse gas emissions from corporate owned facilities, including the retail stores, distribution centers, and offices, by focusing on four key areas: electricity and natural gas consumption, refrigerant leaks, transportation fuel consumption, and waste disposal.

Table 5.4 Transformation of the focus areas into targets, action plans, and KPIs

Focus area	*Quantitative sub-target*	*Action Plan*	*Key Performance Indicators*
Energy Efficiency	35% reduction in emissions associated with electricity use by 2030	* LED conversions for refrigerated cases, task lighting, underground parking areas, and distribution centers * Improve efficiencies in lighting, evaporators, battery charges and door seals in distribution centers * Optimize energy consumption through energy management systems	* Electricity emissions per square foot ($tCO_2e/sqft^2$)
Refrigerants	* 15% absolute emission reduction by 2020 * 50% absolute emission reduction by 2030	* Replace high Global Warming Potential (GWP) refrigerants with lower GWP Hydrofluoro-olefin (HFO) blend * Reduce refrigerant leaks in corporate stores and distribution centers	* KGs refrigerants * GWP of refrigerants * Leakage in KGs
Waste	* 80% diversion rate by 2030 in corporate stores * 95% diversion rate in distribution centers by 2030	* Reduce waste to landfill by increasing organic diversion using mechanical separation or third-party separation.	* Organic waste diversion rate (%)
Transportation and Logistics Freight	* Reduce the intensity of transportation emissions to 0.087 gCO_2 e/t-km by 2030	* Expand the use of 60-foot trailers to improve the efficiency of transporting goods by road * Convert trucks from diesel to compressed natural gas (CNG) or liquefied natural gas (LNG) where feasible * Assess the feasibility of using CO_2 refrigerants in reefer trailers	* Tonnes of freight by mode of transportation (gCO_2e/t-km) * Fuel efficiency – miles per gallon (MPG)

(*Continued*)

Table 5.4 (Continued) Transformation of the focus areas into targets, action plans, and KPIs

Focus area	*Quantitative sub-target*	*Action Plan*	*Key Performance Indicators*
Transportation and Logistics Corporate Fleet	* Combined fuel economy rating of less than 13 l/100 km.	* Review fuel economy for all new corporate fleet vehicles * Remove low-efficiency vehicles from corporate fleet	* Fuel efficiency – miles per gallon (MPG) or L/100 km

For each area of focus we will deliver specific operational efficienciesCorporate target: We will reduce absolute emissions 20% by 2020 and 30% by 2030 relative to a 2011 baseline

Source: Loblaw Report 2017 "Reducing our Carbon Footprint 30% by 2030"

www.loblaw.ca/content/dam/lclcorp/pdfs/Responsibility/Loblaw%20Carbon%20Reduction%20Strategy_EN.pdf

Table 5.5 Origins of CO_2 production

Electricity	33.7%
Refrigerant releases	30.7%
Building fuel consumption	13.1%
Waste	10.8%
Fleet fuel consumption	10.1%
Corporate travel	1.7%

Total: 900,491.7 tons CO_2

Corporate carbon reduction progress: Loblaw achieved a 21.9% decrease in 2017 in absolute greenhouse gas emissions against its 2011 baseline.

5.2.12 Improving Energy Efficiency and Cutting Carbon Emissions

Electricity use and fuel consumption at the stores and other properties account for 47% of the overall measured carbon emissions in 2017. Because it is the largest segment in the carbon footprint, Loblaw continues to explore opportunities for developing improved energy management systems that will enable them to increase energy efficiency and reduce carbon emissions across their operations. The goal is to reduce emissions associated with electricity in the stores and distribution centers by 35% by 2030, based on a 2011 baseline.

5.2.13 Converting Refrigerants and Reducing Leak Intensity

In 2011, Loblaw launched a robust refrigerant leak-checking program in all corporate stores, which enables them to find leaks faster and reduce the amount of refrigerant leaked. Loblaw also launched a program to convert the refrigerant in the systems from high global warming potential hydrofluorocarbon (HFC) refrigerants to lower global warming potential hydrofluoro-olefin (HFO) blends, which cuts the potential environmental impact of future leaks by half. In 2017, Loblaw converted the refrigerant at 28 stores.

5.2.14 Building Energy Consumption

In 2017, Loblaw reduced electricity use per square foot in existing corporate grocery stores by 4.27%. Loblaw continued the lighting retrofit program and converted ambient lighting from fluorescent to LED at 180 locations and added doors to otherwise open-air refrigeration units at 36 stores.

5.2.15 Converting Fleet to Electric

The electrification of the corporate owned trucking fleet is part of the goal to reduce the overall transportation emissions by 25% by 2030. In November 2017, Loblaw unveiled a first-of-its-kind fully electric Class 8 truck and hybrid refrigerated trailer capable of making commercial grocery deliveries with zero carbon emissions. A new order of 25 heavy-duty electric Tesla semi-trucks will contribute to eliminating the carbon output. Removing diesel from transport trucks and refrigerated trailers will cut CO_2 emissions by 94,000 tons per year, which is equivalent to taking more than 20,000 cars off the road. Loblaw is committed to reducing transportation emissions and will continue to introduce technological advancements throughout the supply chain.

5.2.16 Reducing and Diverting Waste

Loblaw's business generates a lot of organic, paper, and plastic waste. Therefore, Loblaw set as a first priority the improvement of waste diversion in operations. It set targets for each of the regions along with a long-term goal of achieving national diversion rates of 80% at corporate stores and 95%

at distribution centers by 2030. In 2017, Loblaw achieved the national diversion rates of 66% for corporate stores and 90% at distribution centers.

Additionally, Loblaw made progress on reducing food waste and used several different downstream processes to divert food waste from landfills.

Loblaw also recognizes that it has a role to play in the issue of textile waste. That's why Loblaw is working with sector leaders and academics to find innovative and scalable solutions to this major challenge.

5.2.17 Important Preliminary Remark

A note to the reader before we begin the assessment of CSR approaches and results at Loblaw.

We found this case study on the Internet. We are pleased to have the opportunity to prove how the BEST-methodology works in practice. Since the authors of the Loblaw case study were not aware of the criteria and characteristics of the BEST-tool, it is understandable that there will be some areas in the case study where information is identified as "missing."

The CSR reports reflect the use of Loblaw values, e.g. the establishment of the CSR reports shows the application of the value "Excellence." The Loblaw CSR reports we downloaded are of high quality. If we compare these reports with the submission documents for the European Excellence Award (assessed by "criterion 8 *Society Results*" of the EFQM model*) we may say that these reports are of world class level.

5.2.18 Assessment of the Loblaw CSR Case Study†

This section applies the full BEST-tool to the Loblaw case study. The main subject of comparison is the management of Corporate Social Responsibility. As explained above, this is based upon three pillars (environment, sourcing, and community). We will mainly treat the pillar Environment and the objective of CO_2 reduction.

As described in Chapter 3, The BEST-tool consists of ***four building blocks***:

1 Enabler
2 Results

---

* For details of the EFQM-model, see www.efqm.org. EFQM-model consists of nine criteria, where criterion 8 shows the Society Results.

† www.loblaw.ca/en/responsibility.html.

3 Management of process
4 Process format

5.2.19 Building Block 1: Enabler (22 criteria and 44 characteristics)

This consists of four parts: Plan, Do, Check, and Act.

5.2.19.1 Analyze the Plan *Phase of the BEST-Method*

The highest score can be assigned for nearly all characteristics (Figure 5.14).

		Element	0%	25%	50%	75%	100%	Not described	Comments
1	Plan	**Description**							
		• The approach is repeatable and based on reliable data and							
		• The core process are identified and described					x		
		• The methods are documented					x		
		• The process is the reflection of common sense and is well thought out (logical sequence, clearly linked to organizational strategy, interactions with other processes and sub-processes)					x		
2		**Stakeholders**							
		• The process is tailored to the needs, requirements and expectations of interested parties (stakeholders)					x		Every two years, we consult a panel of stakeholders to assess the quality and value of our CSR report. This includes surveys and interviews with senior representatives from key vendors, academic institutions and non-governmental organizations (NGOs), as well as CSR/ sustainability research and advisory
		• The indicators and targets are set and the relationship with the core process is clearly defined					x		
3		**Responsibilities**							
		• The responsibilities and accountabilities are clearly defined					x	x	Indirectly, not explicitely
		• Each process has a process owner					x	x	Indirectly, not explicitely
		• The process description takes into account the skills and experiences required by the persons responsible for carrying out the process and approaches					x	x	Indirectly, not explicitely
4		**KPI's and PI's**							
		• Each process contains one or more KPI's (Key Performance Indicator) and one or more PI's (Performance Indicator)					x		
5		**Deployment and Segmentation**							
		• The description of the process and approaches considers the specificities of all segments of the organization (division, department, work unit) and the variety of products and services					x		See example of segmentation in CO_2 reduction process
6		**Prevention**							
		• Prevention is built into the process					x		
		• The core process description takes into account the specific circumstances of the organization and prevention is integrated into the daily work					x		
7		**Benchmarking**							
		• The process description takes into account similar benchmarks and best-in-class examples					x		Our **carbon strategy**, including targets and action plans, is informed by Science-Based Targets. Working with our partners like WWF-Canada (a key driver of Science-Based Targets) we intend to deliver emission reductions in line with industry standards.
8		**Data**							
		• The measurement methods are described clearly and unambiguously, including securing the relevance, integrity and reliability of the measurement results					x		
		• The data are presented at the proper level of segmentation to effectively reflect performance and results at different levels of the organization.					x		

Figure 5.14 Assessment of the *Plan* phase.

5.2.19.1.1 Description

The processes are described at a high level and demonstrated in a comprehensive illustration on the Loblaw website. See also the introductory text to this chapter.

5.2.19.1.2 Stakeholders

Every 2 years, Loblaw consults a panel of stakeholders to assess the quality and value of the CSR report. This includes surveys and interviews with senior representatives from key vendors, academic institutions, and NGOs, as well as CSR and sustainability research and advisory firms. They also routinely conduct ad-hoc conversations with major ethical fund managers.

The CSR report 2013 mentions no less than 38 partners and stakeholders!

5.2.19.1.3 Responsibilities

This is indirectly present, but not explicitly described in the document. Ownership is one of the key values of Loblaw. The report is not detailed enough to include names of the people responsible for the large number of (sub)processes, objectives, and KPIs.

5.2.19.1.4 KPIs and PIs

Table 5.4 shows the transformation of the focus areas into targets, action plans, and KPIs. Targets and results achieved (from the CSR Annual Report 2017) are described in Table 5.6.

5.2.19.1.5 Segmentation

See Table 5.5 Origins of CO_2 production.

Segmentation: all results of energy consumption from the different stores are consolidated. The same is done for the different types of vehicles (cars and trucks, trailers).

5.2.19.1.6 Prevention

Identification and evaluation of the risks of business is a key responsibility that is managed through the Board's various committees, such as the Audit Committee and the Environment, Health and Safety Committee, which exercise specific oversight on a range of environmental, health and social (EH&S) matters.

As part of its fiduciary responsibility, the Board oversees the company's management of EH&S issues and opportunities. Prioritization of efforts

Table 5.6 Targets set, and the results achieved for the three pillars at the end of 2017

TARGET	*PROGRESS SUMMARY*
Environment	
Reduce our operational carbon footprint by 20% by 2020 and 30% by 2030.	20% by 2020 achieved in 2017. Making good progress to reduce carbon emissions 30% by 2030. Carbon emissions in corporate operations have been reduced 21.9% relative to a 2011 baseline.
Source fiber used in corrugated boxes and trays, folding cartons and paperboard trays from recycled material and/or certified sustainably managed forests by year-end 2018.	Target in progress. We are working with vendors to collect product packaging specifications and tracking compliance.
Sourcing	
Source all fresh veal from suppliers that have transitioned to group housing by year-end 2018.	Target in progress. We continue to engage and receive status updates from our fresh veal suppliers.
Source all fresh pork from suppliers that have transitioned to group housing by year-end 2022.	Target in progress. We continue to engage and receive status updates from our fresh pork suppliers.
Transition all shell eggs to cage-free by year-end 2025.	Target in progress. In 2017, *our President's Choice* free-run egg offering was extended to include PC Blue Menu Omega-3 Free-Run white eggs. This new offering was rolled out in all Fortinos banner stores in Ontario, transitioning these stores to be our first banner to offer only free-run eggs under the President's Choice and PC Blue Menu brands. PC Organics eggs continue to be free-range.
Formulate our Life Brand and President's Choice household, beauty, and cosmetic products without triclosan, phthalates, or plastic micro beads by year-end 2018, and encourage our suppliers to identify and eliminate phthalates that may come from other sources, such as manufacturing equipment and packaging.	Successfully stopped manufacturing products formulated with plastic micro beads, triclosan, and phthalates by year-end 2017. We continue to encourage our suppliers to identify and eliminate phthalates that may come from manufacturing equipment and packaging.

(*Continued*)

Table 5.6 (Continued) Targets set, and the results achieved for the three pillars at the end of 2017

TARGET	*PROGRESS SUMMARY*
Disclose on our corporate website the list of offshore apparel factories we do direct business with and update the list twice a year.	List of factories is disclosed and updated twice a year.
Transition three farms in Ontario and Quebec to grow five ethnic products to help increase our multicultural product offering by year-end 2017.	Three farms in Ontario and Quebec were transitioned in 2017 with three new ethnic products grown.
Community	
With the help of our customers, colleagues, employees and business partners, we will contribute more than $65 million to charities and non-profit organizations across Canada, which includes support to programs benefiting women and children's health through SHOPPERS LOVE. YOU. and President's Choice® Children's Charity, by year-end 2017.	Donated more than $74 million to charities and non-profit organizations across Canada, benefiting women and children's health through SHOPPERS LOVE. YOU. and President's Choice® Children's Charity.
Educate 500,000 children about food and food sustainability in market stores by year-end 2017.	Educated 297,246 children through in-store events, school tours, and child-focused cooking classes.
Raise and donate $3 million to various charities as part of our "Save It Forward" program in discount stores by year-end 2018.	Raised $2.2 million in 2017 through three events, as part of the "Save It Forward" program in discount stores.
Launch a health and wellness platform for colleagues and customers by year-end 2017.	Launched a health and wellness pilot app for colleagues.

within the three CSR pillars based on the urgency of an issue, its importance to customers and Canadians, its relevance to business and the potential for Loblaw to make a meaningful impact.

5.2.19.1.7 Benchmarking

The carbon strategy, including targets and action plans, is informed by Science-Based Targets. Working with partners like WWF-Canada (a key driver of Science-Based Targets) Loblaw intends to deliver emission reductions in line with industry standards.

The 2017 CSR report mentions that the target for the corporate fleet must be lower than 13 L/100 km (see Table 5.4 Transformation of the focus areas into targets, action plans, and KPIs). However, European middle cars already have a fuel consumption which is lower than 10 L/km. This is an illustration of the importance of using (external) comparisons to be sure that you achieve the best possible results.

5.2.19.1.8 Data

This is indirectly present, but not explicitly described in the document.

5.2.19.2 Analyze the Do-*Step of the BEST-Method*

5.2.19.2.1 Implementation

It is not possible to achieve the results described in the CSR report without implementation of the enablers and processes.

5.2.19.2.2 Cause-Effect

The illustration on the website explaining the whole CSR approach explains the cause and effect between enabler and results achieved.

5.2.19.2.3 Accountability

This is indirectly present, but not explicitly described in the document.

Be reminded that ownership is one of the Loblaw values (Figure 5.15).

5.2.19.2.4 SMART

This is clearly present in the reports.

5.2.19.3 Analysis of the Check *Step of the BEST-Method*

5.2.19.3.1 Monitoring

From the different CSR reports (2007–2017) we conclude that Loblaw makes use of a monitoring system (Figure 5.16).

The reports mention the targets, but also the degree to which targets are achieved. There are three categories: 1) target met, 2) target almost met or on track, and 3) target not met or at the initial stage.

		Criteria and characteristics	0%	25%	50%	75%	100%	Not described	Comments
1	DO	**Implementation**							
		• The daily activities are in conformance with the process descriptions and documented methods					x		
		• The implementation of the core process is integrated into the					x		
2		**Deployment**							
		• The approach is used by all appropriate work units					x		
3		**Cause-effect**							
		• The use of the key process leads to concrete and measurable					x		
4		**Accountability**							
		• All employees and managers clearly exhibit how they are responsible and accountable for their assigned tasks					x		Indirectly, not explicitely
5		**SMART**							
		• KPI's and PI's are used systematically					x		
		• SMART decisions are taken and action plans are developed					x		

SMART This is an acronym and stands for Specific, Measurable, Assignable (Accountable), Relevant and Timely executed

Figure 5.15 Assessment of the *Do* phase.

		Criteria and characteristics	0%	25%	50%	75%	100%	Not described	Comments
1	Check	**Integration**							
		• Plans, process, results, analysis, learning and actions are harmonized across the process and work units to support organization-wide goals					x		
2		**Monitoring**							
		• The performance of each core process is regularly measured and monitored					x		Indirectly, not explicitely
		• The obtained results related to a core process are regularly discussed with all relevant stakeholders					x		Indirectly, not explicitely
		• The method to determine the target value of the KPI (target) is validated and opportunities for improvement are recorded					x		Indirectly, not explicitely
		• Relevance, integrity, completeness and reliability of the results achieved are checked					x		
3		**Audit**							
		• Each process owner audits his or her core process regularly	x						
		• The process owner examines what can be done to bring the core process to a higher maturity level (to determine improvement opportunities)	x						
4		**Adjustment and Learning**							
		• Deviations from the desired and/or planned results serve as input for the improvement and revision of the core process and/or approaches					x		Indirectly, not explicitely
		• Identification of problems related to the sufficient availability and appropriate resources such as budget, machinery, equipment, provisions, tools, and Information Technology (software, hardware, networking, security, etc.)					x		Indirectly, not explicitely
		• Identification of an adequate number of employees and/or of shortcomings of skills and experiences of employees in the process and/or approaches					x		Indirectly, not explicitely
		• Comparison of the results obtained with the benchmark and Best-in-Class	x						
		• Prioritization of opportunities for improvement					x		Indirectly, not explicitely
		• Encouragement of breakthrough change to the approach applied through innovation					?		

Figure 5.16 Assessment of *Check* phase.

5.2.19.3.2 Audit

No evidence of application of a systematic audit of approaches, processes, and results.

5.2.19.3.3 Adjustment and Learning

From the different CSR reports (2007–2017) we conclude that Loblaw applies adjustment and learning topics.

5.2.19.4 Analysis of the Act *Step of the BEST-Method*

See Figure 5.17.

5.2.19.4.1 Improvement

Through the reading of the CSR reports we see that improvement is present in the Loblaw culture.

5.2.19.4.2 Processes

Description is done on a high level.

		Criteria and characteristics	0%	25%	50%	75%	100%	Not described	Comments
1	Act	**Improvement** • The output of the measurement and learning is analyzed and used to identify additional improvements; to prioritize, to plan and to implement these further opportunities for improvement					x		Indirectly, not explicitely
2		**Process** • The process, methods and approaches are revised and improved in response to the findings gained in the Check phase					x		Indirectly, not explicitely
3		**Resources** • The amount and nature of the resources that were adjusted because of the findings in the Check phase are documented					x		Indirectly, not explicitely
		• The number of employees assigned to the process is adjusted considering the opportunities of improvement and the outcome of the process, methods and approaches					x		Indirectly, not explicitely
4		**Knowledge and Experience** • New training and/or refresher training is given to meet the findings gained in the Check phase					x		Indirectly, not explicitely
		• Sharing of refinements and innovations with other relevant work units and processes					?		
		• The Knowledge and experience of those involved in the process are documented and validated as Best-in-Class or Benchmark level					x		Indirectly, not explicitely
5		**Benchmark** • The organization can be set as a model for other organizations					x		

Figure 5.17 Assessment of *Act* phase.

5.2.19.4.3 Resources

This is indirectly present, but not explicitly described in the document.

We believe that it is impossible to achieve such excellent results without the necessary resources present (budget, people, and time).

5.2.19.4.4 Knowledge and Experience

This is indirectly present, but not explicitly described in the document.

We believe that it is impossible to achieve such excellent results *without an active development of knowledge and continuous gain in experience.*

5.2.19.4.5 Benchmark

These reports are impressive. CSR at Loblaw can be considered as a benchmark for other organizations.

In this case study the enablers are well developed, and much evidence is given. Let us now assess the *results* of the case study.

5.2.20 Results (7 criteria and 20 characteristics)

These results are excellent, according to the results assessment in Figure 5.18.

The next step is the assessment of the *process.*

5.2.21 Management of Process (nine criteria)

Finally, we can analyze the last item in the BEST-tool, i.e. *process format.* Here we assess to what extent the process is fully *described.* More information would certainly be gained by an on-site visit (Figure 5.19).

About half of the characteristics are not described in the report. We could expect this finding because Loblaw is not aware of the requirements of the BEST-method.

5.2.22 Maturity of the Management of the Process

Next is an assessment of the maturity of the management of the CSR process at Loblaw.

We assign a score of 4 for the process of management of CSR at Loblaw. This is a good, working level for a successful organization (Figure 5.20).

	Element	0%	25%	50%	75%	100%	Not described	Comments
1	**Scope and Relevance**							
	• The results are aligned with the expectations and needs of the relevant stakeholders					x		
	• The results are aligned with policy and strategy of the organization					x		
	• The most important key results are identified and prioritized					x		
	• The relation between the results is understood					x		
2	**Integrity of data**							
	• Results are timely					x		
	• Results are reliable and accurate					x		
3	**Segmentation**							
	• Results are segmented in a suitable manner					x		
	o By region, country					x		
	o By department, business line, division, unit					x		
	o By product and service type					x		
4	**Trends**							
	• Trends are positive for 5 years or more					x		
	• Results are sustainable and show good performance					x		
5	**Targets**							
	• Targets for core results are set					x		
	• Targets are suitable					x		
	• Targets are achieved					x		
6	**Comparisons with targets and benchmarks**							
	• Comparisons for core results are made					x		
	• Comparisons are suitable					x		Comparison with own targets
	• Comparisons are favorable					x		
7	**Cause-effect**							
	• The results are clearly achieved through the chosen approach (cause - effect)					x		
	• The relations between results achieved and the approaches are understood					x		
	* Based on the evidence presented, it is assured that the positive performance will continue in the future, i.e. the results are sustainable					x		

Figure 5.18 Assessment of *Results* for CSR Loblaw case study.

5.2.23 Assessment of the Format *of the Best Practice of Loblaw*

The Best Practice report needs to fulfill a series of requirements, i.e. the format. This allows the reader to have a full and detailed picture of the Best Practice (Figure 5.21).

5.2.24 Summary of the Assessment of the CSR Loblaw Case Study and Conclusion

There are suggested improvement areas only for the process description and the case study format. This case study fulfills the criteria and characteristics of a Best Practice in a large part for the enablers (PDCA) and results.

	Subject	NOK	OK	Comment
1	Owner of key process	x		Not explicitely described in the text. However ownership is one of the values of Loblaw
2	Integrity		x	
3	Risk management	x		Not described in the text
4	Relation with strategic plan		x	
5	Adding value		x	
6	Systematic simplification	x		Not described in the text
7	KPI		x	
8	Audit	x		Not described in the text
9	Maturity level of process		x	

Figure 5.19 Assessment of the *management of the process* of Loblaw's CSR Best Practice.

It is impressive that Loblaw has already published 11 CSR reports. There is clear evidence of sustainability of the results.

This case study can be considered as a Best Practice. There is also a high probability that much more detail, interesting approaches, and corresponding results would be discovered through an on-site visit.

5.2.25 Good Practice

It is probable that a first assessment will identify characteristics with a 75% score and some with a 100% score. In that case the process owner has recognized a "good practice." However, this assessment allows the process owner to make further improvements for those characteristics at the 75% (or below) level.

Note:

With the aid of the BEST-method a company or process owner can prove the existence of a Best Practice for a subject like CSR. It is absolutely necessary, however, to keep in mind that the whole organization needs to be healthy, not only one process, i.e. a systematic achievement of excellent results for all stakeholders. The use of the BEST-method on a continuing basis across all key processes will drive system-wide improvement for organizational excellence.

Levels		Description	Assessment
0		**Non-existent** Within the organization there are no or very little management measures. Control awareness is rather low and only few actions are taken to achieve an adequate system of organizational management (internal control system).	
1		**Ad-hoc basis** Only ad-hoc management measures are in place within the organization. The awareness of the need for appropriate management (internal control) is growing, but there is still no structured or standardized approach present. The system of organizational management (internal control) is more focused on people than on systems.	
2		**Structured start** A structured impetus is given to the development of management measures. The management tools are therefore being developed but are not yet applied (Plan)	
3		**Defined** (= level 2 + ...) Control measures are provided. These are standardized, documented, communicated and implemented (Do).	
4		**Management system** (= level 3 + ...) The control measures are internally assessed and adjusted (Check & Act). There is a "living" adequate and effective system of organizational management.	
5		**Optimized** (= level 4 + ...) The control measures are continuously optimized through benchmarking and obtaining quality certificates or external evaluations (PDCA).	

Figure 5.20 Assessment of the *maturity of the management of the process* of CSR Loblaw's Best Practice.

The authors believe that it would be useful, after two concrete and real case studies, to give an example of an ideal case study where nearly all criteria of the BEST-tool are met. The Dream Hotel case study gives the reader an example of a "perfect" Best Practice case study. It follows all the criteria and characteristics required for a Best Practice process. Be aware that few if any real processes will achieve 100% adherence to the BEST-assessment model. If you are not interested in this didactic example, you can skip this case study and go to the next chapter.

	Subject	NOK	OK	Comments
1	Title		x	
2	Subject		x	Corporate Social Responsibility, annual reports from 2007 to 2017
3	Author (name, title, company, contact)	x		Not explicitly mentioned in the reports
4	Context (sector, country restrictions)		x	
5	Description of the method and results		x	
6	Measurement method		x	
7	Process description and maturity	x		Not explicitly mentioned in the reports
8	KPIs (Key Performance Indicator) and results		x	
9	Distribution of the results		x	
10	Cause and effect		x	
11	Measurement: RADAR, PDCA, or other		x	
12	Limiting conditions	x		Not explicitly mentioned in the reports
13	Date and Revision Level		x	Annual report

Figure 5.21 Assessment of the description of the *format* of a Best Practice for Loblaw's management of Corporate Social Responsibility (CSR).

5.3 Case Study 3 Dream Hotel

Dream Hotel was founded in Brussels in 1995. At that time the European Union was expanded to 16 member states. In 2013 28 European countries already were members of the European Union. Several European institutions are based in Brussels, i.e. the European Commission which is the European Government, European Parliament and European Council. It is also the political and economic capital of the European Union. Brussels also houses the headquarters of NATO. It has, of course, embassies from all countries around the world.

The European Union contains 513 million people, which is the third largest "country," after China (1,433 million people) and India (1,366 million people), but before the USA (329 million people). However, the USA is stronger in political and economic power. Brussels has gradually become more and more attractive for many international organizations (trade unions, employers, farmers, consumers, etc.).

The founder of Dream Hotel wanted to be the first choice for his customers among the 800 hotels situated in the Brussels region. He did not only use customer satisfaction surveys, but also tried to find out what customers valued and would influence them to return. One of the strengths is that all staff members fluently speak at least three languages. More than half of the staff speak five languages or more fluently. Because the hotel is a four star hotel, it offers a wide variety of services to its customers, such as premier class food in its restaurants, a large variety of food (breakfast, lunch, and dinner), a premium service for guests and organizers of events, a large variety of services such as a swimming pool, fitness center, bar, garden, laundry, free Wi-Fi, safety deposit box, satellite channels, wake up service, coffee machine, minibar, and free airport shuttle. Regular guests recognize Dream Hotel as one of the best in Brussels.

After the retirement of the founder Joseph Johnson, 5 years ago, his son Peter took the lead.

Composition of the management team:

- Peter Johnson, General Manager, son of the founder Joseph Johnson
- Ian Nicholson, Sales and Marketing Manager
- Nick Posner, Operational Manager
- Diana Ferguson, Administrative, Purchasing, and Financial Manager
- Josephine Peters, Maintenance and Facility Manager
- John Williams, Quality and Customer Service Manager
- William Stevens, HR and IT Manager

The Dream Hotel has 300 beds, 180 bedrooms, 4 event rooms. The hotel has 250 staff members (205 FTE).

5.3.1 Organization of the Company

In Table 5.7 the key processes are grouped according to their influence in the realization of the activities; i.e. these can be considered as inputs, processes, outputs, and/or outcome results. The table also shows who is accountable for which key process and corresponding KPIs.

This figure shows the result of many learning points from the last years. Indeed, once a year a self-assessment is made by the expanded management team, i.e. all the members of the management team together with five middle managers. From this yearly exercise, an annual action plan is established. The follow up of this plan is reviewed monthly by the management team.

Each manager is accountable for one or more key processes and corresponding KPIs. Each manager monitors at least one output or outcome KPI.

The top management of the Dream Hotel developed their operating strategy in 1996. Every 5 years the strategy is completely revised. The strategy 2018 is explained in Figure 5.22.

Table 5.7 Relationship of the key processes and KPIs with the type of achievement results

Type of results → *Owner of key process*	*Input*	*Process*	*Output*	*Outcome*
Sales Mgr		Sales	Sales	Turnover/FTE
Purchasing Mgr	Purchasing		Costs	
Marketing Mgr	Marketing			Increase in market share
Events Mgr		Events	Profitability	
Facility Mgr	Facility mgt	Facility mgt	Costs	
Maintenance Mgt	Maintenance	Maintenance	Costs	
Customer Service Mgr		Surveys	Customer satisfaction Repeat business	Customer satisfaction
Customer Service Mgr			Complaints	Customer satisfaction
Operational Mgr		Check-in		
Operational Mgr		Check-out Invoicing	Check-out Occupancy of bedrooms Turnover	Turnover EBITDA
Facility Mgr		Environment	Energy reduction CO_2 reduction	
General Mgr	Leadership		Managerial competencies	
HR Mgr	Training Number training days per staff member	Training	Number languages/ staff member Number of technical and people competencies/staff member	People satisfaction

(Continued)

Table 5.7 (Continued) Relationship of the key processes and KPIs with the type of achievement results

Type of results ? Owner of key process	*Input*	*Process*	*Output*	*Outcome*
Customer Service Mgr		Kaizen applied to key processes	Reduction of costs Reduction of cycle time Increase in reliability of products and services	Operational Efficiency
General Manager	Policy and Strategy development			Achievement of Strategy

Vision : First choice

We will be the first choice for people who need a hotel

Strategies

Employer of choice

Engagement of all employees

* Leadership development
* Competency development
* Community development

Culture of innovation

* Empowerment
* Continuous improvement (kaizen)
* Process Excellence
* New value added services

Value chain Optimization

Asset utilization

* Occupancy of rooms
* Occupancy of event facilities
* Profitable growth, EBITDA

Customer focus

* Product quality
* Service quality
* Value added services
* Recognition as an Excellent Hotel

Figure 5.22 Strategy 2018, Dream Hotel.

Since 1999, the Dream Hotel has used the European Excellence model Self-Assessment method, i.e. EFQM model. This annual Self-Assessment leads to an action plan that is monitored by the management team.

Each key process owner makes an inventory of the expectations and requirements of their stakeholder. The stakeholder map in Figure 5.23 gives an overview of these expectations and requirements.

The founder was a strong believer that an investment in people contributes to a positive evolution of the company. The number of training days per collaborator increased over the last 10 years from 2–8 days per staff member

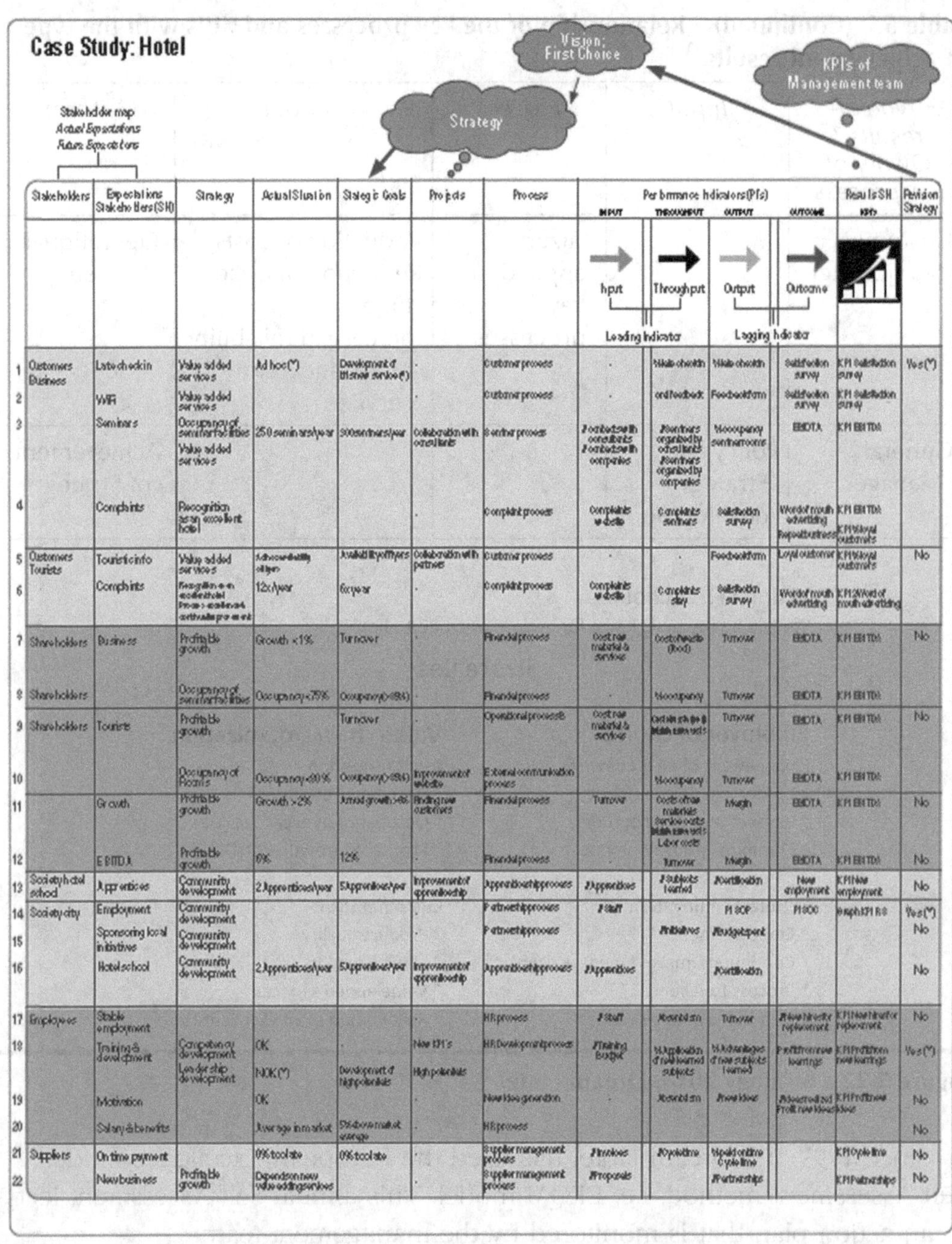

	Stakeholders	Expectations Stakeholders (SH)	Strategy	Actual Situation	Strategic Goals	Projects	Process	Performance Indicators (PIs) INPUT	THROUGHPUT	OUTPUT	OUTCOME	Results SH KPIs	Revision Strategy
1	Customers Business	Late check-in	Value added services	Ad hoc(*)	Development of this new service(*)	-	Customer process	-	% late checkin	% late checkin	Satisfaction survey	KPI Satisfaction survey	Yes(*)
2		WiFi	Value added services			-	Customer process	-	and feedback	Feedback form	Satisfaction survey	KPI Satisfaction survey	
3		Seminars	Occupancy of seminar facilities Value added services	250 seminars/year	300 seminars/year	Collaboration with consultants	Seminar process	# contacts with consultants # contacts with companies	# seminars organized by consultants # seminars organized by companies	% occupancy seminar rooms	EBIDTA	KPI EBITDA	
4		Complaints	Recognition as an excellent hotel			-	Complaint process	Complaints website	Complaints seminars	Satisfaction survey	Word of mouth advertising Repeat business	KPI EBITDA KPI % loyal customers	
5	Customers Tourists	Touristic info	Value added services	[illegible]	Availability of flyers	Collaboration with partners	Customer process	-	-	Feedback form	Loyal customer	KPI % loyal customers	No
6		Complaints	[illegible]	12x/year	6x/year	-	Complaint process	Complaints website	Complaints stay	Satisfaction survey	Word of mouth advertising	KPI 2 Word of mouth advertising	
7	Shareholders	Business	Profitable growth	Growth <1%	Turnover	-	Financial process	Cost raw material & services	Cost of waste (food)	Turnover	EBIDTA	KPI EBITDA	No
8	Shareholders		Occupancy of seminar facilities	Occupancy <75%	Occupancy(>85%)	-	Financial process	-	% occupancy	Turnover	EBIDTA	KPI EBITDA	
9	Shareholders	Tourists	Profitable growth		Turnover	-	Operational process	Cost raw material & services	[illegible]	Turnover	EBIDTA	KPI EBITDA	No
10			Occupancy of Rooms	Occupancy <80%	Occupancy(>85%)	Improvement of website	External communication process		% occupancy	Turnover	EBIDTA	KPI EBITDA	
11		Growth	Profitable growth	Growth >2%	Annual growth >4%	Finding new customers	Financial process	Turnover	Costs of raw materials Service costs [illegible] Labor costs	Margin	EBIDTA	KPI EBITDA	No
12		EBITDA	Profitable growth	6%	12%	-	Financial process	-	Turnover	Margin	EBIDTA	KPI EBITDA	No
13	Society hotel school	Apprentices	Community development	2 Apprentices/year	5 Apprentices/year	Improvement of apprenticeship	Apprenticeship process	# Apprentices	# Subjects learned	# Certification	New employment	KPI New employment	No
14	Society city	Employment	Community development			-	Partnership process	# Staff	-	PI SOP	PI SOC	[illegible] KPI RS	Yes(*)
15		Sponsoring local initiatives	Community development			-	Partnership process		# Initiatives	# Budget spent			No
16		Hotel school	Community development	2 Apprentices/year	5 Apprentices/year	Improvement of apprenticeship	Apprenticeship process	# Apprentices		# Certification			No
17	Employees	Stable employment				-	HR process	# Staff	Absenteeism	Turnover	# new hires for replacement	KPI New hires for replacement	No
18		Training & development	Competency development Leadership development	OK NOK(*)	- Development of high potentials	New KPI's High potentials	HR Development process	# Training Budget	% Application of new learned subjects	% Advantages of new subjects learned	Profit from new learnings	KPI Profit from new learnings	Yes(*)
19		Motivation		OK		-	New idea generation	-	Absenteeism	# new ideas	Achieved realized profit new ideas	KPI Profit new ideas	No
20		Salary & benefits		Average in market	5% above market average	-	HR process						No
21	Suppliers	On time payment		0% too late	0% too late	-	Supplier management process	# Invoices	# Cycle time	% paid on time Cycle time		KPI Cycle time	No
22		New business	Profitable growth	Depends on new value adding services		-	Supplier management process	# Proposals		# Partnerships		KPI Partnerships	No

Figure 5.23 Stakeholder map and the corresponding KPIs and results. See Yves Van Nuland and Grace L. Duffy, *Professional Process Management*, The Quality Management Forum, 2019, 45(4), 5–12.

per year. The number of newly developed competencies per staff member is considered as a measure for the future development of the company. Not only is on-the-job training important, but staff training is also provided by external professionals.

The documentation method for the description of the key processes is based upon the experience of the quality manager. The basis is a flowchart for each key process; details of every step in the flowchart are put into a second parallel page where the details are contained in four columns, i.e. who, where, when, and how. This approach minimizes the bureaucracy and is complete and transparent. Everyone knows at every moment what and how to execute an activity of the flowchart. For details of the flowchart see Figure 5.24.

The owner of the key process audits his process once a year. He studies how he can shorten the key process by eliminating the non-value-added steps. To improve the work instructions where necessary, he checks whether the lessons learned are integrated into the key process and finally, how the process

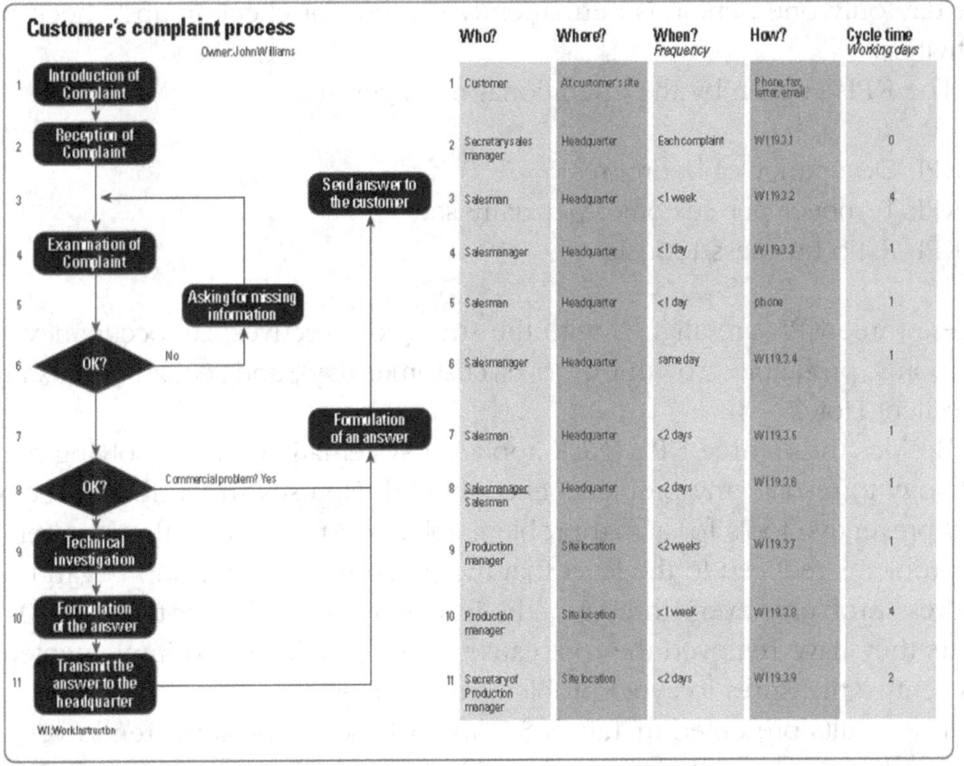

Figure 5.24 Description of the flowchart approach for the key process Customer Complaints.

can be improved by a further increase in the competencies of the collaborators. All these initiatives serve to reduce the cycle time of the key process, which is also a measure of operational efficiency (see strategy: process excellence).

In order to demonstrate the way Dream Hotel applies the management of key processes, the quality manager checks once a year that all the key processes have been audited and reviewed. He also checks the revision number of each key process. Twenty years ago, it was hard to convince every member of the management team. Now that they have seen the positive effects of their efforts and reviews, they review the processes spontaneously on an annual basis.

5.3.2 Description of the Key Process Check-out

The description of the Check-out process is similar to the description given in Figure 5.24. Nick Posner, Operational Manager, is the process owner. The majority of the check-out activities happen between 7 am and 9 am for businesspeople and between 9 am and 11 am for tourists. Between 7 am and 9 am two persons are available at the check-out counter. For the rest of the day only one person is permanently present for check-in and check-out activities.

The KPIs chosen by the operational manager are:

KPI: Occupancy of bedrooms
KPI: Turnover per customer per daily stay
KPI: Ratio business/tourists

These three KPIs are aligned with the strategic objectives, i.e. occupancy of rooms, profitable growth (turnover/customer/day), and recognition as an Excellent Hotel.

Besides these three KPIs, Nick applies a systematic problem-solving methodology to resolve any problems encountered. He uses structured corrective and preventive tools for actual problem solving. After 5 years the number of problems reduced to the level that the problem-solving group began to address problems every three months instead of monthly. For the past 10 years they have removed the root cause of the problems and implemented preventive measures to avoid problem recurrence.

The results presented in Tables 5.8 and 5.9 show a positive trend over a period of 8 years. The low results in 2016 and 2017 are due to the bomb attack at the airport in 2016. From 2018 on the trend returned to positive growth. The dip in results during 2016–2017 is present for the whole hotel

Table 5.8 Occupancy bedrooms (%), Turnover/customer/day (Euro) and Business travelers (%)

Year	*Occupancy bedrooms (%)*	*Target (%)*	*Turnover/ customer/day*	*Target*	*Business (%)*	*Target*
2012	75	78	205	210	72	75
2013	78	78	211	210	75	75
2014	79	80	213	215	74	75
2015	81	80	215	215	78	75
2016	74	82	190	220	77	75
2017	75	82	195	220	76	75
2018	84	82	225	220	75	75
2019	86	85	235	230	75	75

Table 5.9 Monthly details of the year 2019

Year 2019	*Occupancy bedrooms (%)*	*Target (%)*	*Turnover/ customer/ day*	*Target*	*Business*	*Target*
January	86	85	225	230	74	75
February	85	85	237	230	77	75
March	86	85	220	230	76	75
April	83	85	233	230	72	75
May	87	85	241	230	73	75
June	86	85	225	230	75	75
July	84	85	230	230	74	75
August	86	85	235	230	74	75
September	88	85	237	230	77	75
October	88	85	247	230	78	75
November	89	85	246	230	77	75
December	89	85	245	230	73	75

sector in the Brussels region. The management team discussed many times which extra preventive measures could be taken in order to avoid critical incidents such as a bomb attack. Management initiated a marketing effort to provide positive signals to their customers that safety is taken seriously at Dream Hotel. The counter measures instituted are:

- The local police are invited to take their breakfast (for free) in the hotel. This gives a psychological signal to the customers.
- The elevators are secured. The elevator can only be activated with a badge.
- Housekeeping people are trained on early warning signs and to alert the safety and quality manager immediately.

The check-out person will not only perform the check-out formalities, but also ask the guest if everything was OK during their stay. Most importantly, every customer is asked the following question: "Assume you are the general manager of this hotel, what would you change or improve in order of priority?" All the answers are entered into a computer application. At the end of the month, the quality manager runs a short report with the findings and proposals for action/improvement. This report is discussed among the management team and followed up with an improvement plan.

Every time a process is improved the question is asked: "What do we need to design into the software system, e.g. with pop up screens and drop-down menus, in order to avoid making the same mistake?" Working in that way over the last 7 years the number of typing errors dropped to a very low frequency. Today the error rate is lower than 50 ppm (parts per million).

By combining the customer data (from the check-out data base) and prospects (from sales database) with AI (artificial intelligence) it is now possible to anticipate what new customers expect. This analysis is made beginning in August, when it is a calm period in the hotel. One of the new subjects that appeared from this analysis was an automated check-out. Regular customers can, with their smart-phone, easily check-in and check-out. The automated device delivers and accepts the QR-code of the customer. With this QR-code he can enter the hotel, enter the elevator, and enter his bedroom. Payment is also done with the smart-phone. The customer contacts the staff member at check-in or check-out when he has special requirements, specific questions, or when he encounters problems.

Newly hired personnel work with an experienced staff member for three months so he or she can learn the job of check-out in real time. After 3 months, the experienced person makes a short report of the competencies of the trainee that need to be further developed. The HR manager and the operational manager together establish a training plan to fill any gaps in the new employee's competencies.

The management team takes the vision "We will be the first choice for people who need a hotel" seriously. For that reason, every manager tries to have a short interview with at least five customers per month, e.g. during the breakfast or dinner period. The manager then creates a small report that is discussed along with the monthly check-out report.

Finally, at least three times per year, one or more managers take a hotel room for at least two nights in another capital in Europe to discover new ideas for improvement or added values for their own customers. One of the learning points was that the variety of services and products of the Dream Hotel were not well communicated or presented. These features are now much better highlighted at check-in and in a folder in every bedroom. Some examples created over the last 4 years:

- Order tickets for a concert or museum.
- Contact information for a guided visit of the city of Brussels (every Friday and Saturday).
- Assistance to arrange a trip outside Brussels (African museum in Tervuren, a visit to the university in the city of Leuven, etc.).
- Connect with guests who want to discover the city together.

From the benchmarks the managers conducted, it appears that Dream Hotel is the real best-in-class for the check-out process.

At least once in 2 years the in-house check-out process and that of a benchmark (best hotel of the year in Europe) is investigated in detail. An action plan is established to fill any gaps in performance at Dream Hotel. The management team makes a follow up of the plan.

Dream Hotel participated at the Belgian Excellence Award in 2018. It won the Award. In the feedback report of the assessors, two key processes were considered as best practices, i.e. check-out process and sales process.

Although the management team of Dream Hotel has a number of indications that it is an excellent hotel and a benchmark in its sector, the general manager wanted to know to what extent their key process "check-out" can

	Criteria and characteristics	0%	25%	50%	75%	100%	Not described	Comments
1	**Scope and Relevance**							
	• The results are aligned with the expectations and needs of the relevant stakeholders					x		
	• The results are aligned with policy and strategy of the organization					x		
	• The most important key results are identified and prioritized					x		
	• The relation between the results is understood					x		
2	**Integrity of data**							
	• Results are timely					x		
	• Results are reliable and accurate					x		
3	**Segmentation**							
	• Results are segmented in a suitable manner						x	This is not described in the text. Probably it is present, but it is necessary to check it during a site visit. We expect to see results for business and tourists
	o By region, country						NA	
	o By department, business line, division, unit						x	
	o By product and service type						x	
4	**Trends**							
	• Trends are positive for 5 years or more					x		
	• Results are sustainable and show good performance					x		
5	**Targets**							
	• Targets for core results are set					x		
	• Targets are suitable					x		
	• Targets are achieved					x		
6	**Comparisons with targets and benchmarks**							
	• Comparisons for core results are made					x		
	• Comparisons are suitable					x		
	• Comparisons are favorable					x		
7	**Cause-effect**							
	• The results are clearly achieved through the chosen approach (cause - effect)					x		
	• The relations between results achieved and the approaches are understood					x		
	* Based on the evidence presented, it is assured that the positive performance will continue in the future, i.e. the results are sustainable					x		

Figure 5.25 Assessment of the *results* of the key process *Check-out*

be considered as a Best Practice. For this reason, the detailed BEST-method was applied. The assessment starts with the first building block *results*. In Figure 5.25 an overview of the assessment for the results is given.

All criteria are well described, with the exception of segmentation. Probably segmentation is done; however, the text doesn't mention any detail. Therefore, we need to verify this during a site visit.

The description of the key process Check-out is so detailed and complete that we may expect that Dream Hotel has more to let us see. This is also confirmed with the assessment of the following building block, i.e. the *enablers* (PDCA) (Figure 5.26).

		Criteria and characteristics	0%	25%	50%	75%	100%	Not described	Comments
1	Plan	**Description**							
		· The approach is repeatable and based on reliable data and information					x		
		· The core process are identified and described					x		
		· The methods are documented					x		
		· The process is the reflection of common sense and is well thought out (logical sequence, clearly linked to organizational strategy, interactions with other processes and sub-processes)					x		
2		**Stakeholders**							
		• The process is tailored to the needs, requirements and expectations of interested parties (stakeholders)					x		
		• The indicators and targets are set and the relationship with the core process is clearly defined					x		
3		**Responsibilities**							
		• The responsibilities and accountabilities are clearly defined					x		
		• Each process has a process owner					x		
		• The process description takes into account the skills and experiences required by the persons responsible for carrying out the process and approaches					x		
4		**KPI's and PI's**							
		• Each process contains one or more KPI's (Key Performance Indicator) and one or more PI's (Performance Indicator)					x		
5		**Deployment and Segmentation**							
		• The description of the process and approaches considers the specificities of all segments of the organization (division, department, work unit) and the variety of products and services					x		
6		**Prevention**							
		• Prevention is built into the process					x		
		• The core process description takes into account the specific circumstances of the organization and prevention is integrated into the daily work					x		
7		**Benchmarking**							
		• The process description takes into account similar benchmarks and best-in-class examples					x		
8		**Data**							
		• The measurement methods are described clearly and					x		
		• The data are presented at the proper level of segmentation to effectively reflect performance and results at different levels of the organization.					x		

		Criteria and characteristics	0%	25%	50%	75%	100%	Not described	Comments
1	DO	**Implementation**							
		• The daily activities are in conformance with the process descriptions and documented methods					x		
		• The implementation of the core process is integrated into the daily work					x		
		Deployment							
		• The approach is used by all appropriate work units					x		
2		**Cause-effect**							
		• The use of the key process leads to concrete and measurable results					x		
3		**Accountability**							
		• All employees and managers clearly exhibit how they are responsible and accountable for their assigned tasks					x		
4		**SMART**							
		• KPI's and PI's are used systematically					x		
		• SMART decisions are taken and action plans are developed					x		

Figure 5.26 Assessment of the *approaches (enablers)* of the key process Check-out.

		Criteria and characteristics	0%	25%	50%	75%	100%	Not described	Comments
1	Check	**Integration**							
		• Plans, process, results, analysis, learning and actions are harmonized across the process and work units to support organization-wide goals					x		
		Monitoring							
		• The performance of each core process is regularly measured and monitored					x		
		• The obtained results related to a core process are regularly discussed with all relevant stakeholders					x		
		• The method to determine the target value of the KPI (target) is validated and opportunities for improvement are recorded					x		
		• Relevance, integrity, completeness and reliability of the results achieved are checked					x		
2		**Audit**							
		• Each process owner audits his or her core process regularly					x		
		• The process owner examines what can be done to bring the core process to a higher maturity level (to determine improvement opportunities)					x		
3		**Adjustment and Learning**							
		• Deviations from the desired and/or planned results serve as input for the improvement and revision of the core process and/or approaches					x		
		• Identification of problems related to the sufficient availability and appropriate resources such as budget, machinery, equipment, provisions, tools, and Information Technology (software, hardware, networking, security, etc.)					x		
		• Identification of an adequate number of employees and/or of shortcomings of skills and experiences of employees in the process and/or approaches					x		
		• Comparison of the results obtained with the benchmark and Best-in-Class					x		
		• Prioritization of opportunities for improvement					x		
		• Encouragement of breakthrough change to the approach applied through innovation					x		

		Criteria and characteristics	0%	25%	50%	75%	100%	Not described	Comments
1	Act	**Improvement**							
		• The output of the measurement and learning is analyzed and used to identify additional improvements; to prioritize, to plan and to implement these further opportunities for improvement					x		
2		**Process**							
		• The process, methods and approaches are revised and improved in response to the findings gained in the Check phase					x		
3		**Resources**							
		• The amount and nature of the resources that were adjusted because of the findings in the Check phase are documented					x		
		• The number of employees assigned to the process is adjusted considering the opportunities of improvement and the outcome of the process, methods and approaches					x		
4		**Knowledge and Experience**							
		• New training and/or refresher training is given to meet the findings gained in the Check phase					x		
		• Sharing of refinements and innovations with other relevant work units and processes					x		
		• The Knowledge and experience of those involved in the process are documented and validated as Best-in-Class or Benchmark level					x		
5		**Benchmark**							
		• The organization can be set as a model for other organizations					x		

Figure 5.26 (Continued) Assessment of the *approaches (enablers)* of the key process Check-out.

	Subject	NOK	OK	Comment
1	Owner of key process		x	
2	Integrity		x	
3	Risk management		x	
4	Relation with strategic plan		x	
5	Adding value		x	
6	Systematic simplification		x	
7	KPI		x	
8	Audit		x	
9	Maturity level of process		x	

Figure 5.27 Assessment of the *management of key process* Check-out.

All four parts of the building block PDCA (Plan, Do, Check, and Adjust) are complete. This is an exceptional situation.

Let us have a look at the two next building blocks, i.e. how the key process is managed and how the documentation of the key process is done (Figure 5.27).

The management of the key process Check-out may be considered as excellent. The maturity matrix also gives us a very nice picture (Figure 5.28).

As described in the presentation of the Dream Hotel, we see that the building blocks results, enablers, and management of the process Check-out are completely done. When we put the messages of these four building blocks in the maturity index table, we can conclude that we are dealing with an organization at Level 5, "Optimized." This means that the process Check-out at Dream Hotel may be considered as excellent and a Best-in-Class or Best Practice. It can serve as a benchmark for other organizations.

Finally, the last building block is the assessment of the format (Figure 5.29).

Dream Hotel has not only a Best Practice for the key process Check-out, but it would be interesting to investigate other key processes with the detailed BEST-method. There probably are more Best Practices present.

Levels		Description	Assessment
0		**Non-existent** Within the organization there are no or very little management measures. Control awareness is rather low and only few actions are taken to achieve an adequate system of organizational management (internal control system).	
1		**Ad-hoc basis** Only ad-hoc management measures are in place within the organization. The awareness of the need for appropriate management (internal control) is growing, but there is still no structured or standardized approach present. The system of organizational management (internal control) is more focused on people than on systems.	
2		**Structured start** A structured impetus is given to the development of management measures. The management tools are therefore being developed but are not yet applied (Plan)	
3		**Defined** (= level 2 + ...) Control measures are provided. These are standardized, documented, communicated and implemented (Do).	
4		**Management system** (= level 3 + ...) The control measures are internally assessed and adjusted (Check & Act). There is a "living" adequate and effective system of organizational management.	
5		**Optimized** (= level 4 + ...) The control measures are continuously optimized through benchmarking and obtaining quality certificates or external evaluations (PDCA).	

Figure 5.28 Assessment of the Organizational *Maturity* of Check-out process.

	Subject	NOK	OK	Comments
1	Title		x	
2	Subject		x	This could be better, because there are only a few details available
3	Author (name, title, company, contact)		x	
4	Context (sector, country restrictions)		x	
5	Description of the method and results		x	
6	Measurement method		x	
7	Process description and maturity		x	
8	KPIs (Key Performance Indicator) and results		x	
9	Distribution of the results		x	
10	Cause and effect		x	
11	Measurement: RADAR, PDCA, or other		x	
12	Limiting conditions			Not Applicable
13	Date and Revision Level		x	

Figure 5.29 Assessment of the description of the *format* of the key process Check-out.

5.3.3 Conclusion

When we look at the complete assessment of the key process Check-out, we can conclude that Dream Hotel has a real Best Practice.

If you read the whole case study again, you'll find that it sounds logical and practical. This is indeed a last check of common sense, i.e. does it sound realistic, doable and pragmatic If you can answer with a full yes, then you can say that you not only have a Best Practice, but this case study can also serve as a benchmark for others.

Chapter 6

Application of BEST Quick Scan Tool on Case Studies

As stated in Chapter 2, the BEST-method can be used in two ways:

1. The tool provides an assessment as to what extent the process highlighted is a Best Practice. The approach, the results, and the process management are each assessed.
2. It provides an approximate verification that the description contains all the characteristics of a Best Practice and can be effectively used as a benchmark for comparison and improvement.

As noted in previous chapters, the authors must base any assessment using the BEST-tool on the evidence presented, i.e. the material available in texts and on websites from which the examples are drawn. Although we expect that these companies have substantially more information about the practice than documented in an article, we can only use what is published. For reasons of confidentiality, not everything can be published. Since competitors may also consult these materials, the case studies are often intentionally incomplete. Nevertheless, we think that the use of these materials is valuable, as it allows the BEST-method to be demonstrated. It is not the intention of the authors to make value judgments on the quality of the case studies selected for this chapter. Each of the studies chosen represents a successful activity. Most materials published to recognize a company for their performance are not written to be used as a Best Practice. They are used here to show the effectiveness of the Quick Scan BEST-tool.

Most Best Practices found in books and online are not described in sufficient detail to be used for benchmarking. Much detailed information critical to getting the most out of a benchmarking activity may be missing from resources available on the open market. It would be wasted effort to assess all the characteristics of a Best Practice from articles not intended as a complete benchmark.

In 2019 APQC surveyed organizations that use process frameworks for organizational improvement. The results of an associated case study observed that:

> organizations understand that to improve their processes, they need to understand their current state. However, they are missing out on opportunities to objectively prioritize their improvement opportunities through benchmarking.*

The APQC survey report relates that 87.5% of respondents assess the current state of processes as part of a gap analysis. 83.3% determine the "to be" state of processes, 61.1% prioritize process improvement opportunities, 38.9% benchmark processes internally to identify improvement opportunities, and 34.7% benchmark processes externally to identify improvement opportunities.

The simplified BEST-tool (Quick Scan BEST-tool) provides a framework by which organizations can systematically determine the current and "to be" state of their process and document them sufficiently for improvement gap analysis.

We found that only a small number of the investigated cases can be considered as a Best Practice. In the early development of this book we assessed the available case studies with the complete and detailed BEST-tool. However, we discovered that only a small number of the case studies satisfy the conditions of the (detailed) BEST-tool. Therefore, we developed a Quick Scan BEST-tool. This high-level assessment can be done in less than 20 minutes. If this assessment reveals that the case study is probably a Best Practice, you can then use the detailed BEST-tool (see Chapter 5 for examples) to check whether the case study is a real Best Practice.

The BEST-tool was simplified to accommodate the most common information provided in the examples drawn for assessment. In the assessment of the Best Practices for this BEST Quick Scan chapter, only 32 of the total 73 criteria associated with the BEST-tool have been considered.

---

* Lyke-Ho-Gland, Holly and Morgan, Lochlyn, Putting Process Frameworks into Action, APQC Survey Summary Report Announcement materials. May 2019, APQC, slide 20.

The case studies selected for this Quick Scan BEST-tool descriptive chapter are taken from published texts or from pdf files available on a not-for-profit website. The authors employ a publicly available reference to eliminate the need to reproduce the whole text of the case studies. Introductory paragraphs provide a short discussion of each of these case studies followed by an assessment and main conclusions.

The following lists the sources of the ten case studies and the names of the referenced companies mentioned in these publications.

Case study from the book *Business Process Benchmarking: Finding and Implementing Best Practices*

Author: Robert C. Camp, Editor: ASQC Quality Press (1995), ISBN: 0-87389-296-8

Case study 1: Housekeeping system cycle time reduction at The Ritz-Carlton Hotel Company

Case studies from *Healthy Workplaces: A Selection of Global Good Practices*

Author: Wolf Kirsten, Editor: Global Centre for Healthy Workplaces (1995)

Website: www.globalhealthyworkplace.org/documents/Healthy-Workplaces-Good-Practices.pdf

Case study 2: Lån Spar Bank Denmark
Case study 3: GlaxoSmithKline UK
Case study 4: Baxter International Inc. USA

Case studies from APQC's *Connecting People to Content: Create, Surface, and Share Knowledge for a Smarter Organization*

Author: Lauren Trees, Elizabeth Kaigh, Mercy Harper, and Darcy Lemons, Editor: APQC (2015) Best Practices Report

Website: www.scribd.com/document/253772719/2015-APQC-Connecting-People-to-Content-Report

Case study 5: Nalco
Case study 6: MWH Global Inc.

Case study from the book *The Public Health Quality Improvement Handbook*, pp. 139–144

Author: Stephanie Bailey M.D., MSHSA
Editor: ASQ Quality Press (2009)
ISBN: 978-0-87389-758-7

Case study 7: Already Doing It and Not Knowing It (Chapter 12)
Case study 8: Why is Singapore's School System So Successful, and Is It a Model for the West?

Author: David Hogan, Honorary Professor, The University of Queensland
Website: http://theconversation.com/why-is-singapores-school-system-so-successful-and-is-it-a-model-for-the-west-22917

Case study 9: HR Certification Institute & Top Employers Institute

Title: Emerging Evidence: Business Performance and the Validation of HR Best Practices
Website: www.hrci.org/docs/default-source/web-files/validation-of-hr-best-practices.pdf

Case study 10: ExxonMobil

Title: Corporate Citizenship Report: Safety, Health, and the Workplace
Website: http://corporate.exxonmobil.com/en/community/corporate-citizenship-report

We selected these ten case studies because we believe these could indeed be Best Practices. The more we use the Quick Scan BEST-tool, the more we realize that authors on the Internet use the term Best Practice too loosely. When a process description is attractive or may impress the reader, the authors refer to it as a "Best Practice." There is no use of a *measurement system* or an instrument to verify whether the so-called Best Practice is indeed a Best Practice. This explains why we found only a few real Best Practices among the case studies publicly available on the Internet.

A significant advantage of the BEST-tool is that it gives the user an immediate overview of where additional improvements are possible. This advantage contributes directly to the achievement of excellence for the organization or company.

The authors have organized the Quick Scans in Chapter 6 into sections for ease of description. We examined a variety of activities described in ten case studies from across the globe. Each of the sections begins with a short introduction to the anthology, followed by the BEST Quick Scan table, and an interpretation of the findings. Chapter 3 in this book provides explanations of each of the criteria included in the BEST Quick Scan table.

6.1 *Business Process Benchmarking: Finding and Implementing Best Practices* (Robert Camp)

Robert C. Camp's best-selling book, *Benchmarking: The Search for Industry Best Practices that Lead to Superior Performance* served as the premier resource on measuring corporate performance. The book *Business Process Benchmarking* provides information to show readers how to conduct successful benchmarking projects. Readers will discover how to 1) use Camp's renowned ten-step benchmarking process to achieve peak performance; 2) analyze the performance gap and ensure that every employee contributes toward enhanced corporate performance; and 3) train employees to use benchmarking tools to maximize the company's results.

The book provides a wealth of case studies from organizations that have won the Malcolm Baldrige National Quality Award that illustrate how leading-edge organizations have conducted their most productive benchmarking projects.

We analyzed The Ritz-Carlton Hotel case study from Camp's book by applying the Quick Scan BEST-tool.

6.1.1 Case Study: Housekeeping System Cycle Time Reduction at The Ritz-Carlton Hotel Company

6.1.1.1 Who Is The Ritz-Carlton Hotel Company?

The Ritz-Carlton Hotel Company successfully operates in one of the most logistically complex service businesses. Targeting primarily industry executives, meeting and corporate travel planners, and affluent travelers, the Atlanta-based company manages 91 luxury hotels in 30 countries* while pursuing the distinction of being the best in each market. The hotel builds its success on the strength of a comprehensive service quality initiative, which is integrated into its marketing and business objectives.

Winner of the 1992 Malcolm Baldrige National Quality Award, The Ritz-Carlton Hotel Company operates business and resort hotels in the USA, Europe, Middle East, Africa, Asia, Latin America, and Australia. It has 14 international sales offices and employs 40,000 people. Restaurants and banquets are also marketed heavily to local residents. The company claims

* www.ritzcarlton.com/ accessed 12/29/2019.

distinctive facilities and environments, highly personalized anticipatory services, and exceptional food and beverages.

6.1.1.2 Assessment of the Case Study The Ritz-Carlton Hotel Company

Chapter 11, Pages 273–292

Process: Housekeeping system cycle time reduction

Summary assessment of the case study (see Figure 6.1)

- Results
  - Five criteria are complete, and one criterion is incomplete. There is no information available for one criterion ("Trends").
- Enabler
  - Plan phase: seven criteria are complete, and one criterion is incomplete.
  - Do phase: all five criteria are complete.
  - Check phase: three criteria are complete, and there is no information available for one criterion.
  - Act phase: all five criteria are complete.
- Process: the process description and KPIs are described.
- Format: there is a systematic approach to describe the Best Practice in all its aspects and details.

6.1.1.3 Conclusion

This case study can be considered as a Best Practice. *It would be good to confirm this finding by applying the detailed BEST-tool, i.e. the complete and detailed checklist. This can't be done on this text, because this isn't detailed enough.*

6.2 Case Studies from Healthy Workplaces: A Selection of Global Good Practices

A growing number of employers worldwide are starting to invest in the health and well-being of their employees (Global Survey of Workforce Well-being Strategies, 2016). Leading global reasons for implementing employee health strategies are: improving performance and productivity and improving workforce morale and engagement.

		Criteria	Case study
Results		Scope and relevance	Complete
		Integrity of data	Complete
		Segmentation	Incomplete
		Trends	Not Available
		Targets	Complete
		Comparison with benchmarks	Complete
		Cause - Effect	Complete
Enabler	Plan	Description	Complete
		Stakeholders	Complete
		Responsibilities	Complete
		KPI's and PI's	Complete
		Deployment and Segmentation	Complete
		Prevention	Incomplete
		Benchmarking	Complete
		Data	Complete
	Do	Implementation	Complete
		Deployment	Complete
		Cause - Effect	Complete
		Accountability	Complete
		SMART	Complete
	Check	Integration	Complete
		Monitoring	Complete
		Audit	Not Available
		Adjustment & Learning	Complete
	Act	Improvement	Complete
		Process	Complete
		Resources	Complete
		Knowledge & Experience	Complete
		Benchmark	Complete
Process		Process description	Complete
		KPI's	Complete
Format		13 elements	Complete

Figure 6.1 Assessment of The Ritz-Carlton Hotel Company.

However, while the evidence for both the financial and health-related benefits of implementing programs is increasing, many organizations do not develop cohesive strategies and merely offer fragmented activities without proof of effectiveness or outcomes. A lively discussion has transpired across the globe on what constitutes a healthy workplace and how to craft a successful program to produce positive outcomes for business and employees.

Reference: www.globalhealthyworkplace.org/documents/Healthy-Workplaces-Good-Practices.pdf

This publication is intended to contribute to the discussion and illustrate how a healthy workplace can be created by showcasing real-life strategies and programs from employers in 15 different countries on six continents. All the case studies are considered "good practices" as they have been selected from the growing pool of Global Healthy Workplace Award winners and finalists as well as certified "Healthy Workplaces."*

We investigated six case studies.

- Case study: Unilever Brazil
- Case study: Lån Spar Bank Denmark
- Case study: SAP Germany
- Case study: Mercedes Benz South Africa
- Case study: GlaxoSmithKline UK
- Case study: Baxter International Inc. USA

We describe below the results of the application of the Quick Scan on three of the six case studies, i.e. Lån Spar Bank Denmark, GlaxoSmithKline UK, and Baxter International Inc. USA. For the three other cases only a minority of the criteria of the Quick Scan are adequately covered.

Only the Glaxo Smith Kline UK case passes the Quick Scan and can be considered as a case study which is worthwhile to examine further with the detailed BEST-method.

6.2.1 Case study: Lån & Spar Bank Denmark

6.2.1.1 Who Is Lån & Spar Bank?

Headquartered in Copenhagen, Denmark

Savings and loan bank

380 employees

* http://globalhealthyworkplace.org/awards.html

Vision: We want to be the customer's personal bank by entering into close and relevant partnerships.

6.2.1.2 Health in Business Strategy

Lån & Spar Bank's Healthy Workplace program, "Bank I Bevægelse" (bank in motion), has been a deeply integrated and important part of the Lån & Spar Bank business strategy since 2009. This program has demonstrated positive results in multiple areas, including an increase in turnover, productivity, and customer satisfaction. Lån & Spar Bank focuses on improving the mental, social, and physical well-being of employees based on senior management's belief that balanced and satisfied employees create the best business.

6.2.1.3 Assessment of Case Study Lån & Spar Bank

Summary assessment of the case study (see Figure 6.2)

- Results
  - Five criteria are complete, and two criteria are incomplete.
- Enabler
  - Plan phase: two criteria are complete, and four criteria are incomplete. No information is available for two criteria.
  - Do phase: four criteria are complete. No information is available for one criterion.
  - Check phase: two criteria are complete. No information is available for two criteria.
  - Act phase: two criteria are incomplete. No information is available for three criteria.
- Process: the document does not mention or describe the process or KPIs.
- Format: there is no systematic approach used to describe the Best Practice in all its aspects and details.

6.2.1.4 Conclusion

The case study Lån & Spar Bank is probably not a Best Practice. Some additional on-site verification or documentation would complete the missing elements.

	Criteria	Lan Spar Bank	GSK	Baxter
		Case study		
Results	Scope and relevance	Complete	Complete	Complete
	Integrity of data	Complete	Complete	Complete
	Segmentation	Complete	Complete	Complete
	Trends	Not available	Not available	Not available
	Targets	Not available	Complete	Not available
	Comparison with benchmarks	Complete	Complete	Complete
	Cause - Effect	Complete	Complete	Not available
Enabler – Plan	Description	Complete	Complete	Complete
	Stakeholders	Incomplete	Complete	Complete
	Responsibilities	Incomplete	Complete	Incomplete
	KPI's and PI's	Not available	Complete	Incomplete
	Deployment and Segmentation	Incomplete	Complete	Complete
	Prevention	Not available	Complete	Not available
	Benchmarking	Complete	Complete	Complete
	Data	Incomplete	Complete	Complete
Enabler – Do	Implementation	Complete	Complete	Complete
	Deployment	Complete	Complete	Complete
	Cause - Effect	Complete	Complete	Incomplete
	Accountability	Complete	Complete	Incomplete
	SMART	Not available	Not available	Not available
Enabler – Check	Integration	Complete	Complete	Complete
	Monitoring	Complete	Incomplete	Incomplete
	Audit	Not available	Not available	Not available
	Adjustment & Learning	Not available	Not available	Not available
Enabler – Act	Improvement	Incomplete	Incomplete	Incomplete
	Process	Not available	Not available	Not available
	Resources	Not available	Not available	Not available
	Knowledge & Experience	Not available	Incomplete	Incomplete
	Benchmark	Incomplete	Complete	Complete
Process	Process description	Not available	Not available	Not available
	KPI's	Not available	Not available	Not available
Format	13 elements	Not available	Not available	Not available

Figure 6.2 Assessment of three case studies.

6.2.2 Case Study: GlaxoSmithKline UK

6.2.2.1 Who Is GSK?

Headquartered in Brentford, London

Global healthcare company

99,300 employees

Mission: To help people do more, feel better, and live longer.

6.2.2.2 Health in Business Strategy

GSK aspires to foster a healthy, resilient, high-performing workforce and ensure zero harm to people and the planet. Since 2002, GSK has implemented a global environment, health, and safety (EHS) policy, 50+ EHS standards, and high impact, enterprise-wide health programs. GSK's EHS policy and standards are aligned to the core aims of the World Health Organization's Healthy Workplace Model, ISO/OHSAS, and create minimum, performance-based health standards worldwide.*

6.2.2.3 Assessment of Case Study GSK

Summary assessment of the case study (see Figure 6.2)

- Results
  - Six criteria are complete. No information is available for one criterion.
- Enabler
  - Plan phase: all criteria are complete.
  - Do phase: four criteria are complete. No information is available for one criterion.
  - Check phase: one criterion is complete, and one criterion is incomplete. No information is available for two criteria.
  - Act phase: one criterion is complete, and two criteria are incomplete. No information is available for two criteria.
- Process: the document does not mention or describe the process or KPIs.
- Format: there is no systematic approach used to describe the Best Practice in all its aspects and details.

---

* ISO/OHSAS 18001, This is a standard for the management of Occupational Health and Safety Assessment. Compliance with it enabled organizations to demonstrate that they had a system in place for occupational health and safety. Source : https://en.wikipedia.org/wiki/OHSAS_18001 accessed April 24, 2020.

6.2.2.4 Conclusion

This case study could be a Best Practice. Some additional on-site verification or documentation would complete the missing elements.

6.2.3 Case Study: Baxter International Inc. USA

6.2.3.1 Who Is Baxter?

Headquartered in Deerfield, Illinois.

Provides a broad portfolio of essential renal and hospital products, pharmacy automation, software, and services.

Employees: 48,000

Mission: To save and sustain lives inspires our work and our commitment to expanding access to care, providing cost-effective healthcare solutions, delivering quality products, and advancing innovations for the world.

6.2.3.2 Health in Business Strategy

As a global healthcare company, Baxter International Inc. has a strong commitment to the health of its employees as well as to its customers and patients. Its vision of a Zero-Harm workplace underpins the company's strategic efforts in safety, industrial hygiene, and employee health promotion. Baxter recognizes that healthy employees are more engaged and productive and are less vulnerable to safety incidents and injuries. Through BeWell@ Baxter, the company's global health and wellness program, Baxter strives to create a culture that promotes health at work and at home, raises awareness about these issues, and supports individual accountability and engagement.

6.2.3.3 Assessment of Case Study Baxter International Inc. USA

Summary assessment of the case study (see Figure 6.2)

- Results
  - Four criteria are complete. No information is available for three criteria.
- Enabler
  - Plan phase: five criteria are complete, and two criteria are incomplete. No information is available for one criterion.
  - Do phase: two criteria are complete, and two criteria are incomplete. No information is available for one criterion.

- Check phase: one criterion is complete, and one criterion is incomplete. No information is available for two criteria.
- Act phase: one criterion is complete, and two criteria are incomplete. No information is available for two criteria.

- Process: the document does not mention or describe the process or KPIs.
- Format: there is no systematic approach used to describe the Best Practice in all its aspects and details.

6.2.3.4 Conclusion

Information is missing or incomplete for most of the Quick Scan criteria. Therefore, this case study isn't a true Best Practice *as described.* Some additional on-site verification or documentation might complete the missing elements.

6.2.3.5 Conclusions from Healthy Workplaces: A Selection of Global Good Practices

None of the six case studies we investigated give a description of the process or a full description of the Best Practice. It is difficult to provide this level of detail in the two pages available for each case. A company wishing to benchmark with these companies would need to go on-site to verify the Best Practice to have enough information against which to compare their own processes for improvement.

6.3 Case Studies from APQC CONNECTING PEOPLE TO CONTENT: Create, Surface, and Share Knowledge for a Smarter Organization

6.3.1 Preface

People looking for a comprehensive, professional, and inspiring text about *Knowledge Management* should consult this APQC study. The impetus for this benchmarking study was questions like:

- What types of content are easiest for employees to use and learn from?
- What are the best tools to help people find what they need among a broad range of sources?

- How can people differentiate authoritative content from unverified ideas and suggestions published by colleagues?
- How can organizations maximize the value of their content by delivering targeted recommendations directly to employees in the context of their work?
- How effective are enterprise content management systems in terms of surfacing relevant content and enabling employees to find and access what they need?

Less than one in four participants rated their organization's content management as effective, whereas 43% said their firms were minimally or not at all effective at managing enterprise content.

Why were their organizations less than effective at content management? Relatively few – approximately one in five – cited poor technology as the root cause. Instead, **the clear majority said their biggest challenges centered on change management and organizational structure and accountability**. In short, employees weren't following the **processes** in place to manage content, or the organizations had not defined sufficient **ownership** models for the tools and approaches.*

The model includes technology as an enabler. The bulk of the attributes focus on people and process-related tactics to engage employees, solicit content, and link people to available resources. **As an organization hones its strategy and processes in alignment with suppliers and consumers of content, it can connect supply to demand, enabling meaningful connections, and generating business value.**†

Although the study aims to encourage "management programs toward more aligned strategies, systematic processes, and user-oriented technologies for content contribution, classification, distribution, and sharing,"‡ we see in the two case studies we examined that the process approach is weakly developed in the text. This might be available in other company documentation but is not described in the publication.

This book is a very good reference on *knowledge management*, mainly from the point of view of how to create, manage, and monitor a knowledge management system. The case studies presented are probably true Best Practices in Knowledge Management. However, with the characteristics

---

* Leavitt, Paige and Trees, Lauren, *Connecting People to Content, Create, Surface, and Share Knowledge for a Smarter Organization*, APQC, Houston, TX, (2015) p. 4.

† Ibid: p. 5.

‡ Ibid: p. 6.

required for fully documenting a Best Practice identified in this book, the case studies investigated and assessed with the BEST-method do not contain enough information to be used as a Best Practice for benchmarking purposes.

Nevertheless, two case studies have been assessed using the BEST Quick Scan: Nalco and MWH Global Inc.

6.3.2 Case study: Nalco

Pages 146–171.

6.3.2.1 Initial Comment

The authors define Best Practices as the best available practice (i.e. a key process) that contributes to the achievement of the strategy and/or business plan of the organization and leads to excellent and sustainable results.

Nalco's case study, although named as a Best Practice, does not correspond to our definition. The text clearly describes the tool "Connections libraries" and software such as Microsoft SharePoint 2010, Microsoft Dynamics Customers Relationship Management platform, etc. What is missing is a detailed description of how Connections libraries, etc., are part of the *key process of knowledge management.* It would be helpful to explain how the application of these (software) tools contributes to a better achievement of the knowledge management *strategy* of Nalco and offers a *better support* to Nalco sales and customer service processes.

The APQC text is very well written and comprehensive from the point of view of management of the tool, but it is *not a description of one of Nalco's key processes.* We think that this tool is a strong instrument in the hands of Nalco's collaborators and even Nalco's customers. Nevertheless, we apply the BEST Quick Scan on this case study to show 1) differences between a description of Nalco's software tool and 2) a full description of a Best Practice.

6.3.2.2 Who Is Nalco?

Nalco, an Ecolab company, specializes in water, energy, and air applications for light and heavy industries. Its products and solutions focus on treating water as it enters a site, preparing it for industrial and institutional uses, and then re-treating it so that it can be discharged safely back into the environment. By optimizing these processes, Nalco helps customers improve productivity and quality, increase the asset life of their equipment, reduce natural resource consumption, and minimize environmental releases.

6.3.2.3 Assessment of Case Study Nalco

Summary assessment of the case study Nalco (see Figure 6.3)

- Results
  - There is no information available for any of the seven criteria.
- Enabler
  - Plan phase: two criteria are complete, and three criteria are incomplete. No information is available for three criteria.
  - Do phase: two criteria are complete, and two criteria are incomplete. No information is available for one criterion.
  - Check phase: four criteria are incomplete.
  - Act phase: two criteria are incomplete. No information is available for three criteria.
- Process: the document does not mention or describe the process or KPIs.
- Format: there is no systematic approach used to describe the Best Practice in all its aspects and details.

6.3.2.4 Conclusion Case Study Nalco

Descriptions of the process and results are both missing. A Best Practice *always* has a description of output and outcome results. Therefore, we conclude that the case study from Nalco would not be adequate to benchmark against as a Best Practice.

An extract of the text on page 148 illustrates how easily the label of "Best Practice" is used:

> Most of Nalco's knowledge environment is built on Microsoft SharePoint 2010. Figure 68 depicts its main components, including: connections libraries – **collections of Best Practices**, guidelines, and other content published by subject matter experts, etc.*

* St. Charles Consulting Group, *APQC CONNECTING PEOPLE TO CONTENT: Create, Surface, and Share Knowledge for a Smarter Organization*, APQC, Houston, TX, (2015) p. 148.

		Criteria	Case studies: Nalco	Case studies: MWH Global
Results		Scope and relevance	Not available	Not available
		Integrity of data	Not available	Not available
		Segmentation	Not available	Not available
		Trends	Not available	Incomplete
		Targets	Not available	Not available
		Comparison with benchmarks	Not available	Not available
		Cause - Effect	Not available	Not available
Enabler	Plan	Description	Incomplete	Incomplete
		Stakeholders	Complete	Incomplete
		Responsibilities	Complete	Complete
		KPI's and PI's	Incomplete	Not available
		Deployment and Segmentation	Incomplete	Not available
		Prevention	Not available	Incomplete
		Benchmarking	Not available	Not available
		Data	Not available	Not available
	Do	Implementation	Incomplete	Incomplete
		Deployment	Incomplete	Incomplete
		Cause - Effect	Complete	Not available
		Accountability	Complete	Complete
		SMART	Not available	Not available
	Check	Integration	Incomplete	Complete
		Monitoring	Incomplete	Incomplete
		Audit	Incomplete	Not available
		Adjustment & Learning	Incomplete	Incomplete
	Act	Improvement	Incomplete	Incomplete
		Process	Not available	Not available
		Resources	Not available	Not available
		Knowledge & Experience	Incomplete	Incomplete
		Benchmark	Not available	Not available
Process		Process description	Not available	Complete
		KPI's	Not available	Not available
Format		13 elements	Not available	Not available

Figure 6.3 BEST Quick Scan applied against Nalco and MWH Global.

6.3.3 Case study: MWH Global Inc.

Pages 122–145.

6.3.3.1 Who Is MWH Global Inc.?

MWH Global Inc. (MWH) is an engineering and consulting firm focused on wet infrastructure, including water treatment, supply, and power. It has approximately 7,000 employees spread across 200 offices in 35 countries. The company consists of consulting engineers, designers, and management consultants focused on all phases of the water cycle. Most of the staff (including knowledge workers) are people with scientific, engineering, design, or technical backgrounds. The type of work that MWH Global does and the skillsets of its work force determine the types of knowledge that the organization needs to manage namely, technical templates, project templates, forms, and checklists for consulting engagements.

MWH's Knowledge Management program focuses on distributing information and expertise to its global workforce and embedding content directly into its processes and tools.

The case study describes the structure and the management of the database. It describes also the project delivery process. An overview of the process is shown in the text in a figure "Process Navigator," where the different phases and project steps are presented.*

6.3.3.2 Assessment of Case Study MWH Global Inc.

Summary assessment of the case study (see Figure 6.3)

- Results
  - One criterion is incomplete. No information is available for six criteria.
- Enabler
  - Plan phase: one criterion is complete, and three criteria are incomplete. No information is available for four criteria.
  - Do phase: one criterion is complete, and two criteria are incomplete. No information is available for two criteria.

* Ibid: p. 124

  - Check phase: one criterion is complete, and two criteria are incomplete. No information is available for one criterion.
  - Act phase: two criteria are incomplete. No information is available for three criteria.
- Process: one criterion is complete, and one criterion is not available.
- Format: there is no systematic approach used to describe the Best Practice in all its aspects and details.

6.3.3.3 Conclusion Case MWH Global Inc.

The text of the case study is 23 pages long. Yet little information relates to the characteristics of a Best Practice listed in the table of the BEST Quick Scan.

The text uses wording which does not describe a Best Practice. Some examples:

- "particularly because content management is often *not* a department's top *priority*."
- "Some of the Yammer groups have popped up because SharePoint became too *cumbersome* for dynamic discussions."
- "training, while the other half of the room says, '*I will never use this*, it's the worst thing ever.'"
- "Standard templates were *not consistently applied*, and project teams were also using decentralized project storage and filing *with inconsistent filing structures*."
- "*not* every global standard was adhered to."*

Best Practices are documented to share performance excellence that serves as benchmarking targets. Affirmative and positive language is expected. In this case, the BEST Quick Scan provides guidance on how the MWH processes can be improved to approach the level of a Best Practice. The Quick Scan does not validate that the process is already at Best Practice level.

6.3.3.4 Global Conclusion on the APQC Case Studies (Nalco and MWH Global Inc.)

It is remarkable that neither case study defines clearly what they want to enter into the knowledge management database and what the minimum

* Ibid: pp. 122–145.

criteria are for an excellent knowledge management database. Without a clear definition of the intended content, the reader could assume that "everything that could be interesting" should be entered into the database.

Although both case studies use the term "Best Practice" several times, these cases do not contain enough information to be used as Best Practices. They focus on a tool (Knowledge Management Database) while a Best Practice focuses on the assessment of a process, including corresponding *results*, which support the achievement of the strategy and/or business plan of the company.

6.3.4 Case Study: Already Doing It and Not Knowing It

Author: Stephanie Bailey M.D., MSHSA

Book: *The Public Health Quality Improvement Handbook*, chapter 12, pp. 139–144.

Editor: ASQ Quality Press (2009)

In 1999, Metropolitan Nashville and Davidson County, Tennessee, was number one in the country for incidence of syphilis. Nashville, according to the study that was eventually done about the epidemic, had been in an epidemic state since 1996. On October 7, 1999, the Centers for Diseases Control and Prevention (CDC) announced a National Plan to Eliminate Syphilis from Nashville's Health Department. At this time in history, less than 1% of US counties accounted for half of the reported syphilis cases. One half of all new syphilis cases were concentrated in 28 counties mainly in the south and select urban regions. Davidson County was one of the ten counties/cities with the highest number of reported syphilis cases. We created STD Free!*

6.3.4.1 Who Is Metro Public Health Department (MPHD) Nashville, Tennessee?

The mission of the Metro Public Health Department is to protect, improve, and sustain the health and well-being of all people in Metropolitan Nashville. Metro Public Health Department (MPHD) serves the Nashville metro and surrounding Davidson County areas and municipalities. Davidson

* Bialek, Ron, Duffy, Grace L. and Moran, John W. *The Public Health Quality Improvement Handbook*, Quality Press, Milwaukee, WI, (2009) pp. 139, 140.

County, Tennessee is 526 square miles in size and has a total population of 679,000 persons.*

6.3.4.2 Assessment of Case Study Metro Public Health Department (MPHD) Nashville, Tennessee

6.3.4.2.1 Summary Assessment of the Case Study (see Figure 6.4)

This is an interesting case because at first view it appears that this is a complete Best Practice. When the BEST Quick Scan is applied, there is not enough information to conclude that this is a true Best Practice. The case study is well written. It is a very good project description. It would not be enough for another Health Department to use for benchmarking to improve their own related processes.

The following overview gives an idea to what extent the case study can be considered a Best Practice.

- Results
  - Five criteria are complete. No information is available for two criteria.
- Enabler
  - Plan phase: three criteria are complete, and four criteria are incomplete. No information is available for one criterion.
  - Do phase: four criteria are complete. No information is available for one criterion.
  - Check phase: two criteria are complete, and one criterion is incomplete. No information is available for one criterion.
  - Act phase: one criterion is complete, and two criteria are incomplete. No information is available for two criteria.
- Process: two criteria are incomplete.
- Format: there is no systematic approach used to describe the Best Practice in all its aspects and details.

6.3.4.3 Conclusion of the Nashville, TN Case Studies

Too many criteria in the enabler component are missing. Therefore, this case study cannot be considered as a Best Practice. We are convinced that the

* www.nashville.gov/Health-Department/About-Us.aspx, Nashville, TN Health Department website, accessed 12/29/2019.

		Criteria	Case study MPHD
Results		Scope and relevance	Complete
		Integrity of data	Complete
		Segmentation	Complete
		Trends	Not available
		Targets	Not available
		Comparison with benchmarks	Complete
		Cause - Effect	Complete
Enabler	Plan	Description	Complete
		Stakeholders	Complete
		Responsibilities	Incomplete
		KPI's and PI's	Incomplete
		Deployment and Segmentation	Complete
		Prevention	Incomplete
		Benchmarking	Not available
		Data	Incomplete
	Do	Implementation	Complete
		Deployment	Complete
		Cause - Effect	Complete
		Accountability	Complete
		SMART	Not available
	Check	Integration	Complete
		Monitoring	Complete
		Audit	Not available
		Adjustment & Learning	Incomplete
	Act	Improvement	Complete
		Process	Incomplete
		Resources	Not available
		Knowledge & Experience	Incomplete
		Benchmark	Not available
Process		Process description	Incomplete
		KPI's	Incomplete
Format		13 elements	Not available

Figure 6.4 BEST Quick Scan Metro Public Health Department (MPHD), Nashville, TN.

case study would qualify as a Best Practice if the author of this chapter had the BEST Quick Scan tool as a guide while writing the case study. One of the authors of this Best Practice text assisted in the editing of this case study when originally written. The data existed in the project files. The BEST Quick Scan tool was not yet available for reference.

6.3.5 Case Study: Why Is Singapore's School System So Successful and Is It a Model for the West?

Author: David Hogan, Honorary Professor, the University of Queensland

Website: http://theconversation.com/why-is-singapores-school-system-so-successful-and-is-it-a-model-for-the-west-22917

This is an interesting case because it concerns a process at a high level, i.e. a countrywide educational system. Singapore is successful in many endeavors. There are very few countries that perform as well on economic plans and educational systems. Singapore has achieved an annual GDP growth of over 4% for more than 40 years. This does not happen by accident. This sustained performance is a result of well-thought planning, organization, and monitoring.*

6.3.5.1 Assessment of Case Study Singapore's School System

Summary assessment of the case study 8 (see Figure 6.5)

- Results
  - Seven criteria are complete.

    The important results here are the international PISA† tests of OECD.‡
- Enabler
  - Plan: seven criteria are complete. No information is available for one criterion.
  - Do: five criteria are complete.

---

* Ghesquire, Henry, *Singapore's Success, Engineering Economic Growth*, Thomson Learning, (a division of Thomson Asia Pte Ltd), Singapore (2007).

† PISA: Programme for International Student Assessment. www.oecd.org/pisa/ accessed 12/29/2019.

‡ The Organisation for Economic Co-operation and Development (OECD): www.oecd.org/about/ accessed 12/29/2019; www.compareyourcountry.org/pisa accessed 12/29/2019. This is an international and standardized test that is executed on a regular basis in 24 Western countries.

		Criteria	Case study Singapore
Results		Scope and relevance	Complete
		Integrity of data	Complete
		Segmentation	Complete
		Trends	Complete
		Targets	Complete
		Comparison with benchmarks	Complete
		Cause - Effect	Complete
Enabler	Plan	Description	Complete
		Stakeholders	Complete
		Responsibilities	Complete
		KPI's and PI's	Complete
		Deployment and Segmentation	Complete
		Prevention	Not available
		Benchmarking	Complete
		Data	Complete
	Do	Implementation	Complete
		Deployment	Complete
		Cause - Effect	Complete
		Accountability	Complete
		SMART	Complete
	Check	Integration	Complete
		Monitoring	Complete
		Audit	Not available
		Adjustment & Learning	Complete
	Act	Improvement	Complete
		Process	Complete
		Resources	Complete
		Knowledge & Experience	Complete
		Benchmark	Complete
Process		Process description	Not available
		KPI's	Not available
Format		13 elements	Not available

Figure 6.5 BEST Quick Scan: Education system in Singapore.

- Check: three criteria are complete. No information is available for one criterion.
- Act: five criteria are complete.

- Process: both criteria are incomplete, although it is possible that the process is well described and reviewed on a regular basis based upon the completeness of other criteria.
- Format: there is no systematic approach used to describe the Best Practice in all its aspects and details.

6.3.5.2 Conclusion

The results and enabler criteria are nearly complete. If the process and format criteria would have been described, we could consider this case study as a Best Practice. Some additional on-site verification or documentation would complete the missing elements.

This case study warrants the application of the detailed BEST-tool because the BEST Quick Scan gives a positive indication that this is truly a Best Practice.

6.3.5.3 Additional Comments

A Best Practice assessment is usually performed by the organization itself. The organization must know its requirements, plans, and objectives. An analysis of the Singapore educational system from a Western point of view (the USA or Europe) could be clouded by cultural differences rather than learning from this case study. The educational system in Singapore differs from the Western context, but nevertheless Singapore's students are performing at high levels. A benchmarking partner should learn from the differences.

An on-site visit would be appropriate to verify that this is truly a Best Practice. The Quick Scan provides the justification for a more in-depth benchmarking partnership. A face-to-face working relationship with the Singapore educational system will provide the details and insight to finalize a complete BEST-assessment.

The BEST Quick Scan would be useful for the Minister of Education in Singapore to identify where further improvements are possible. As this case study is a Best Practice, we recommend the application of the detailed BEST-tool, which will generate an effective gap analysis for continuous improvement.

6.4 Case Study: HR Certification Institute & Top Employers Institute

Title: Emerging Evidence: Business Performance and the Validation of HR Best Practices

Website: www.hrci.org/docs/default-source/web-files/validation-of-hr-best-practices.pdf

HR Certification Institute & Top Employers Institute

6.4.1 About HRCI

HR Certification Institute (HRCI) is the premier professional credentialing organization for the worldwide human resources profession. Founded in 1976 and headquartered in the USA, HRCI is celebrating 40 years of setting the standard for HR mastery and excellence around the globe. An independent non-profit organization, HRCI is dedicated to advancing the HR profession through developing and administering Best-in-Class certifications, including the NCCA-accredited Professional in Human Resources (PHR) and Senior Professional in Human Resources (SPHR). All HRCI's credentials are recognized as the most rigorous, meaningful, and grounded professional certifications demonstrating competency, real-world practical skills, and knowledge in the field. Together with HRCI-certified professionals in 100 countries around the globe, HRCI ensures, strengthens, and advances the strategic value and impact of HR.

6.4.2 About Top Employers Institute

Top Employers Institute (TEI), headquartered in the Netherlands, is an independent organization that certifies excellence in employee offerings, HR practices, and the environment employers have in place for employees to advance their development. Since 1991, Top Employers Institute has recognized exceptional employers around the world with its annual Top Employers Global, Top Employers Continental, and Top Employers Country certifications. In 2016 Top Employers has recognized more than 1,000 Top Employers in 102 countries.

This case study was published in 2016. It is interesting to note that the term "Best Practice" is used 45 times in this case study. Figure 6.6 contains the results of assessing the HRCI & TEI method (i.e. certification of HR departments and individuals) as a Best Practice according to the BEST-method.

		Criteria	Case study HRCI & TEI
Results		Scope and relevance	Complete
		Integrity of data	Complete
		Segmentation	Complete
		Trends	Complete
		Targets	Complete
		Comparison with benchmarks	Complete
		Cause - Effect	Complete
Enabler	Plan	Description	Complete
		Stakeholders	Complete
		Responsibilities	Not available
		KPI's and PI's	Incomplete
		Deployment and Segmentation	Not available
		Prevention	Not available
		Benchmarking	Complete
		Data	Complete
	Do	Implementation	Complete
		Deployment	Complete
		Cause - Effect	Complete
		Accountability	Complete
		SMART	Not available
	Check	Integration	Complete
		Monitoring	Not available
		Audit	Complete
		Adjustment & Learning	Not available
	Act	Improvement	Not available
		Process	Not available
		Resources	Complete
		Knowledge & Experience	Complete
		Benchmark	Complete
Process		Process description	Not available
		KPI's	Not available
Format		13 elements	Not available

Figure 6.6 BEST Quick Scan: HR Certification Institute & Top Employers Institute case study.

6.4.3 Assessment of the Case Study HR Certification Institute & Top Employers Institute

The assessment performed using the BEST Quick Scan method is not intended to criticize the HRCI & TEI method, but to illustrate how the BEST Quick Scan assessment functions and could lead to different conclusions.

6.4.3.1 Summary Assessment of Case Study 9 *(see Figure 6.6)*

- Results
  - Seven criteria are complete.
- Enabler
  - Plan phase: four criteria are complete, and one criterion is incomplete. No information is available for three criteria.
  - Do phase: four criteria are complete. No information is available for one criterion.
  - Check phase: two criteria are complete. No information is available for two criteria.
  - Act phase: three criteria are complete. No information is available for two criteria.
- Process: both criteria are incomplete.
- Format: there is no systematic approach used to describe the Best Practice in all its aspects and details.

The approach is not process-oriented. The approach applied by HRCI & TEI is focused on the development of skills and experiences of staff, building a culture of trust and respect, development of leadership and in creating the right environmental context (workplace flexibility, opportunities for learning, autonomy, etc.).

6.4.4 Conclusion of the Assessment of HRCI & TEI

Only 20 out of the 32 criteria are fulfilled. Too many pieces of information are absent for us to say that this case study is a Best Practice. It would be helpful to investigate the points that are not available in the case study through an on-site visit.

6.5 Case Study: ExxonMobil Safety, Health, and the Workplace

6.5.1 Who Is ExxonMobil?

ExxonMobil Corporation is an American multinational oil and gas corporation headquartered in Irving, Texas. ExxonMobil is the largest of the world's Big Oil companies, or super majors, with daily production of 3.92 million BOE (barrels of oil equivalent); but it is significantly smaller than a number of national companies. With 37 oil refineries in 21 countries, constituting a combined daily refining capacity of 6.3 million barrels (1,000,000 m^3), ExxonMobil is the largest refiner in the world. ExxonMobil consists of upstream, downstream, and chemical activities.

Title: **Corporate Citizenship Report: Safety, Health and the Workplace**

Website: http://corporate.exxonmobil.com/en/community/corporate-citizenship-report/safety-and-health-and-the-workplace

Interesting aspects of this case study: every staff member of ExxonMobil has worldwide access to the experiences and Best Practices of their colleagues. ExxonMobil has a clear goal on safety: "Nobody Gets Hurt." Prevention and lessons learned are characteristics that are clearly present.

6.5.2 Assessment of Case Study ExxonMobil Safety, Health, and the Workplace

Summary assessment of case study 10 (see Figure 6.7)

- Results
  - Five criteria are complete, and two criteria are incomplete.
- Enabler
  - Plan: eight criteria are complete.
  - Do: five criteria are complete.
  - Check: three criteria are complete. No information is available for one criterion.
  - Act: five criteria are complete.
- Process: one criterion is complete. No information is available for one criterion.
- Format: there is no systematic approach used to describe the Best Practice in all its aspects and details.

		Criteria	Case study ExxonMobil
Results		Scope and relevance	Incomplete
		Integrity of data	Complete
		Segmentation	Complete
		Trends	Complete
		Targets	Complete
		Comparison with benchmarks	Incomplete
		Cause - Effect	Complete
Enabler	Plan	Description	Complete
		Stakeholders	Complete
		Responsibilities	Complete
		KPI's and PI's	Complete
		Deployment and Segmentation	Complete
		Prevention	Complete
		Benchmarking	Complete
		Data	Complete
	Do	Implementation	Complete
		Deployment	Complete
		Cause - Effect	Complete
		Accountability	Complete
		SMART	Complete
	Check	Integration	Complete
		Monitoring	Complete
		Audit	Not available
		Adjustment & Learning	Complete
	Act	Improvement	Complete
		Process	Complete
		Resources	Complete
		Knowledge & Experience	Complete
		Benchmark	Complete
Process		Process description	Not available
		KPI's	Complete
Format		13 elements	Not available

Figure 6.7 BEST Quick Scan assessment of ExxonMobil Safety and Health.

6.5.3 Conclusion

Many of the criteria are fulfilled. However, we have no written evidence of the process (exception KPI) and format criteria. If these two criteria would have been present, we could say that the Exxon Safety, Health, and the Workplace case study can be considered as a Best Practice. An on-site visit would be helpful to validate details and confirm the existence of a Best Practice.

6.6 Observations Gained from the Assessment of Ten BEST Quick Scan Studies

Choosing and documenting the approach and method (the Enabler) is generally the easy part of developing a Best Practice. There are many excellence models available based on leadership preferences. The authors use the PDCA model as a universally flexible approach. Other models, such as the US Malcolm Baldrige Performance Model (MBA), the European Foundation for Quality Management Model (EFQM), Hoshin Kanri, or the ISO Quality Management System are also frequently used enablers.

Most important is to see positive results caused by the application of the enabler. Many times, results are not included in Best Practice descriptions. It is challenging to sustain positive results from an improved process. Consider how many organizations publish case studies of their improvement efforts. We reviewed a good many case studies. These studies document methods, procedures, and approaches while including very few output and outcome results. Showing positive, sustained results for at least 5 years after a process improvement is a true indicator of a Best Practice.

The reverse can also be seen. An organization can document the results of their process improvement but not share the enabler they used to achieve the results. The authors observe this omission in private production companies (mainly small- and medium-sized enterprises).

Organizations that are lower on the corporate maturity ladder are just beginning to define their processes. They may not have controls in place to standardize activities and measures. These organizations are small enough that leadership is brute-forcing positive results through intense effort rather than a systematic approach to process improvement.

When we speak about Best Practices, we refer to a formal, documented approach with detailed process descriptions, output and outcome indicators, and corresponding results. Every building block of a Best Practice consists of a series of criteria. A Best Practice is only a Best Practice when at least 80% of the BEST-tool criteria are fulfilled. We experienced over the last year that only a few of investigated case studies fulfill this requirement.

All case studies we investigated have one thing in common: there is no evidence of a process description. Those familiar with MBA or EFQM know that processes, enablers, and results are linked and need to be described explicitly. A process works within a system to effectively meet organizational and customer expectations. All three components, process, enabler, and results are required for the system to function correctly.

The length of the case study is not an important factor. The APQC case studies included in this chapter are each more than 20 pages long. But even these case studies fail to describe or include a flowchart of the processes that are being targeted for improvement.

The ten case studies investigated in this chapter demonstrate that only four of these can be considered as Best Practice. For the six others, as is also true for the hundreds of other case studies we investigated, there is proof only that we need a framework where we can assess the extent to which the case study can be considered as a real Best Practice. Up to now no one has developed such a framework. It is clear why so few published cases can be considered as a Best Practice.

Are we too severe? We think we are not, because what we have done is apply our experience with Total Quality Management and excellence models on one specific process. Once again, note that a process documented as a Best Practice case study must be a core process and critical for the success of the organization.

Do not conclude that the investigated case studies which we find not to be a real Best Practice with the BEST-method are badly managed. This is not the conclusion at all. We can only draw a conclusion from the documents we have at hand. In reality, these cases probably have much more evidence of fulfillment of the BEST-method criteria. That information is simply not in the text available to us without contacting the company.

Each of the descriptions assessed in this chapter was called a Best Practice by their author. However, when applying the BEST Quick Scan tool, only four case studies contained enough information to be considered a Best Practice. How do we explain this discrepancy? The perception and interpretation of the concept of a "Best Practice" vary across organizations. The authors define a Best Practice as an excellent *process* leading to the achievement of the strategy and/or business plan, while most authors have documented the functioning of a *tool* and considered it a Best Practice.

The management of Knowledge Management databases by Nalco and WMH Global Inc. are two clear examples of this disparity. Sharing how these companies use the Knowledge Management database is helpful to another company only if there is enough information for the benchmarking company to integrate the tool into their system of processes to obtain exceptional results.

The value of the BEST-tool is the ability to describe a Best Practice in a complete and objective way that can be understood and translated into the overall system of the benchmarking company. A Best Practice is intended to contribute to the achievement of strategic goals.

Chapter 7

Orange County Health Department Case Study

In 2008 one of the authors participated in an improvement project of the Florida Department of Health in Orange County (DOH-Orange). This case study was published by The American Society for Quality, Quality Press, in *The Public Health Quality Improvement Handbook*, "Orange County Health Department, STD Quality Improvement Case Study" (Chapter 24).*

In this first section, we reprint the initial improvement case study. In the second section, we apply the BEST-method to this case. The BEST-method identifies the gaps and missing information to improve the described process to a best practice level.

7.1 Original Case Study: Orange County Health Department, STD Quality Improvement Case Study

(October 2005–July 2006)

James Hinson, Team Leader and STD Department Manager

The Situation: Using the Seven-Step Plan-Do-Check-Act Problem Solving Model

---

* Bialek, R., Duffy, G. and Moran, J. *The Public Health Quality Improvement Handbook*, Chapter 24, Orange County Health Department, STD Quality Improvement Case Study, ASQ Quality Press, Milwaukee, WI, (2009) pp. 331–346.

PLAN

Step 1: Describe the Problem
Step 2: Describe the Current Process
Step 3: Identify the Root Cause(s) of the Problem
Step 4: Develop a Solution and Action Plan

DO

Step 5: Implement the Solution

CHECK

Step 6: Review and Evaluate the Results of the Change

ACT

Step 7: Reflect and Act on Learnings (Figure 7.1)

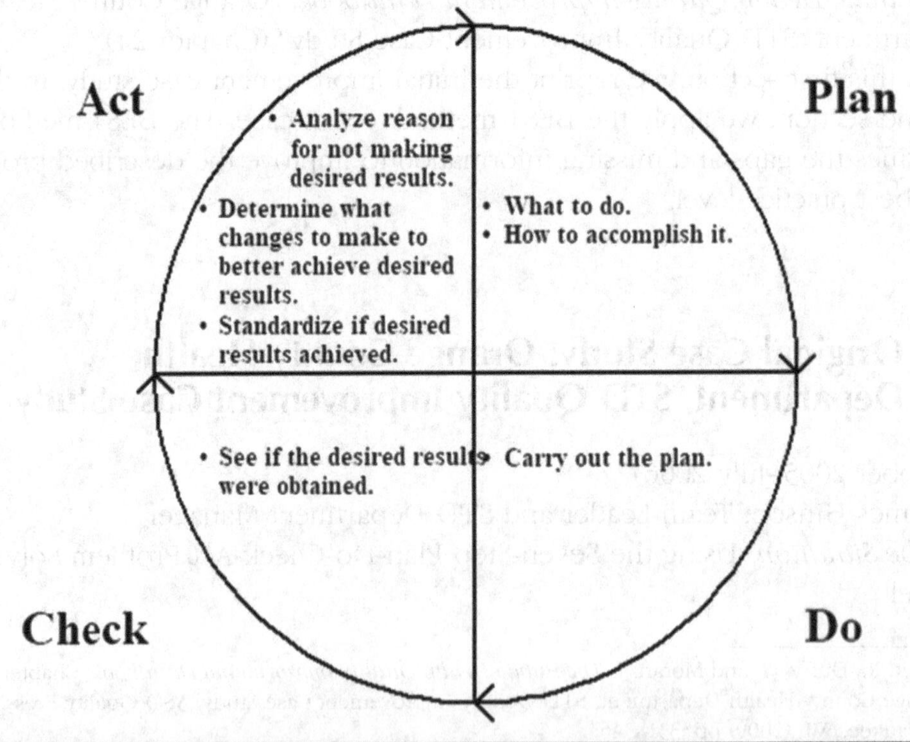

Figure 7.1 Actions taken mapped to the Plan-Do-Check-Act Cycle.

7.2 The Situation

Between 2004 and 2005, the Orange County Health Department (OCHD) saw a sharp increase (45%) in new early syphilis cases in its jurisdiction, from 136 cases per year to 195 cases per year. Following a trend that was seen in Florida and nationwide, these new syphilis cases were mostly seen in the MSM (men who have sex with men) population. Based on the accelerating rate of increase per year since 2001, the STD team knew that syphilis would grow into a larger epidemic if not rapidly controlled.

Short on staff and already feeling stretched to the limit with the many statutory responsibilities, the STD team was not sure what more they could do to stop the spread of the disease in their community. Within the unit, turnover was high, resources were limited, and employee satisfaction was low according to a recent department-wide employee survey.

Because of the urgency of the problem and the need for new solutions, the local health department leaders considered the STD unit ideal for piloting a new quality improvement (QI) project, taking productive QI methodology from the private sector, and using those tools in the public sector. In years past, OCHD had tried to bring QI to the entire health department, by training upper managers in QI methods. However, QI never really "trickled down" to the remainder of departments. Trying a more "bottom up" approach for the STD QI project, the department formed a QI team that consisted mainly of the frontline workers, having a combined 75+ years STD experience. Ultimately, if this model proved successful in addressing the syphilis problem, the health department hoped to expand it throughout the entire agency.

Figure 7.2 provides a snapshot run chart of incidence of early syphilis cases during 2004–2006, the subject of the STD QI project.

To assist the STD QI team, OCHD provided a hands-on training opportunity, and hired a highly recognized consultant to coach the team in applying QI methods in regular team meetings to address the problem. In order to make time available for the staff involved to be able to meet regularly, OCHD Administration was very flexible in allowing the STD Department to focus on the higher priorities during the duration of the initiative. Very critical to the success of the QI team activities was for the other STD Department staff to help "pick up the slack" while the project meetings took place, which they did magnificently.

At the Public Health Foundation led kick-off meeting, the STD team was introduced to QI tools such as the Why Tree, Affinity Diagram, and Fishbone Diagram. In this initial exploration of reasons for the rising syphilis rates, they came up with several potential root causes, including constant turnover of skilled DIS workers, lack of training for DIS workers, and OCHD's poor reputation in the MSM community.

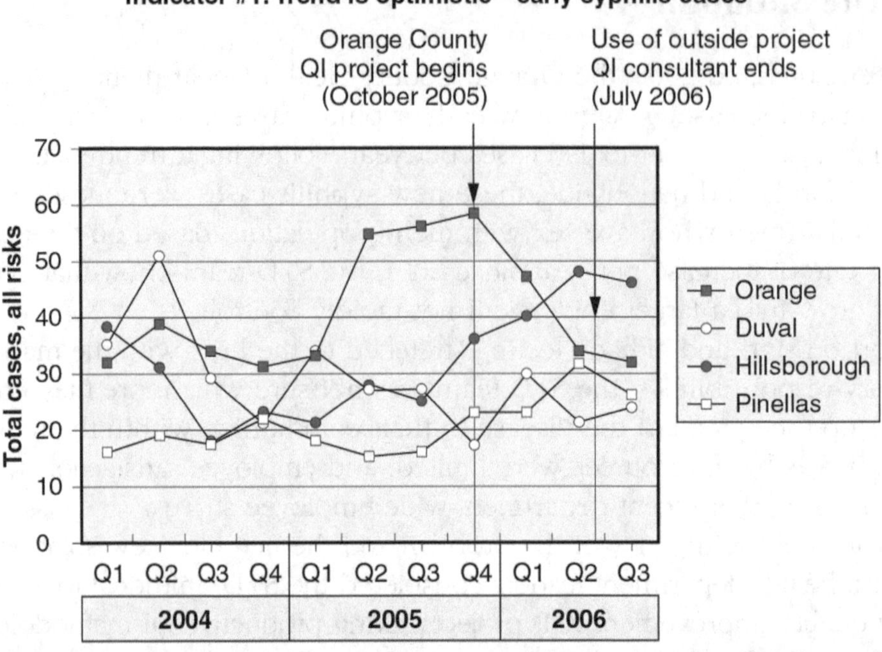

Figure 7.2 Snapshot results of the quality improvement project. Total Reported Early Syphilis Cases by Quarter, 2004–2006: Orange County compared to peer counties* in Florida. Syphilis Data Source: Florida Department of Health, STDMIS system, 2006 data for all four counties provided as of 10/13/2006. *Peer county designation created by Community Health Status indicators (CHSI) Project, HRSA, 2000, based on population density, size, and poverty levels. CHSI data notes are available at www.comunityphind.net/CHSI-CompanionView.pdf.

7.3 Step 1: Describe the Problem

Problem Statement: Early syphilis is increasing in Orange County.

Reason Selected: Surveillance data showed significant increases in early syphilis over the previous 4 years. If not rapidly controlled, early syphilis could become a larger epidemic, costing the community hundreds of thousands of dollars in health-related costs for early, late, and congenital syphilis cases, in addition to potential costs resulting from syphilis-associated HIV transmission.

Measures of project success:

1. Reduce new early syphilis cases by 25% compared to the previous year (Outcome measure).
2. 100% of Disease Intervention Specialists (DIS) will test a minimum of four associates per month for syphilis through DIS-initiated field work.

Table 7.1 Cluster and Contact Index and CDC Goal (situation 2006)

Measure	Team baseline (previous 6 mos.)	State average (previous 6 mos.)	CDC goal
Cluster Index	0.51	0.66	1.0*
Contact Index	0.84	1.41*	2.0

* Team target

3. Increase the quarterly cluster index to 1.0 on early syphilis cases among MSM.
4. Increase the quarterly contact index on all early syphilis cases, including MSM cases, to 1.41.

The team identified four measures of its success: one outcome measure and three performance measures for processes important to reaching the outcome goal. Two process measures – the contact index and cluster index (process measures related to eliciting partner names and testing at-risk individuals) – were identified as areas for improvement because the team performed below the state average and Centers for Disease Control and Prevention (CDC) goals. See Table 7.1 for contact and cluster index measures. The third process measure was a new internal standard for "field blood draws," which could be tracked monthly (Table 7.2).

7.4 Step 2: Describe the Current Process

There are six major processes involved in field blood draws: preparation, acquiring vehicle, field work, field recording, blood handling, and post-test procedures (Figure 7.3 and Table 7.3).

Table 7.2 STD team members and milestones

STD team members	*Milestones*
• Jim Hinson – Team Leader • Earl Boney – QI Lead • Anne Marie Strickland – QI Support • Donna Bouton – Dept Admin Ass't • Preston Boyce – DIS Supervisor • Barbara Carroll – Operations Manager • Shonda Mitchell –Surveillance Supervisor • Rajendra Hiralal – DIS Supervisor • Scott Fryberger – DIS Staff • Isabel Hudson – DIS Staff	• Team committed to problem statement • Identified national and state standards • Defined measures and targets • Completed first working/ learning session • Drafted expectations for members on QI team

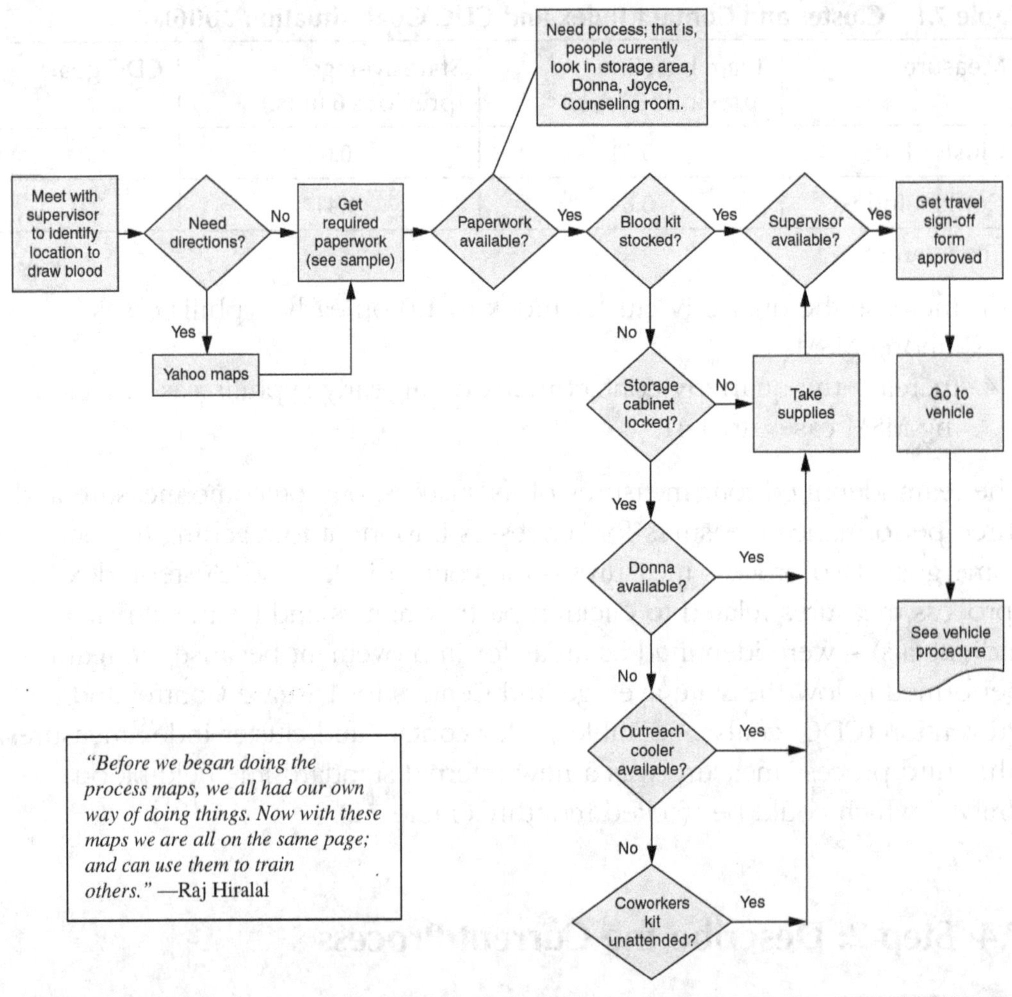

Figure 7.3 Sample process map for field blood draws: preparation.

Table 7.3 Interpretation of flow chart, milestones, and QI tools used in this step

1. Examination of the current process for doing blood draws revealed areas of inconsistent DIS practices and inefficiencies in the way the process was currently carried out. 2. The DIS field preparation process took too much time – estimated as much as two hours each time. 3. The two areas that consumed the most time for field preparation were getting the key to unlock the supply cabinet and getting permission to use a vehicle (involving several permission steps).	**Milestones** • Completed 7 process maps (1 overall, 6 detailed) related to carrying out blood draws. • Identified opportunities for cutting down time in 2 major areas of field preparation, as well as improving other processes. **QI tools used in this step** • Process Mapping, • Brainstorming, • Discussion.

7.5 Step 3: Identify Root Cause(s) of the Problem

Problem: Early syphilis is increasing in Orange County.

1. After conducting an initial root cause analysis examining the possible reasons for the increasing rate of early syphilis in Orange County, the DIS saw that an overlapping issue in various categories was high staff turnover (Figure 7.4).
2. By delving deeper into the issue, the team concluded that staff turnover affected their performance indicators.
3. The rate of turnover for DIS workers was high at OCHD, where the average length of stay for DIS new employees was six months or less.

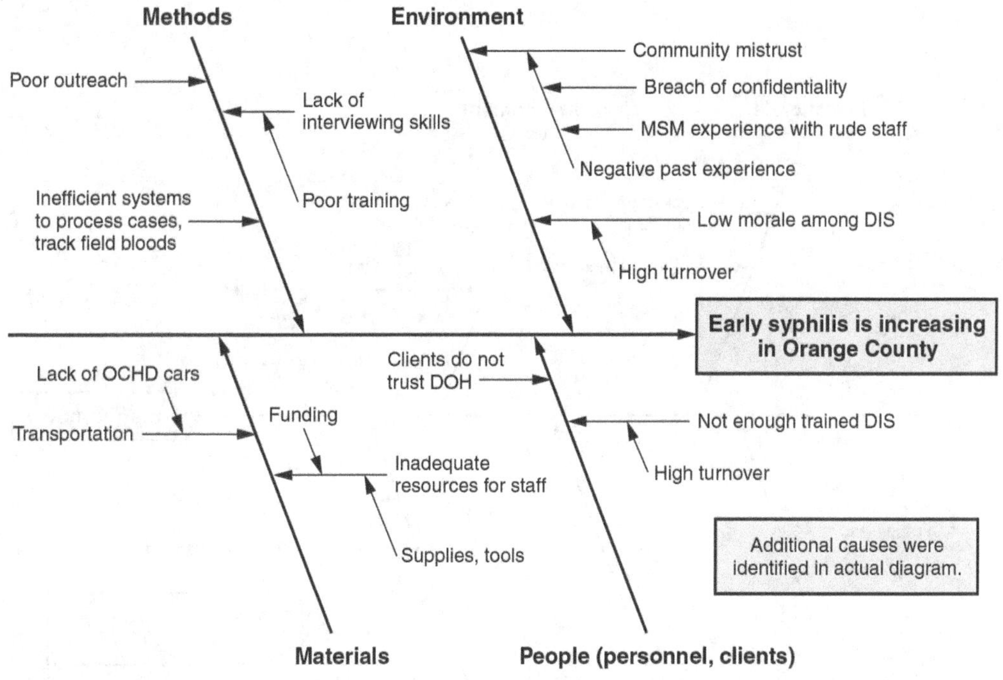

Figure 7.4 Cause and Effect ("Fishbone") Diagram: root causes for rising syphilis cases.

> The contact index relies on information provided from clients, and this is where the experience of DIS workers helps in pushing the contact index up … It takes some time and exposure to develop these relationships [with clients].
>
> **– Scott Fryberger**

The STD QI Team located most of their turnover problems in four main areas (see Figure 7.5):

1. Lack of training
2. Low morale
3. Office environment (including space and interpersonal issues)
4. Lack of good candidates

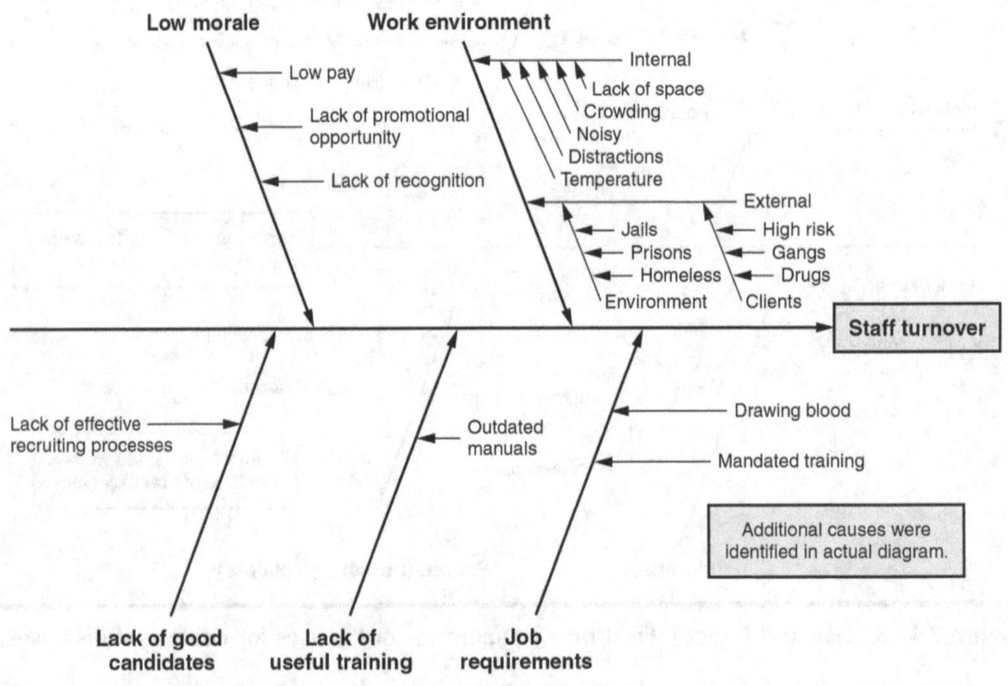

Figure 7.5 Initial Fishbone Diagram for staff turnover.

Milestones

- Completed initial Fishbone Diagram showing major factors in addressing the syphilis problem and identified that staff turnover was underlying most of these causes.
- Created detailed Fishbone and Affinity Diagrams on staff turnover with co-worker input.
- Decided to focus on staff turnover and programmatic processes that are within departmental control.
- Repeated a department SWOT (Strengths, Weaknesses, Opportunities, and Threats) Analysis to take stock in what they had accomplished since the last analysis and identify strengths they could use to address future STD unit needs.

QI tools used in this step: *Brainstorming, Affinity Diagram, Management Survey, SWOT Analysis, Fishbone Diagram, Process Maps/Drill Downs, Priority Setting Matrix* (Tables 7.4 and 7.5).

Table 7.4 Sorting activity: "Lack of Useful Training"

To tackle staff turnover, the team found that there were multiple areas members could work on. Because of this, they had to focus their attention first on the areas they felt were most important. Through multi-voting, the team determined that the three most important areas to address were the following (from most to least important): • Training • Finding good candidates • Low morale In addition, the team set aside time in weekly meetings to improve the processes that were hindering the unit's success.	Identified cause from Fishbone Spine	What is to be done first? *	What do we control?
	Can't do job = Skill	2	Y
	Accountability	3	Y
	Gossip	4	Y
	Logical Decision Making	5	Skills needed = Y (learned)
	Internal Customer Service	1	Y

* Result of *multi-voting* on priority to address
Lowest number = Highest priority

Table 7.5 C/I/C Chart: Staff Turnover

Things within our:		
Control	*Influence*	*(Have)* Concern
• Gossip • Training • Recognition • Process	• Hiring • Inter-departmental relations	• Salary

7.6 Step 4: Develop a Solution and Action Plan

"Control and influence" was an important concept introduced to the team by the team's consultant, which helped the team prioritize what causes they could most directly affect.

Milestones

- Analyzed maps of current processes to pinpoint areas for improvement.
- Identified three priority areas for action plan to address root causes for turnover: lack of useful training, lack of good candidates, and low morale.
- Analyzed each area of the fishbone and categorized potential solutions within the team's control or influence.
- Selected strategies the team could easily control that would affect programmatic processes or environment.
- Submitted proposal for additional vehicles.
- Requested help from HR and outside organizations on behavioral interviewing.
- Submitted a proposal to human resources to increase salary grade.
- Collected information on strategies effective in other jurisdictions.
- Reviewed evidence and recommendations for controlling syphilis in MSM populations.

QI tools used in this step: *Multi-voting, Sorting tool, Benchmarking, Control/Influence/Concern Chart*

7.7 Step 5: Implement the Solution

The team implemented changes by dealing with easily addressed problems first. Among their first successes, they reorganized space and made supplies more readily available to decrease preparation time for field blood draws.

Next, the team implemented several other solutions, such as enhanced DIS training and coaching, recognition of staff accomplishments, obtaining vehicles for the unit, increasing the base rate of pay for DIS, and creating a consistent process for data gathering.

Action registers helped the team track progress (Table 7.6).

Milestones

- Changed assignments for orientation training and initiated regular case review sessions for continuous on-the-job learning.
- Health department approved unit request for three new vehicles.
- DIS workers sent to national STD meeting for training.
- Implemented new interviewing process for DIS candidates.
- Trained newly hired people using improved process maps.
- Clarified and eliminated unnecessary steps in procedures:
  - Centralized location of forms.
  - Made supply cabinet unlocked for all DIS.
  - Eliminated use of certain forms in the preparation process.
- Reorganized space for better work environment.
- Started recognizing DIS workers for their work and contributions.
- Increased base rate of pay for DIS 10%.

***QI tools used in this step**: Action Register*

Table 7.6 Sample from Action Register: "Lack of Good Candidates"

Action	*Owner*	*Due date*	*Comments*
1. Improve Interview/ Hiring Process	Jim/ Barbara	2/16	To include: review people first, information/job specific description/ requirements/etc., qualifying questions, interview questions
2. Conduct informal survey of current field staff	Scott	3/2	Ask how DIS found out about job, what would make you stay

7.8 Step 6: Review and Evaluate Results of the Change

By the end of the nine-month project, new early syphilis cases leveled off and began to decline (Figure 7.6). During the same period, syphilis increased in Florida peer counties.

1. 100% of DIS conformed to minimum blood draw standards for the last two months.
2. Achieved cluster index above CDC standard for four consecutive quarters: attributed by team members to better interviewing skills.

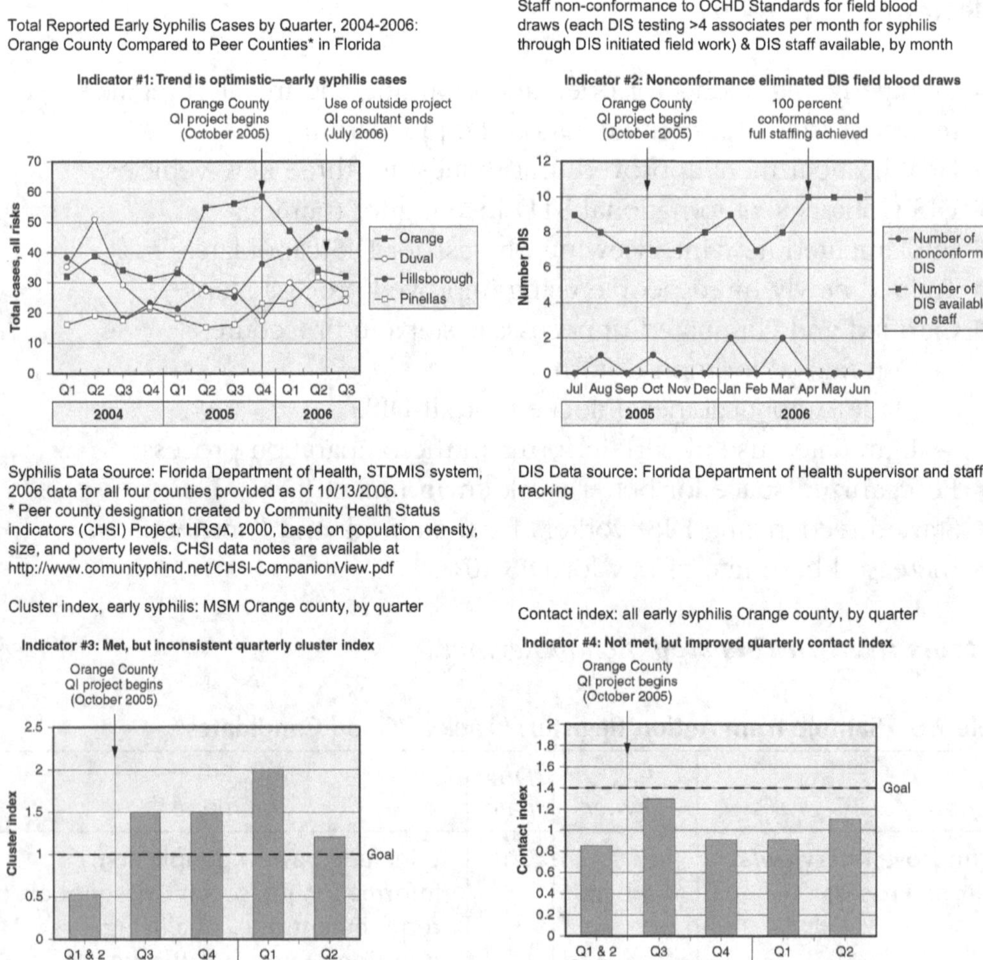

Figure 7.6 Measures of project success after 9-month process improvement efforts.

3. Contact index target was improved but target not met – needs additional action.

Milestones

- Gathered data and charted progress on the indicators.
- Revisited Fishbone Diagram on turnover, and identified that most causes had been addressed, or were being addressed, by the team.

QI tools used in this step: *Control Charts, Fishbone Diagram*

7.9 Step 7: Reflect and Act on Learnings

Secondary Effects of QI Effort: In addition to advances made in their indicators, the team also reported the following successes which grew out of the QI initiative:

- Stopped DIS staff turnover (a root cause)
  - Zero DIS left the unit in the first half of 2006; 6 left in 2005.
  - Fully staffed for the first time in group memory.
- Improved morale and teamwork
  - Increased job satisfaction: STD employee satisfaction surveys show an 18% increase in 2006 compared to the last survey in 2004 (significant at the p = .05 level).
  - More cohesiveness and trust in team.
  - Better morale and teamwork translated into a better ability to work with the community.

> The community is more accepting and receptive to our team because of the improvements we've made within our unit.
>
> **– Jim Hinson**

Team success strengthened OCHD ability to request other project funds.

Implementing QI: Since this was the health department's first QI initiative using this approach, the team learned what support needed to be in place for a successful project. While some team members had previous

QI training, most learned new methods by carrying out the project. One of the most important assets was having a consultant who could be neutral, provide expertise from other fields, and help keep the team focused. The team also identified other practices and expectations they saw as necessary to successfully carry out the QI process; however, they also found that establishing these practices and expectations proved to be a challenge.

Some *challenges* identified by the team:

- Dedicating staff to full attendance at all team meetings.
- Staying focused on priority issues.
- Scheduling subject matter experts for process drill down documentation.
- Using quality tools effectively.
- Securing imbedded consultant with required support skills.

Other Team Lessons: The project gave the team many other insights, such as:

- Most useful tools: Affinity Diagram, Fishbone Diagram, Process Mapping.
- Biggest surprise: The problem is not necessarily what you think it is.
- Maintaining focus on quantitative measures requires discipline and time commitment.
- Barriers and gaps must be documented for action.
- QI projects must be aligned to organization's goals.

Milestones

- Completed evaluation using interviews, quarterly questionnaires, and data review.
- Recognized team members with letters of commendation from the local health officer, certificates of accomplishment, and a placard with team members' photos in the lobby.
- Shared successes through agency presentations, newsletters, and milestone meetings.
- Other units became interested in QI and requested project participation.

7.10 Looking Back: Fall 2008

Two years have passed since the Orange County Health Department (OCHD) undertook the STD Improvement Project. Like many health departments, Orange County is facing challenges of funding, manpower, scarce resources, and increasing community needs. OCHD senior management remains committed to quality improvement as the path to increased community service and organizational performance, and the vision of "A Healthier Future for the People of Florida." Orange County Florida has a population of over 1 million residents, and over 40 million visitors a year come to the area attractions, including Disney, Universal, and the Convention Center. With this large, transient population, consistent monitoring of STD incidence is imperative to achieve appropriate Plan/Do/Check/Act processes and control STDs.

As the Winter Park Health Foundation project was having its successes, two other STDs were increasing in Orange County, as well as Statewide – chlamydia and gonorrhea. These bacterial infections, while easily treatable, many times go unrecognized (asymptomatic) by an infected person, thus leading to medical complications and spreading of the diseases in the community. Seeing this increase, STD management moved more manpower towards this growing issue, especially focusing on infected pregnant females. During 2007 in Orange County, over 1200 pregnant females had Chlamydia or Gonorrhea. Increased effort was placed on assuring these medically at-risk individuals were adequately treated, and an effort made to notify their partners of possible exposure and infection so they could seek evaluation and treatment, and not re-infect the pregnant female in order to have a favorable outcome of a healthy baby and mother. Though this move of personnel caused efforts with syphilis to be somewhat lowered, the lessons learned during the project served to help the STD Department to look at the increasing STD situation in Orange County in a different manner, and to begin to take steps to manage the increasing numbers of STDs using tools and methodology learned in the syphilis initiative.

One example of action taken was that the STD clinic flow was analyzed, and the decision was made to focus on the clinic flow process to increase the number of clients that could be seen as well as improve client satisfaction. The entire clinic process was mapped, with improvements initiated at many stages of the operation. The clinic went from 22.5 to 37 hours being available to the public for care, thus providing the opportunity to see more clients. Staff morale improved with alternative flexible work schedules, and revenues have increased. The waiting area and intake areas are being renovated to a modern professional appearance. The result of using the QI process is that persons with or exposed to STDs have a better chance of getting rapid quality care, and the community will be healthier with this opportunity to reduce the spread of STDs, thus helping us reach our vision.

Critical to the improvements has been the continual support of Senior Management in providing the necessary resources to meet the growing demands of the program. Six vehicles are now available to the DIS field staff. DIS morale has improved. On-going surveys are showing that client satisfaction is improving, and the results of using the QI tools as presented by the consultant have well served and will continue to be used by the OCHD STD Program.

The return on the initial investment of time and resources to train staff in the use of QI tools has more than paid for itself in the continuation of use of the tools in the different processes in the program, providing a proven process that permits optimal resolution to our challenges.

Seeing the success that this initiative had with the STD program, the Orange County Health Department launched an internally funded major quality initiative to improve Septic System Permitting in spring 2008. This project achieved the following outcomes:

Wins for the Process Performance Action Team:

- Date stamping of all paperwork received.
- Comment Form in each green folder and utilized.
- Green Folder labeled with Re-host number for tracking.
- Updated instructions (in process).
  - Spanish and English versions (in process).
- Immediate Line Locator input by clerical staff.
- Workload rebalancing for management file reviews.
- SharePoint site established for project documentation.
- Adjusting front counter hours at Mercy Drive location to meet state guidelines (8 – 4). Shorter hours allow staff to address paperwork requirements before end of day.

OCHD embarked on the development of a department-wide quality system in fall 2008. The department has again retained the imbedded consultant involved in the 2006 STD and the 2008 Septic System Permitting improvement team activities. The consultant is tasked with coaching senior leadership, the department QI coordinator and selected teams in the skills necessary to become totally self-supporting in their quality and performance improvement efforts.

OCHD is committed to the use of quality tools and techniques to provide an ever-increasing level of service to the public health community in Orange County, Florida. The team outcomes, community acceptance, fact-based decision making, and improved morale resulting from OCHD quality efforts have convinced senior management in the department that quality improvement is a core element of their organizational culture.

7.11 Apply the BEST-Method: Updating to 2019

The authors were curious about how closely the Orange County Health Department (OCHD) best practice of 2008 is, compared to a real Best Practice. We applied the Quick Scan tool to the OCHD STD Quality Improvement process description. As documented in Figure 7.7, the missing parts are: trends, stakeholders, and audit. One of the authors contacted the Department of Health – Orange County again to update the figures.

Figure 7.7 is the result of using the BEST Quick Scan to assess the *original 2008* case study. The reader will see that although the Quick Scan tool was not available to the case study author in 2008, most of the characteristics of a Best Practice were included in this original document.

- Results
  - Six criteria are complete, and one criterion is incomplete.
- Enabler
  - Plan: seven criteria are complete, and one criterion is incomplete.
  - Do: five criteria are complete.
  - Check: three criteria are complete. One criterion is incomplete.
  - Act: five criteria are complete.
- Process: both criteria are complete. In fact, there are two processes described: Quality Improvement Process and Sample Process for Field Blood Draws.
- Format: complete, although the format differs from the Quick Scan format description.

One of the authors of the present text was the consultant to the original case study written in 2008. Once the Quick Scan was complete, it was a simple task to identify the areas of the case study that needed either more

		Criteria	
Results		Scope and relevance	Complete
		Integrity of data	Complete
		Segmentation	Complete
		Trends	Incomplete
		Targets	Complete
		Comparison with benchmarks	Complete
		Cause - Effect	Complete
Enabler	Plan	Description	Complete
		Stakeholders	Incomplete
		Responsibilities	Complete
		KPI's and PI's	Complete
		Deployment and Segmentation	Complete
		Prevention	Complete
		Benchmarking	Complete
		Data	Complete
	Do	Implementation	Complete
		Deployment	Complete
		Cause - Effect	Complete
		Accountability	Complete
		SMART	Complete
	Check	Integration	Complete
		Monitoring	Complete
		Audit	Incomplete
		Adjustment & Learning	Complete
	Act	Improvement	Complete
		Process	Complete
		Resources	Complete
		Knowledge & Experience	Complete
		Benchmark	Complete
Process		Process description	Complete
		KPI's	Complete
Format		13 criteria	Complete

Figure 7.7 ***Quick Scan assessment*** **of OCHD STD Quality Improvement process (situation 2008). Case Study from chapter 24, *The Public Health Quality Improvement Handbook* 2009. Author: Jim Hinson. Editor: Bialek, Duffy and Moran. Assessment is done on only criteria level, not on characteristic level.**

description or for which there was an opportunity for improvement. Those areas were:

- Results
  - Trends from 2006 to 2019 for STD testing and comparison with comparative Florida counties.
- Enabler
  - Plan: Stakeholder descriptions.
  - Check: Evidence of systematic process audits.

7.11.1 Improvement: Trends

Table 7.7 gives the 2019 Orange County indices showing new CDC goals. State averages for syphilis tracking have been changed to reporting of Area 07 (Brevard, Orange, Osceola, Seminole counties) averages due to centralization of Health Departments within Florida. Orange County tracking over multiple years allows the local team to calculate their baseline.

The team continues to track the four measures of its success from 2006:

1. Reduce new early syphilis cases by 25% compared to the previous year. (Outcome measure).
2. 100% of Disease Intervention Specialists (DIS) will test a minimum of four associates per month for syphilis through DIS-initiated field work.

Table 7.7 Orange County, Florida Syphilis Cluster and Contact Index summary (situation 2019)

Measure	*Team baseline (6 yr average)*	*Area 07 Average (6 yr average)*	*CDC goal*
Cluster Index*	0.13	.10	.50 Change from 1.0
Contact Index**	1.2	.94	1.0 Change from 2.0

* Cluster Index tracks the identification of other persons who are potentially connected to a case as well as the standard inquiries such as pregnant females, intravenous drug users, roommates, etc. The goal is to obtain information from a contact about at least one other individual the Health Department can communicate with for the purpose of syphilis testing and tracking. The current CDC (Centers for Disease Control and Prevention) goal is to obtain one additional name from at least every other contact (e.g. 1/2 = .50 index).

** Contact Index records the average number of partners identified by an individual exhibiting early syphilis symptoms. The current CDC goal is to obtain the name and contact information for at least one partner for each contact made (e.g. 1/1 = 1.0 index).

(Performance measure) – Now tracked on an annual basis with a goal of 12 draws per DIS per year.

3. Increase the quarterly cluster index to 1.0 on early syphilis cases among MSM. (Performance measure) – Now of lower priority due to capacity issues.
4. Increase the quarterly contact index on all early syphilis cases, including MSM cases, to 1.41. (Performance measure).

One outcome measure and three performance measures are tracked for processes important to reaching the outcome goal. Two process measures – the contact index and cluster index (process measures related to eliciting partner names and testing at-risk individuals) – were identified as areas for improvement because the team performed below the state average and CDC goals. The third process measure remains "field blood draws," which is now tracked on an annual basis.

These indicators are tracked the same way, but due to the significant increase in syphilis, the Cluster Index is given less priority than treatment and partner tracking (Contact Index). This lower priority within Area 07 and Orange County can be seen in Table 7.7 as neither index is close to the .50 CDC goal.

The goals from the CDC have been reduced over the years to reflect reduced capacity of health departments to handle the increased workload of rising STD cases. The measures are tracked through a new database called STARS. Syphilis monitoring and partner contact are also tracked through a monthly surveillance reporting system.

Figure 7.8 is an evolved report from the 2006 Reported Early Cases of Syphilis graph. Due to centralization of Florida Health Departments, the counties are now grouped by Areas and Orange is not compared with the same counties as in 2006. The graph now tracks number of interviewed contacts which lead to data then reflected in Indicators 3 and 4 in Figure 7.6, Cluster and Contact Indices. Note that the number of Early Syphilis Cases in Orange County is significantly higher than in proximate counties in the 2019 graph. The 2006 graph (Indicator #1, Figure 7.6) of all cases compared to other major population centers in Florida shows Orange as the highest incidence of morbidity. Figure 7.9 is the current trend of morbidity in Orange County from 2014 to 2019. This chart shows all identified cases of Early Syphilis, where Figure 7.8 records number of contacts interviewed.

Several factors beyond the control of the Health Department influence the growing number of cases in Orange County. Measure #1: Reduce new

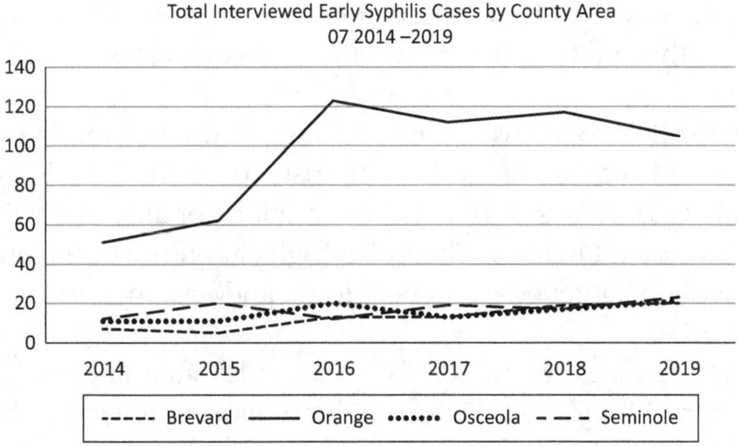

Figure 7.8 Total interviewed early syphilis cases by county area 07.

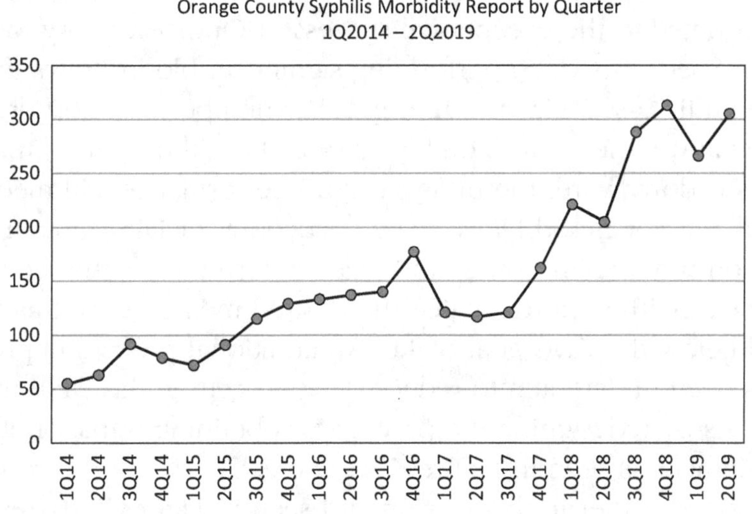

Figure 7.9 Orange County syphilis report by quarter.

early syphilis cases by 25% compared to the previous year (Outcome measure) from 2006 and still in effect for 2019, states a goal of a 25% reduction of cases year over year. Figure 7.9 shows this has not been attained. One of the impacting factors is the general increase of syphilis within the population because of changes in how individuals meet others for intimate purposes. In the past, the Health Department established working relationships with local gathering spots where liaisons were initiated. Contacting and testing of individuals could be geographically focused. The rise of social media applications allows anonymous introduction of partners that cannot be easily tracked by the Health Department. The anonymity of social media also precludes the ability to assess whether the contacts are MSM or other pairings.

Two additional factors have arisen in Orange County, Florida over the past 13 years. At least one of the large tourist attractions outside Orlando holds annual LGBTQ days. Scheduled celebrations of alternative lifestyles are hosted in downtown Orlando. The Pulse Nightclub terrorist tragedy on June 12, 2016 brought heightened awareness to Orlando as an alternate lifestyle destination.

Figure 7.11 illustrates the trend of Contact Index attainment of goals for the 5 years from 2014 to 2019. Orange County has improved its ability to contact infected individuals despite the increase in social media applications bringing individuals together anonymously. Measurement #4: Increase the quarterly contact index on all early syphilis cases, including MSM, ranges just above or below the CDC goal for the years 2014–2019. This success is partially attributed to the exceptional success of Orange County for Disease Intervention Specialists (DIS) performing significant blood draws to identify early syphilis cases. Figure 7.12 trends the number of blood draws now tracked annually, rather than monthly as in 2006. Although the trend of the past 6 years is downward, the mid-year 2019 performance still meets the total annual goal for Blood Draws. The headcount for DIS varies from 5 – 10 depending on funding and program focus. Performance to the goal of a 1.41 Contact Index in 2018 approximated the desired metric. As of this writing, 2019 is still below the CDC goal of 1.0. An additional process improvement activity has been undertaken to reduce delay in getting the DIS out on blood draw missions by redesigning the process for obtaining transportation and testing equipment as seen in Figures 7.21 and 7.22.

As mentioned earlier in this section and seen in Figure 7.10, trending for Orange County Cluster Index has not had heavy focus. There is no attempt to attain the CDC goal of .5 referrals per infected individual. The emphasis is on treating the original individual and any direct partners to contain the spread of the disease.

7.11.2 Area for Improvement: Stakeholders

The Orange County Health Department managers used the BEST-tool to identify the missing section of Enabler: Stakeholders

Identifying and treating the symptoms of early syphilis cases involves a complex set of stakeholders. Already introduced are:

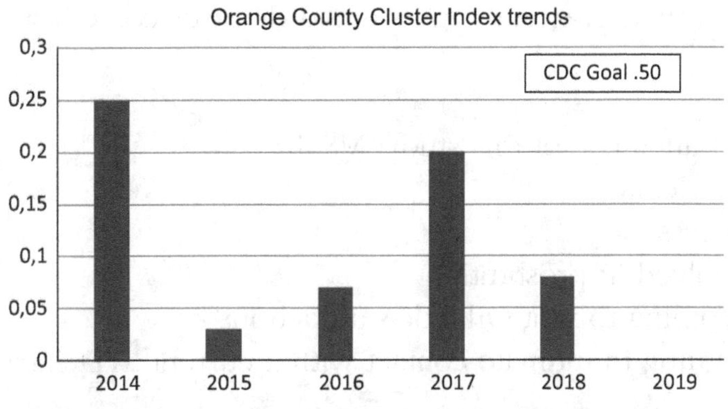

Figure 7.10 Cluster Index Orange County 2014–2019.

Orange County Health Department stakeholders

- Disease Intervention Specialists
- Quality Manager
- Quality Improvement team
- STD unit leadership
- Other STD unit professionals covering for QI team members
- Department administrative support staff

The individuals displaying symptoms involve another set of stakeholders:

- The individual
- The individual's partners
- Family
- Friends and associates
- Employers
- Caregivers

Government and agency stakeholders beyond the Orange County Health Department include:

- Peer health departments grouped in a common measurement cohort
- Community support agencies
- State health agencies
- Centers for Medicare and Medicaid
- Health and Human Services

Individuals contracting sexually transmitted diseases come from all walks of life:

- The target audience of this study: MSM
- College students
- The homeless
- Those involved in prostitution
- Tourists coming to visit Orlando's attractions
- Others coming in intimate contact with a current STD carrier

We have identified one stakeholder for each cluster for which a KPI and results can be reported (Tables 7.8 and 7.9).

7.11.3 Improvement Audit

Although the concept of audit is a familiar method within TQM, nobody thought 13 years ago to include this in the case study. The Quick Scan revealed that it is necessary to document the audit and to take

Table 7.8 Overview of stakeholders, KPI, and results

Stakeholder	*KPI (name)*	*Results*
Disease intervention specialists	Minimum number of blood draws/year	Figure 7.12
The individual's partners	Contact index	Figure 7.11
Peer health departments	Compared to area index average	Table 7.7
Individuals contacted	# contacted per period	Figure 7.8

Table 7.9 Number of individuals interviewed and referrals

1Q Year X	*County*	*# of Interviews*	*# of Linked partners*	*Partner index*
2014	Orange	51	35	0.69
2015	Orange	62	65	1.05
2016	Orange	123	128	1.04
2017	Orange	112	106	0.95
2018	Orange	117	152	1.3
2019 YTD	Orange	105	102	0.97

corresponding corrective actions. In 2019 we applied the same QI methodology as in 2008. Monthly audits are performed by the local Operations and Management Consultant Manager and results documented to the Area 07 Manager of Community Health. The measures from these audits are reflected in the reports from which Figures 7.9–7.12 are created.

7.12 Looking Back: Experiences from 2008 till 2019

7.12.1 2019 Assessment of Case Study Orange County Health Department, STD Quality Improvement

The major challenge was to access data from the last 13 years to show the evolution of reporting. Like many government programs, measurement and reporting requirements change over time. Fortunately, one of the original

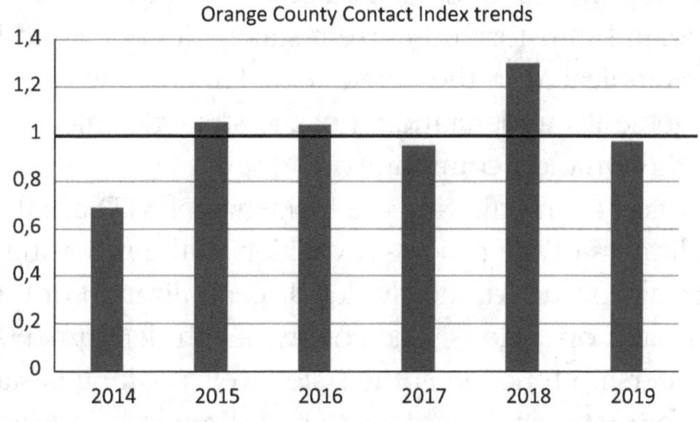

Figure 7.11 Contact Index Orange County 2014–2019.

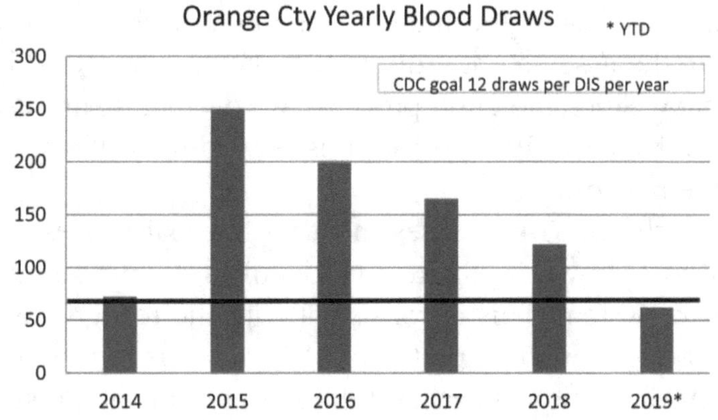

Figure 7.12 Orange County Yearly DIS Blood Draws.

supervisors is now the Area 07 Manager of Community Health and was able to work closely with the Orange County Department and Quality Managers to illustrate the evolution of the tracking systems used as the Florida Public Health system was centralized. Priorities have changed at both the Federal and State level, and epidemic focus moved from one disease to another.

The Enabler omissions were easy to include, since the stakeholders of the STD programs remain relatively constant. Audits have been performed during the entire life of the program. The original case study authors neglected to include this information in their 2008 document.

7.12.2 Full BEST-Tool Assessment of Orange County Health Department STD Blood Draw Process Case Study

A closer assessment using the detailed BEST-tool further clarified improvements suggested in the Quick Scan. Figure 7.7: the Results section of the BEST-tool, identified the need to list stakeholders of the Blood Draw process. The 2019 team brainstormed current stakeholders and added a comprehensive list as indicated in the above text. This review of stakeholders refreshed management's understanding of the strategic value of the process as a support to the Orlando community.

Trends and targets for monitoring the incidence of STD are the Key Performance Indicators of the process. Evolution of the reporting process over the past 13 years has occurred, mostly due to centralization of the Florida Department of Health operations. The county health departments now report to a common leadership function at the state level. Tracking is standardized across locations for better analysis. This standardization increases the opportunity that positive performance will continue in the future (Figure 7.13).

The Enabler section of the BEST-tool reflects the Plan – Do – Check – Act cycle of process design and implementation as seen in Figures 7.14–7.17. Comments from the assessment indicate that the case study addresses each area appropriately. Since the 2006 process improvement team used the PDCA cycle as a base for their project, it is rewarding to have the BEST-tool validation of their success.

In addition to the BEST-tool assessment for internal process performance, the Maturity Model shown in Figure 7.18 identifies the process at level 4; part of a Management System. This is consistent with the recognition the Orange County office of the Florida Department of Health has received through the Public Health Accreditation Board and the high performing results of their Quality Management System.

	Criteria and characteristics	0%	25%	50%	75%	100%	Not described	Comments
1	**Scope and Relevance**							
	• The results are aligned with the expectations and needs of the relevant stakeholders					X		Verify all Stakeholders - 3/24/18
	• The results are aligned with policy and strategy of the organization					X		
	• The most important key results are identified and prioritized					X		
	• The relation between the results is understood					X		
2	**Integrity of data**							
	• Results are timely					X		
	• Results are reliable and accurate					X		
3	**Segmentation**							
	• Results are segmented in a suitable manner							
	o By region, country					X		
	o By department, business line, division, unit					X		
	o By product and service type					X		
4	**Trends**							
	• Trends are positive for 5 years or more						X	To be verified with process owner 3/24/18
	• Results are sustainable and show good performance						X	To be verified with process owner 3/24/18
5	**Targets**							
	• Targets for core results are set					X		
	• Targets are suitable					X		
	• Targets are achieved				X			To be verified from reporting of trends
6	**Comparisons with targets and benchmarks**							
	• Comparisons for core results are made					X		
	• Comparisons are suitable					X		
	• Comparisons are favorable				X			To be verified from reporting of trends
7	**Cause-effect**							
	• The results are clearly achieved through the chosen approach (cause - effect)					X		
	• The relations between results achieved and the approaches are understood					X		
	* Based on the evidence presented, it is assured that the positive performance will continue in the future, i.e. the results are sustainable				X			Based on budget and priority of programs

Source: Orange County Health Department STD QI project. Assessment of the results of the Best Practice of STD testing.

Figure 7.13 STD Quality Improvement Best Practice OCHD case study, application of the detailed BEST-method: assessment of the results.

The management of the process, as reflected in Figure 7.19 prompted the documentation of the audit activities to the original 2006 text. Process ownership remains with the Area 07 Manager, Community Health. That the current Area 07 manager was part of the original 2006 process improvement team provides strong continuity of monitoring and results. Risk management, which was only informally addressed in 2006, is now a formal part of the Orange County Health Department Quality Management System in 2019.

The Format section of the BEST-tool reinforced the strength of the original PDCA structure of the 2006 case study. Using a standardized improvement model automatically guided the process improvement team

#		Criteria and characteristics	0%	25%	50%	75%	100%	Not described	Comments
1	Plan	**Description**							
		• The approach is repeatable and based on reliable data and information					X		
		• The core process are identified and described					X		
		• The methods are documented					X		
		• The process is the reflection of common sense and is well thought out (logical sequence, clearly linked to organizational strategy, interactions with other processes and sub-processes)					X		
2		**Stakeholders**							
		• The process is tailored to the needs, requirements and expectations of interested parties (stakeholders)				X			Identify stakeholders of process
		• The indicators and targets are set and the relationship with the core process is clearly defined					X		
3		**Responsibilities**							
		• The responsibilities and accountabilities are clearly defined					X		
		• Each process has a process owner					X		
		• The process description takes into account the skills and experiences required by the persons responsible for carrying out the process and approaches					X		Part of implementation actions
4		**KPI's and PI's**							
		• Each process contains one or more KPI's (Key Performance Indicator) and one or more PI's (Performance Indicator)					X		
5		**Deployment and Segmentation**							
		• The description of the process and approaches considers the specificities of all segments of the organization (division, department, work unit) and the variety of products and services					X		
6		**Prevention**							
		• Prevention is built into the process					X		
		• The core process description takes into account the specific circumstances of the organization and prevention is integrated into the daily work					X		
7		**Benchmarking**							
		• The process description takes into account similar benchmarks and best-in-class examples			x				Benchmark against State established goals
8		**Data**							
		• The measurement methods are described clearly and unambiguously, including securing the relevance, integrity and reliability of the measurement results					X		
		• The data are presented at the proper level of segmentation to effectively reflect performance and results at different levels of the organization.					X		At operational level

KPI : Key Performance Indicator (this has a direct relationship with the strategy of the organization)

PI : Performance Indicator (several performance indicators contribute to the validity of a KPI)

Figure 7.14 STD Quality Improvement Best Practice case study, application of the detailed BEST-method. Assessment of the ENABLERS (PDCA) PLAN. Source: Orange County Health Department STD QI project report. Assessment of the enabler of the Best Practice of STD testing: PLAN. KPI: Key Performance Indicator (this has a direct relationship with the strategy of the organization). PI: Performance Indicator (several performance indicators contribute to the validity of a KPI).

		Criteria and characteristics	0%	25%	50%	75%	100%	Not described	Comments
1	DO	**Implementation**							
		• The daily activities are in conformance with the process descriptions and documented methods					X		
		• The implementation of the core process is integrated into the daily work					X		
		Deployment							
		• The approach is used by all appropriate work units					X		
2		**Cause-effect**							
		• The use of the key process leads to concrete and measurable results					X		
3		**Accountability**							
		• All employees and managers clearly exhibit how they are responsible and accountable for their assigned tasks				x			Processes are defined. KPIs monitored and reported quarterly.
4		**SMART**							
		• KPI's and PI's are used systematically					X		
		• SMART decisions are taken and action plans are developed					X		

SMART: This is an acronym and stands for Specific, Measurable, Assignable (Accountable), Relevant and Timely executed

Figure 7.15 STD Quality Improvement Best Practice case study, application of the detailed BEST-method. Assessment of the ENABLERs (PDCA) DO. Source: Orange County Health Department STD QI project report. Assessment of the enabler of the Best Practice of STD testing: DO. SMART: This is an acronym and stands for Specific, Measurable, Assignable (Accountable), Relevant and Timely executed.

to include most of the components of a best practice. The BEST-tool served as a clarifying instrument to identify those few items omitted from the 2006 report and the 2008 update. The 2019 BEST-assessment alerted the process owner to areas for additional improvement (Figure 7.20). The addition of these missing components truly elevates this process to that of a Best Practice.

7.12.3 Current Status of Best Practice: Summer 2019

Figures 7.21 and 7.22 show the updated flowchart of the Blood Draw Preparation process. The BEST-method suggests a more complete process that identifies the Who, What, Where and How of each process step. The exercise of updating the 2006 process flow with the current process owner and supervisor provided a refresh of the value of the process and identified some areas of the flow that had changed over the years. Inconsistencies emerged and opportunities for further cycle time improvement were discovered.

Assessment of the **enabler** of the Best Practice of STD testing: **CHECK**

		Criteria and characteristics	0%	25%	50%	75%	100%	Not described	Comments
1	Check	**Integration**							
		• Plans, process, results, analysis, learning and actions are harmonized across the process and work units to support organization-wide goals					X		
		Monitoring							
		• The performance of each core process is regularly measured and monitored					X		On a quarterly basis
		• The obtained results related to a core process are regularly discussed with all relevant stakeholders					X		
		• The method to determine the target value of the KPI (target) is validated and opportunities for improvement are recorded					X		
		• Relevance, integrity, completeness and reliability of the results achieved are checked					X		
2		**Audit**							
		• Each process owner audits his or her core process regularly						X	
		• The process owner examines what can be done to bring the core process to a higher maturity level (to determine improvement opportunities)						X	
3		**Adjustment and Learning**							
		• Deviations from the desired and/or planned results serve as input for the improvement and revision of the core process and/or approaches					X		
		• Identification of problems related to the sufficient availability and appropriate resources such as budget, machinery, equipment, provisions, tools, and Information Technology (software, hardware, networking, security, etc.)					X		
		• Identification of an adequate number of employees and/or of shortcomings of skills and experiences of employees in the process and/or approaches					X		Major target of QI project
		• Comparison of the results obtained with the benchmark and Best-in-Class					X		
		• Prioritization of opportunities for improvement					X		
		• Encouragement of breakthrough change to the approach applied through innovation					X		

Figure 7.16 STD Quality Improvement Best Practice case study, application of the detailed BEST-method. Assessment of the ENABLERs (PDCA) CHECK. Source: Orange County Health Department STD QI project report. Assessment of the enabler of the Best Practice of STD testing: CHECK.

7.12.4 Conclusion

This case study, as improved from the original version in 2008 is a Best Practice. As further evidence of the effectiveness of the overall system managed by this organization, the Orange County locations received full Public Health Accreditation Board recognition in 2017. The first re-accreditation audit process is occurring as of this writing.

This chapter is written by a quality professional, with the support of the current STD department and quality managers. The spontaneous presentation in 2008 of most of the criteria included in the BEST Quick Scan tool reinforces the credibility of the BEST-tool. The same quality professional

Assessment of the **enabler** of the Best Practice of STD testing: **ACT**

		Criteria and characteristics	0%	25%	50%	75%	100%	Not described	Comments
1	Act	**Improvement**							
		• The output of the measurement and learning is analyzed and used to identify additional improvements; to prioritize, to plan and to implement these further opportunities for improvement					X		
2		**Process**							
		• The process, methods and approaches are revised and improved in response to the findings gained in the Check phase					X		
3		**Resources**							
		• The amount and nature of the resources that were adjusted because of the findings in the Check phase are documented					X		
		• The number of employees assigned to the process is adjusted considering the opportunities of improvement and the outcome of the process, methods and approaches					X		Balanced across projects by priority
4		**Knowledge and Experience**							
		• New training and/or refresher training is given to meet the findings gained in the Check phase					X		
		• Sharing of refinements and innovations with other relevant work units and processes					X		
		• The Knowledge and experience of those involved in the process are documented and validated as Best-in-Class or Benchmark level					X		This case study is the recognition
5		**Benchmark**							
		• The organization can be set as a model for other organizations					X		

Figure 7.17 STD Quality Improvement Best Practice case study, application of the detailed BEST-method. Assessment of the ENABLERs (PDCA) ACT. Source: Orange County Health Department STD QI project report. Assessment of the enabler of the Best Practice of STD testing: ACT.

who edited the case study in 2008 used the results of the BEST Quick Scan in writing this chapter to identify missing information that would be critical for continuous improvement within the Health Department or to those using this case study as a benchmark for their own operations. This case is the basis for writing a Best Practice as described in Chapter 4.

The Florida Health Department – Orange County is a benchmark within Florida for process definition, improvement and the implementation of an effective Quality Management System. One major factor in the continued process strength of Orange County Health Department is that their Quality Manager is an ISO Lead Auditor with extensive experience with General Electric, one of the earliest implementers of Six Sigma statistical process improvement methods. The Quality Manager developed the first Quality Management System in the Florida Health Department System and continues to be instrumental in assisting other state health departments and the centralized organization in process definition, standards compliance, and strategic benchmarking.

Assessment of the maturity of the process of Best Practice: STD testing

Levels	Description	Assessment	Comments
0	**Non-existent** Within the organization there are no or very little management measures. Control awareness is rather low and only few actions are taken to achieve an adequate system of organizational management (internal control system).		
1	**Ad-hoc basis** Only ad-hoc management measures are in place within the organization. The awareness of the need for appropriate management (internal control) is growing, but there is still no structured or standardized approach present. The system of organizational management (internal control) is more focused on people than on systems.		
2	**Structured start** A structured impetus is given to the development of management measures. The management tools are therefore being developed but are not yet applied (Plan)		
3	**Defined** (= level 2 + ...) Control measures are provided. These are standardized, documented, communicated and implemented (Do).		
4	**Management system** (= level 3 + ...) The control measures are internally assessed and adjusted (Check & Act). There is a "living" adequate and effective system of organizational management.		Based on emerging process and systems definition and integration: 2006
5	**Optimized** (= level 4 + ...) The control measures are continuously optimized through benchmarking and obtaining quality certificates or external evaluations (PDCA).		

Figure 7.18 Assessment of the Organizational Maturity of the STD testing process. Source: Orange County Health Department STD QI project report. Assessment of the maturity of the process of Best Practice: STD testing.

	Subject	NOK	OK	Comment
1	Owner of key process		X	Who is this now?
2	Integrity		X	
3	Risk management		X	ISO QMS
4	Relation with strategic plan		X	
5	Adding value		X	
6	Systematic simplification		X	
7	KPI		X	
8	Audit	X		Verify
9	Maturity level of process		X	

Source: Orange County Health Department STD QI project report

Figure 7.19 Assessment of the management of the STD testing process.

	Subject	NOK	OK	Comments
1	Title		X	
2	Subject		X	
3	Author (name, title, company, contact)		X	
4	Context (sector, country restrictions)		X	
5	Description of the method and results		X	
6	Measurement method		X	
7	Process description and maturity		X	Added Maturity Model assessment 3/24/18
8	KPIs (Key Performance Indicator) and results		X	
9	Distribution of the results		X	
10	Cause and effect		X	
11	Measurement: RADAR, PDCA, or other		X	
12	Limiting conditions		X	
13	Date and Revision Level		X	

Source: Orange County Health Department STD QI project report.

Figure 7.20 Assessment of the format of the STD testing process.

7.13 Lessons Learned

The Quick Scan tool facilitated several major learning points for Orange County. The assessment immediately identified the need to study performance trends from the original case study writing. Although reporting requirements had changed at the State and National level from 2006 to 2019, the local and area managers were able to access data to recognize trends in disease patterns and demographics necessary to revisit key processes. This trend data was even more valuable considering that the area manager in 2019 was the local leader in 2006 when the original process improvement effort was chartered. His memory of the evolution of disease tracking and treatment over the ensuing 13 years was instrumental in prioritizing improvement efforts in 2019.

Another significant lesson from the Quick Scan assessment was the omission of identified stakeholders in the original case study. It was a mistake on the part of the original case study authors to only focus on the internal processes. The Orange County Health Department works closely with community, state and, national partners to anticipate changes in demographics, regulations, and resource requirements to meet a growing disease epidemic. Fortunately, the local and area managers have an excellent rapport with the stakeholders identified. This updated case study now recognizes the

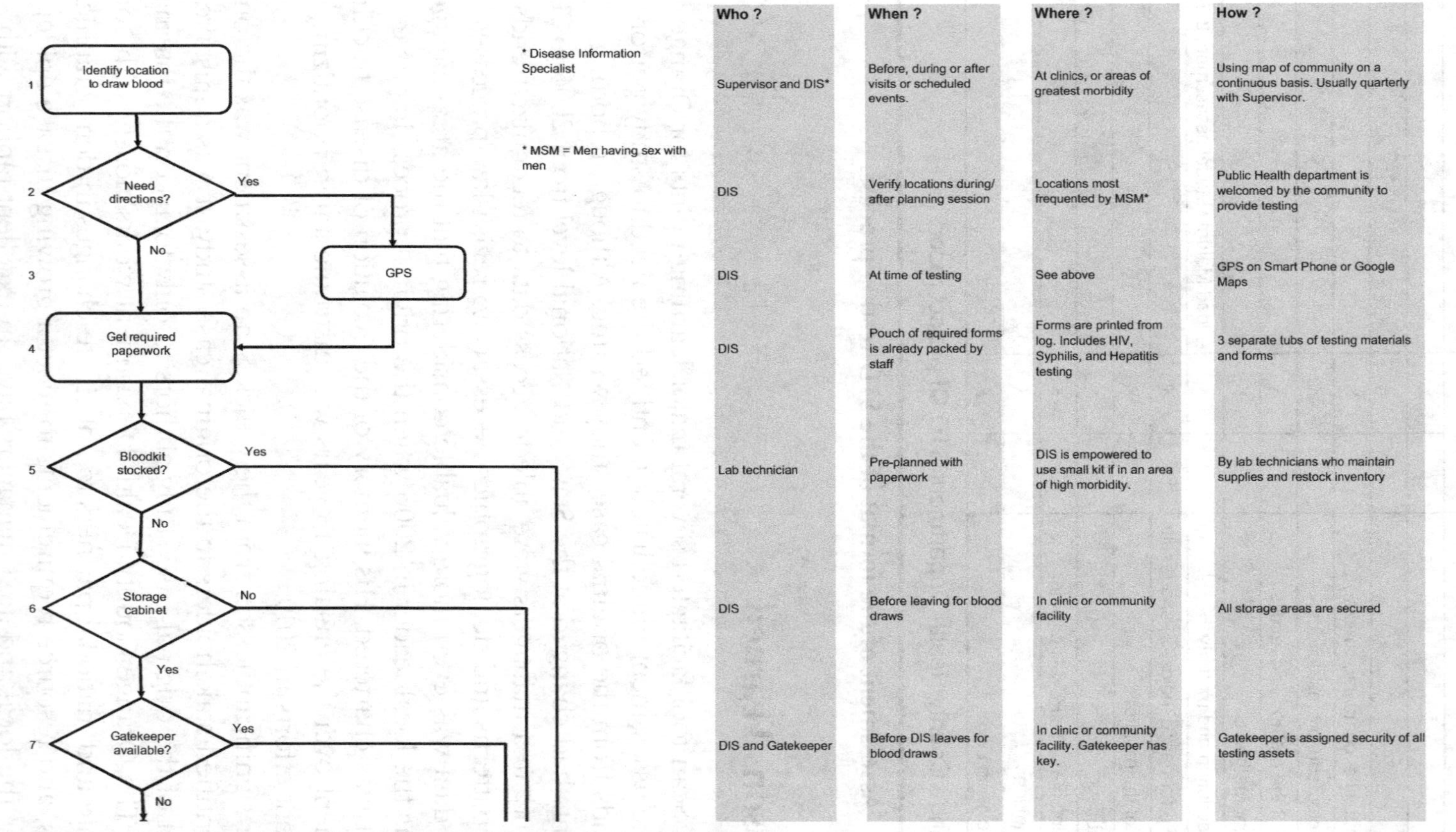

1
Identify location to draw blood
2
Need directions?
Yes
No
3
GPS
4
Get required paperwork
5
Bloodkit stocked?
Yes
No
6
Storage cabinet
No
Yes
7
Gatekeeper available?
Yes
No
* Disease Information Specialist
* MSM = Men having sex with men
Who ?
Supervisor and DIS*
DIS
DIS
DIS
Lab technician
DIS
DIS and Gatekeeper
When ?
Before, during or after visits or scheduled events.
Verify locations during/after planning session
At time of testing
Pouch of required forms is already packed by staff
Pre-planned with paperwork
Before leaving for blood draws
Before DIS leaves for blood draws
Where ?
At clinics, or areas of greatest morbidity
Locations most frequented by MSM*
See above
Forms are printed from log. Includes HIV, Syphilis, and Hepatitis testing
DIS is empowered to use small kit if in an area of high morbidity.
In clinic or community facility
In clinic or community facility. Gatekeeper has key.
How ?
Using map of community on a continuous basis. Usually quarterly with Supervisor.
Public Health department is welcomed by the community to provide testing
GPS on Smart Phone or Google Maps
3 separate tubs of testing materials and forms
By lab technicians who maintain supplies and restock inventory
All storage areas are secured
Gatekeeper is assigned security of all testing assets

Figure 7.21 Improved Blood Draw process using BEST-tool flowcharting format: part 1. Sample Process Map for Field Blood Draws, Preparation – updated April 20, 2018.

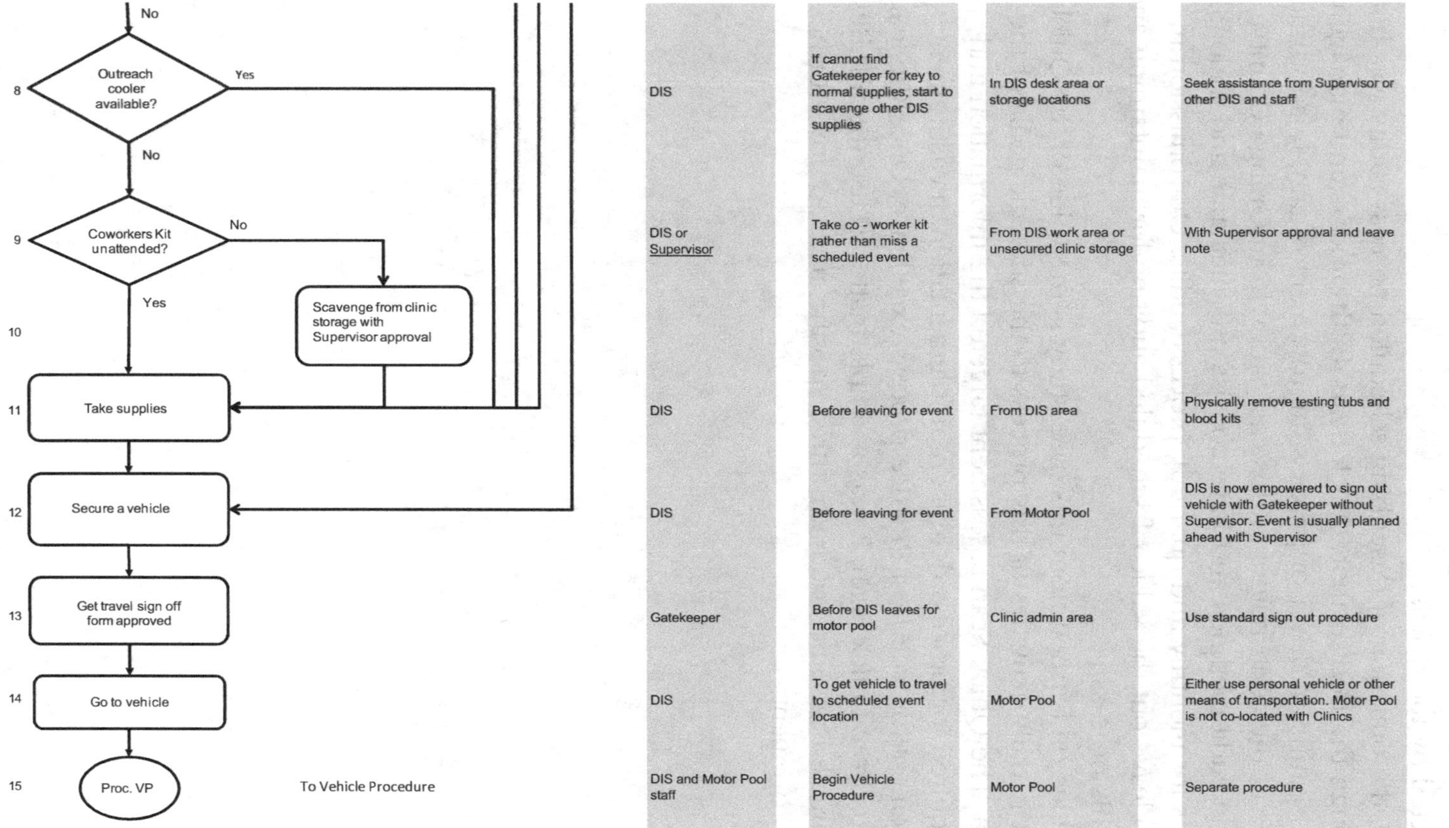

Figure 7.22 Improved Blood Draw process using BEST-tool flowcharting format, part 2. Sample Process Map for Field Blood Draws, Preparation – updated April 20, 2018.

importance of these stakeholders to the ability of Orange County to support those impacted by the disease.

Likewise, the omission of describing scheduled process audits was highlighted through the Best-method Quick Scan. Both process and management audits are a significant driver of process improvement. Again, it is fortunate that all three of the contributors to this case study from Orange County are trained in audit methods and have consistently met state and national requirements for monthly and quarterly process audits. Our omission in 2006 was to leave out the value of scheduled auditing for maintaining and improving this process.

The final lesson learned from this case study is the value of the Quick Scan to tie the daily activities of this process to the strategic goals of the organization. The Quick Scan assessment targeted the information and activities required for process definition, implementation, measurement and improvement for true Best Practice process excellence. Once the team had the focus from Quick Scan, it was a simple matter to use the full Best-method characteristics and criteria in three specific areas to drive further process improvement.

Chapter 8

Conclusion

The BEST-methodology is a vehicle to know whether a process is truly a Best Practice. It answers the question "*To what extent* is this Best Practice a true Best Practice?" It provides valuable information on which specific subjects in the process under consideration can benefit from improvement.

The BEST-method consists of four building blocks: process, results, enabler, and format. Figure 8.1 illustrates the interaction of these building blocks in documenting a Best Practice. All four building blocks must be present in a Best Practice. When you review a case study, you can quickly see that one or more of these building blocks are missing. Results that are achieved without an enabler or process are only achieved by accident or in spite of management. An enabler without results is only a "nice theory." Documenting a Best Practice without a precise process description can be an indicator that the company is throwing resources, tools, and skills at an objective without a structured plan. This is not at all a guarantee of sustainable results.

The BEST-method supports top management in attaining process excellence and continuous improvement. In our experience merely copying a Best Practice is not the best way to improve the business. Every company has its own unique identity, which must be safeguarded. Using a Best Practice as a comparison against a company's own process using the BEST-method allows for fine tuning relative to the culture, strategies, and goals of the benchmarking organization. Simply overlaying another company's Best Practice onto another organization may cause disruption with related processes both upstream and downstream from the transplanted process.

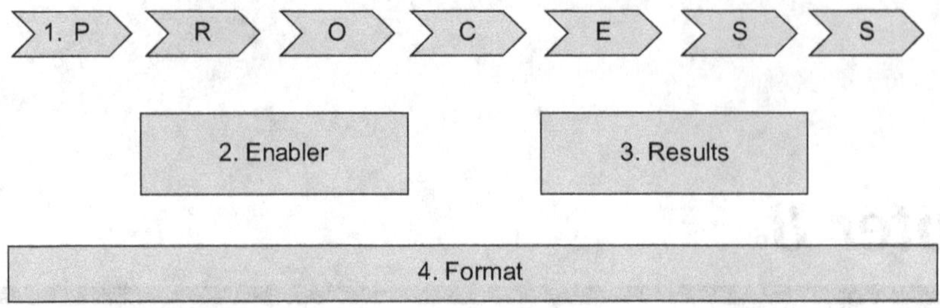

Figure 8.1 Four building blocks of the BEST-method.

Many leaders rely on perceptions, attitudes, and opinions. We call this intuition management. There is no proof that this type of management is superior to the more systematic approaches such as the Malcolm Baldrige Performance Model (MBA), European Foundation for Quality Management (EFQM) model, Lean approach, Six Sigma methodology, or other process management enablers. The authors are convinced that a disciplined and rigorous application of the BEST-method will lead to better and *sustainable* results for *all stakeholders* of the organization.

Best Practices are found mostly in departments such as production, sales, logistics, IT, purchasing, facility management, and finance. The processes for these departments are easier to describe than the "non-tangible" departments such as human resources, public relations, and marketing. The BEST-method, however, is also applicable to these departments. There simply are few examples of these Best Practice case studies available in management literature.

8.1 Lessons Learned

What we have learned in our work and in writing this text is that the majority of so-called Best Practices are marketing publications. A case study appeals to a broader audience when labeled a Best or Good Practice. No one can verify the designation because in the past there was no instrument to check to what extent the advertised process is really a Best Practice. Now the BEST-tool provides this verification.

The authors caution that the objective of using the BEST-tool is not to score 100% for all criteria and all characteristics. Even US, Canadian, and European winners of their Excellence Awards have scores of about 60%–70%, never 100%.

Best Practice is a way of doing something in a sustainable way that yields the best results.

But two factors must be considered:

1) *Context*: every organization has a different history, different leaders, different products, different workforces. It is impossible to say that one solution is the best across every industry and every business. There is simply too much variation.
2) *Change*: the world changes so quickly that it is not possible to achieve the ultimate improvement of a Best Practice before it becomes obsolete. Someone always finds a better way.

8.2 Complete Best Practice

Published Best Practices in literature or on the Internet are often incomplete. In many cases there is much more information available on site than published. Probably for confidential reasons the companies are reticent to show their detailed results and process description. Nevertheless, we found regularly that even the key performance indicators (KPIs) weren't mentioned. Therefore, we must question whether those measures are fully in place.

A Best Practice is only complete when the four building blocks (enabler, process, corresponding results, and format) are described *in detail.* In practice we find that generally the enabler is described. The other three components are only partially documented or not described at all. Even the enabler is often incomplete. The Plan and Do phases are quite well described, but the Check and Act phases are often poorly or not described at all.

As identified in Table 8.1, the American Productivity and Quality Center reported in the 2019 Survey the top five reasons surveyed organizations did

Table 8.1 Top five reasons why organizations don't adopt a framework for process improvement

	Reason	*Percentage*
1	No formal process management available	62.5
2	No support from management	45.8
3	Internal political or cultural resistance	37.5
4	Do not understand how it can be used	16.7
5	Do not know how to get started	16.7

not adopt a framework for process improvement.* The BEST-method provides a systematic framework of criteria and characteristics for organizations to define and manage their processes. The four building blocks of the BEST-method guide senior leadership to align process management to the strategic goals of the organization. The Excel worksheets for both the Quick Scan and detailed assessment BEST-tool clearly explain the components for effective process definition and provide a tangible place to start to achieve organizational excellence. Political or cultural resistance is minimized through objective criteria directly related to evidence-based measures and outcomes.

8.3 Facts and Figures

When a Best Practice starts with the detailed description of the objectives and then the results, the reader becomes curious about how these results were achieved. None of the case studies (see Chapter 6, Quick Scan) discussed in this text use this sequenced approach. Consequently, the reader either assumes what the results were or becomes distracted by task-level activities that may not have had any influence on process results. This is the antithesis of one of the requirements of a Best Practice: **to be factual and evidence based**.

It is strange that nearly all the Best Practices we have seen lack corresponding results. We can only say that the described methods (enablers) are effective and lead to excellent results when the results are also documented. Otherwise we are only dealing with *intentions*. The lesson learned here is that when you look for a Best Practice, ask first about the objectives of the Best Practice and the results achieved. If these two subjects are weak, you can stop looking at that specific Best Practice (outside your organization) or plan corrective actions (if you are analyzing a Best Practice inside your own organization).

8.4 Definitions

We cannot stress enough that definitions of words and concepts (see Chapter 1) are important in order to avoid misunderstandings. When you

* Lyke-Ho-Gland, Holly and Morgan, Lochlyn, *Putting Process Frameworks into Action*, APQC Survey Summary Report Announcement materials. May 2019, APQC, slide 36.

look at management literature and mainly the marketing texts, you see that the words *Best Practices*, *Best-in-Class*, and *World-Class practices* are used too loosely. Now that you have the BEST-tool, you know better.

8.5 Is This Approach Bureaucracy?

It is not possible to describe a full Best Practice in two pages. There are too many criteria and characteristics that must be clarified. For the skeptical reader among us, this is not a bureaucratic system. Every organization or company has only a few Best Practices. Obviously, you must choose carefully those Best Practices you want to develop. After all **the Best Practice contributes in a positive and significant way to the achievement of the company's strategy**.

Don't think that a Best Practice text is a lengthy, detailed, and complex text. No, it must be concise and yet detailed. The more it corresponds to the criteria and characteristics of the BEST-tool, the better. You only need to give evidence on how the criteria and characteristics are put into practice. The best way to start is with a clear and detailed description of what you want to achieve with that Best Practice process.

8.6 "Poor" Best Practices

The reader might think the requirements of the BEST-tool are not realistic. The objective is *not* to find weaknesses nor to make judgments in the style of "this is a poor Best Practice." The real objective of this book is to discover where improvements are feasible (compared with the ideal situation) and how to document a Best Practice.

An unexpected advantage of the BEST-tool is to validate that the management world needs a professional tool to measure the degree of excellence of a Best Practice. Most of the so-called Best Practices have not yet achieved that degree of excellence. Most need significant improvement.

8.7 Journey toward Excellence

The authors are not implying that once a Best Practice is achieved the company or organization has reached its final goal, i.e. a state of excellence.

Even winners of the MBA and EFQM Awards must continue their journey toward excellence. If these organizations stop developing their business and making improvements, they can end up in situations like Kodak, Nokia, Fokker, and others who no longer are recognized industry leaders or have even disappeared.

8.8 Pitfalls

Here are some quick Don'ts and Dos in the use of Best Practice:

Don't:

- Pretend that you have a Best Practice without evidence of the four building blocks of a Best Practice.
- Create a lengthy document lacking precision and using only slogan language.
- Consider as a Best Practice a process that has no alignment with the strategy and business plan of the organization.

Do

- Verify that the Best Practice supports the realization of the strategy and the achievement of business results.
- Require that process improvement is led by the owner of the process and with the active involvement of all people concerned.
- Start with an inventory of the expectations and needs of all process stakeholders.

8.9 Super Quick Assessment

Finally, we want to give the reader a final tool to check very *quickly* (Super Quick Assessment) where he stands with his Best Practice (Figure 8.2). This tool gives a quick overview of the current situation. If you want a precise diagnosis, you can then proceed to use the BEST-tool.

If you can verify that 17 or more of the items have "Evidence present," you can then apply the detailed BEST-tool and check where you still have opportunities for improvement or confirm that you have indeed achieved a Best Practice.

	Questions	Evidence present	Documented	I don't know
1	The objective of the Best Practice is fully described in detail			
2	The results achieved are mainly output and outcome results			
3	The measurement methods are described clearly and unambiguously, including securing the relevance, integrity and reliability of the measurement results			
4	The process is fully described			
5	The results contribute to the achievement of the organization's strategy			
6	There is a clear cause and effect between enabler and results			
7	The results are aligned with the expectations and needs of all relevant stakeholders			
8	There is a positive trend in results for more than 5 years			
9	The comparison of the results with targets and benchmark are favorable			
10	The results presented are deployed and segmented			
11	The processes are tailored to the needs, requirements and expectations of interested parties (stakeholders)			
12	The responsibilities and accountabilities are clearly defined			
13	Prevention is built into the processes			
14	The approach (enabler) is used by all appropriate work units			
15	The performance of each core process is regularly measured and monitored			
16	Each process owner audits his core process regularly			
17	Deviations from the desired and/or planned results serve as input for the improvement and revision of the core processes and/or approaches			
18	The output of the measurement and learning is analyzed and used to identify additional improvements to prioritize, to plan and to implement these further opportunities for improvement			
19	There is an application of knowledge development and sharing of experiences between all members of the organization			
20	The organization can be set as a model for other organizations			
	Total			

Figure 8.2 Checklist: Super Quick Assessment of a Best Practice.

In all situations where you cannot verify that evidence is present, you know where further improvements can be made. We wish you good luck and many excellent results with this tool.

8.10 Choice of the CEO

Top management commitment, engagement, and support in the development of Best Practices are essential. Without these elements it is very difficult to have Best Practices and to achieve excellent results.

A CEO could expect his organization to have at least one new Best Practice every year. If the organization is not working on a Best Practice, is it due to a lack of priority, resources, training, etc.? The CEO has the responsibility to demand continuous improvement within the organization. Therefore, it is up to him or her to make the necessary decisions and request an action plan from the core process owners to cyclically assess and improve their processes, outputs, and outcomes toward Best Practice status.

8.11 Static or Dynamic?

Don't think that once you have a Best Practice, that it is a Best Practice forever. The world is constantly changing. It could be that after 10 years your Best Practice is no longer the best because of new technological innovations and improvements. If you create a new Best Practice in your organization annually, you will always be at the forefront of successful organizations.

Once you have realized a Best Practice, it doesn't mean that this is for perpetuity. After 5 years or so you need to verify that your Best Practice is still a Best Practice.

BOX 8.1 Origin of the Physical Dimension of Newspapers*

In 1712 the British authority introduced a new tax on newspapers. The more pages in the newspaper, the higher the tax. Consequently, the editors decided to increase the size of the newspaper, because it became possible to put the same content onto a smaller number of pages. Even when the tax was stopped, they continue to use the same non-user-friendly size.

Three hundred years later when newspaper editors are asked why the (paper) size is so large, they react all in the same way: "That's the way we've always done it."

What can we learn from this example? This example illustrates the effect of complacency. People do things because they are used to doing them and are comfortable with the status quo.

* Vermeulen Freek, *Breaking Bad Habits: why best practices are killing your business*, Harvard Business Review Press (2018) Boston Massachusetts.

A correct application of the BEST-methodology can overcome this complacency. After all, each Best Practice consists of a process together with a key performance indicator. The latter is always aligned with the strategy and business plan of the organization. This alignment avoids the rigidity of maintaining processes that are no longer effective.

Rethink your long-held beliefs about organizational norms while reinvigorating your business by breaking out of the status quo. We are convinced that once people use the BEST-method in a structured and systematic way, a number of truly Best Practices will become available. Excellent and sustainable results will follow.

We wish you good luck and success in the application of the BEST-methodology in your organization.

Appendix

Abbreviations

6S DFSS	Six Sigma Design for Six Sigma
6S DMAIC	Six Sigma Define-Measure-Analyze-Improve-Control
AI	Artificial Intelligence
APQC	American Productivity & Quality Center
BEST	a **B**etter way to **E**xcellent results and **S**uccess through the application of an appropriate **T**ool
BOE	Barrels of oil equivalent
BSC	Balanced Score Card
C	Complete
CDC	Centers for Disease Control and Prevention
C/I/C	Control – Influence – (Have) Concern
CMM	Capability Maturity Model
CNG	Compressed natural gas
CoQ	Cost of quality
CSR	Corporate social responsibility
Customer Sat.	Customer satisfaction
D/M	Decision making
DFSS	Design for Six Sigma
DIS	Disease intervention specialists
DMAIC	Define, measure, analyze, improve, and control (from lean and Six Sigma)
DOH	Department of Health
EFQM	European Foundation for Quality Management
EH&S	Environmental, health, and social
GDP	Gross domestic product
GWP	Global warming potential
HFC	Hydrofluorocarbon

HFO	Hydrofluoroolefin
HRCI	HR Certification Institute & Top Employers Institute
I	Incomplete
ISO	ISO 9001
Kaizen	Japanese word for Continuous Improvement
KPI	Key performance indicator
Lean	Lean enterprise system
LED	Light-emitting diode
LNG	Liquefied natural gas
MBA	Malcolm Baldrige Award
MBNQA	Malcolm Baldrige National Quality Award
Mgt. Audit	Management audit
MPG	Miles per gallon
MPHD	Metro Public Health Department
MSM	Men who have sex with men
NA	Not available
NCCA	National Commission for Certifying Agencies
NGO	Non-governmental organizations
OCHD	Orange County Health Department
PDCA	Plan-Do-Check-Act cycle, also called Deming circle
PHR	Professional in human resources
PI	Performance indicator
ppm	Part per million
P/S	Problem solving
P&S Syphilis	Primary and secondary syphilis
QFD	Quality function deployment
QI	Quality Improvement
QMS	Quality Management System
QR code	Quick Response code
SCM	Supply chain management
SDT	Sexually transmitted disease
SMART	Specific, Measurable, Assignable (Accountable), Relevant and Timely executed
SOP	Standard operating procedure
Spec. Registrations	Specific Registrations
SPHR	Senior Professional in Human Resources
SWOT	Strengths, weaknesses, opportunities, and threats
TEI	Top Employers Institute
TQM	Total Quality Management
WWF	World Wildlife Fund

Frequently Asked Questions (FAQ)

Although we tried to describe the BEST-method and the BEST-tools in detail, there could be some subjects we didn't develop enough. The answers to the following questions may be helpful to fill the gap.

1. Can you also apply the BEST-method to "Good Practices"?

Yes, of course you can. A process is considered a *Best Practice* when all characteristics in the BEST-tool are satisfied to a 75% or higher level. For a *good practice* there will be a number of criteria and/or characteristics which will score lower than 75%. Nevertheless, a good practice still contributes to some (or to a large) extent to the achievement of organizational strategic goals. The application of the BEST-tool allows you to see quickly where opportunities for improvement are present.

2. Is the BEST-method only applicable for profit-oriented organizations?

No, not at all. *Every* organization tries to achieve excellent results for all its stakeholders. Therefore, all key processes need to be developed in a professional way. A systematic improvement of the management of a key process leads to a Best Practice. This is true for profit and not-for-profit organizations.

3. What is the advantage of the BEST-method for government organizations?

Government organizations are financed by tax funds. The citizens expect to receive an excellent service for their money, but also at the lowest possible cost. This expectation is met by applying the BEST-method across all aspects of the public organization. What is valid for citizens who pay the taxes, is also valid for the government functions that support them (think about different types of permits, licenses, services, etc.).

4. Is the development of a Best Practice a costly project?

It shouldn't be. If you apply Kaizen in a systematic way, you're able to reduce costs while the quality of the process is improved. A Best Practice is, by definition, a process that leads to excellent results. It contributes also to the achievement of the strategic goals at minimal cost.

5. Is the BEST-method applicable to every process?

Yes, it is. You can apply the BEST-method on every *key process* of the organization. However technological processes in a process industry (chemistry, petrochemical, steel, paper, electronics, …) and health sector (medicine, hospitals, pharmaceuticals, …) have their own typical best performance processes. The main applications of the BEST-method are the processes which are less "tangible," such as human resources (recruitment, promotion, training, rewarding, …), customer service and satisfaction, supplier processes, information management (IT, data protection, data security, …), facility management, supplier management, logistics, sustainable management processes, etc.

6. Can the BEST-method be used by a Process Improvement Team?

Yes. An improvement team, sponsored by the key process owner, is an excellent way to apply the BEST-tool and recommend priority process improvements. The authors have used PDCA, lean, Six Sigma, simple problem-solving, Modular Kaizen, and other enabling methods to address the gaps identified from using the BEST-tool.

7. Can the BEST-method also be applied against product development?

No, product design doesn't belong within the scope of the BEST-method.

8. Does the BEST-method replace other assessment methods such as MBA or EFQM?

No, this is a complementary method. Organizations that use assessment methods such as MBA and EFQM can reinforce their approach by applying the BEST-methodology.

9. Do you need to apply the BEST-method on all key processes?

No, you don't. If you apply the Pareto-principle you would know which 20% of the key processes lead to 80% of the planned results. You need only to apply the BEST-method to this 20% of key processes.

10. Is it really necessary to do such a detailed analysis?

Only when you want to do a complete assessment of a Best Practice, do you need to apply the complete BEST-assessment. We developed the BEST-Quick Scan which allows the user to perform a more restricted assessment in a very short time (less than 20 minutes). If the practice under study "passes" the BEST-Quick Scan, then the complete BEST-assessment should be used to focus on details necessary for benchmarking and process improvement.

11. How does the BEST-method support the concept of benchmarking?

Benchmarking seeks to find the best processes for achieving desired results. Process benchmarking identifies the most effective practices in companies that perform similar functions, no matter in what industry. When benchmarks are adopted from outside the industry, a company may learn ideas and processes as well as new applications that allow it to surpass the best within its own industry and to achieve distinctive superiority. The BEST-method describes the criteria and characteristics of a Best Practice that qualifies for process benchmarking.

12. Doesn't it take too much time? I don't have much time available.

Once you are familiar with the method, you can perform a complete detailed assessment in less than 1 hour. If you can't spend that much time on a strategic issue, then you must ask yourself a different question about your situation.

13. Can I develop my own assessment method for a Best Practice?

Yes, you can. But why should you spend time to develop something new, when there is already a fully described method available and described in detail in this book?

14. Is the BEST-method applicable in every country and every culture?

Yes, it is. Management of processes is a universal function. The assessment of the Best Practice is likewise a universal method. The criteria and characteristics are worded to transcend cultural differences.

15. May I shorten the method because some parts of the method are not applicable in my situation?

Why should you? Ask yourself first why you think that some parts are not applicable. You'll discover that some areas of organizational management are missing in your business planning or not well enough understood. The BEST-assessment provides an excellent basis for strategic planning and organizational design.

16. How can I convince top management to apply the BEST-method?

Start by asking the CEO what he/she believes is important and what he/she wants to achieve. Next, look for the key processes which support the CEO's expectations and desired results. Then ask the CEO whether he/she is interested in further improvement and enhancement of these results. Normally, the CEO should say yes. Then you can apply the BEST-method on these key processes and demonstrate to the CEO where you can achieve further improvement and hence achieve better results.

17. Are there no other methods available in (management) literature to assess a Best Practice?

As far as we know, there are no other methods available.

18. What is the added value of the BEST-method?

There are several advantages, to mention some:

- The assessment of a Best Practice shows you immediately where you can make improvements in the management of the investigated key process.
- A systematic use of the BEST-method leads to progressively better results for the stakeholders of the organization.
- It recognizes all employees who have contributed to the achievement of that Best Practice.
- You can obtain recognition from a global professional audience for your excellent performance.

19. Can the BEST-method be used as a standard to create a world benchmarking database?

In principle, yes. The authors have discovered through their previous work that some organizations are not willing to give a detailed description of their Best Practices to the manager of that database. The BEST-method is comprehensive and, as such, addresses issues of competitive advantage for the organization.

Thanks to the application of the BEST-method in a systematic way, feeding the database with the results of the BEST-assessments allows the users of that database to have data which are reliable and comparable.

20. Who is best placed to assess the Best Practice?

The owner of the key process, because he will also develop specific action plans to improve the management of that key process. The process owner and stakeholders of that process will be the first beneficiaries of further improvement in organizational results. If the organization has a Quality Management Department, those subject matter experts are skilled in cross functional assessment and certainly are viable partners in the assessment process.

21. Does the application of the BEST-method hinder the innovation process?

Not at all. The BEST-method can be applied to the innovation process as it does for other management processes. The innovation process can be done in three ways: a continuous improvement of the products or services, a breakthrough improvement of products or services and a radical new way of producing/delivering products or services. In the latter situation the process will be redesigned. In all three cases the BEST-method can be used. You need first to describe the way you achieve innovation. Innovation is an end-to-end *process* that starts with a problem, issue, or opportunity and ends in the creation of value. Therefore, you start with the question: which expectations or needs of customers are not yet fulfilled? Once you have the answer to this question, you can describe the process. Then you can start to apply the BEST-tools.

22. We are using Cost of Quality as an approach to identify priority key process improvements. Can I use the BEST-method at the same time?

Most certainly. The Cost of Quality approach to continuous improvement and performance excellence identifies the top dollar losses within the organization. Top management assesses the priority of financial exposure of process failure and identifies the key processes in most need of improvement. The criteria and characteristics of the BEST-tool are exactly the items within a process that, when improved, eliminate external failures and customer dissatisfaction. A Process Improvement team lead by process executives uses financial results to direct reduction of internal waste and failure, using lean or PDCA. The BEST-method requires audit (appraisal) as a function of the Check phase of the Enabler component. Finally, the continued use of the BEST-tool highlights areas for prevention of errors and waste in the future.

23. Why may I not copy a Best Practice from a benchmark?

There are at least three reasons why it isn't a good idea to copy some-one's else Best Practice. First, the circumstances of the other organization are not identical to yours. Second, both organizations have their own strategic plans, and these are different. Third, the company cultures are also different. What may work in one organization, may perhaps not work in your organization. The leadership styles of leaders may be (very) different. Consequently, the decision processes are also different. From all this, the management of the process under consideration will also be different.

24. Will the application of BEST-method lead to a status quo?

No, not at all. There are four reasons for this. First, the expectations, needs, and requirements of the stakeholders change over time. Therefore, you need to adapt your process to this new situation. Second, the strategy of the organization also changes every 3–5 years. Again, you must adapt the process to this situation or even to put another key process in the forefront of priorities and actions. Third, according to the BEST-method you'll learn from the achieved results and adapt your plans and process. Fourth, you'll also apply benchmarking, i.e. compare your process (enabler and results) with the Best-in-Class. You will learn from this benchmark and improve (change) your process. Consequently, you have a *dynamic change* of your key process which is today a Best Practice and hopefully next year too.

25. Once I have a Best Practice, will it last for at least 5 years?

No, probably not. If you look at the criteria of the BEST-tool, you'll discover that the process will change over time due to changes in the context, changes in society, changes in the business, changes in priorities and strategic plans of the organization. People working in the process learn every day and gaps will be resolved that are discovered during audits. Managing a process is a (very) dynamic process; consequently you need to update and improve your key process.

26. Is a Best Practice only a reflection of past experience?

Yes, a Best Practice is the reflection of what you improved within your key process and what you learned last year. But, be careful! The management of a key process is a dynamic situation. You look forward, you try to understand what your organization needs in the coming months and years. Therefore, the BEST-method is also a future-oriented approach.

27. Can the application of Best Practices dilute the strategic differentiation of a company?

Yes, it can if you copy the Best Practices and strategy of your competitor. However, we stressed several times in our book that the starting point of management of your organization is the strategy of your company. Of course, this is different from your competitors. Once the strategy is defined and the key processes defined, you can improve these processes by applying the BEST-method. But never copy a Best Practice of your competitor! You may lose your competitive advantage. We stressed earlier the point that you have to *learn* from a benchmark, but never to copy it.

28. Can a company culture have an impact on the application and development of Best Practices?

Yes, it can. A company culture is directly related to the mindset of people within the organization. If the organization is people- and process-oriented, or results-oriented, the culture will tend to be positive. If the culture looks for security and avoids taking risks, it will tend toward the defensive. Some cultures will always try to be the best or want to have everything under control. Some put learning and innovation first. These different company cultures will result in different approaches to process organization. Therefore we advise you when you want to improve your Best Practice, don't look only for a benchmark, but investigate also to what extent your company culture may impede the achievement of excellent results or the opposite: how company culture can give a boost to the way you are organized (enablers) and to your results.

29. Can Best Practice approaches limit opportunities for new learning and growth?

Yes, they can. When leaders apply defensive thinking styles by pretending things such as "we are the best," "we know what we have to do," "we are recognized in the market as the best," etc. the learning process stops. It is important that leaders are humble, listen to all stakeholders, accept difficult messages (we don't say that you need to agree with this feedback), learn from others, are eager to discover new ideas, try to implement new methods, etc. By doing this, not only the leaders may learn and grow, the organization as a whole will also benefit.

Finally, you may contact the authors if you still have unresolved questions. We'll try to answer you.

yves.vannuland@comatech.be
grace683@outlook.com

Definitions

BEST

a **B**etter way to **E**xcellent results and **S**uccess through the application of an appropriate **T**ool

Definition of a Best Practice

A Best Practice is a *process* which is regularly reviewed and improved, monitored by KPIs, and incorporating lessons learned. A Best Practice contributes to the concretization of the strategy of the organization and leads to excellent and sustainable results.

Short definition of a Best Practice

A Best Practice delivers excellent and sustainable results based on the systematic management of a key process.

Best Practice documentation

A detailed documentation where all four components must be linked together: 1) enabler (PDCA, lean, Six Sigma, or other), 2) results, 3) process description, and 4) format of the Best Practice.

BEST-tool

The BEST-tool consists of four **components**: Enabler, Results, Process, and Format.

Each component contains several **criteria**.

Each criterion consists of one or more **characteristics.**

BEST-tool (details)

	Phase	*Number of criteria*	*Number of characteristics*
Enabler	Plan	8	16
	Do	5	7
	Check	4	13
	Act	5	8
Results	Results	7	20
Management of process		9	
Format of process		13	

Excellent results

These include results for all the stakeholders of the organization (customers, employees, partners, contractors, suppliers, society, local community, etc.) which exceed the expectations of these stakeholders. These results are positive compared with benchmarks and organizations recognized as Best-in-Class.

Four building blocks

- Enabler (the method for developing the process)
- Results (measures of effectiveness)
- Process (the flow of the activities to be improved)
- Format (the structure of a Best Practice description: the format is the organization of components 1, 2, and 3)

Key process

These are the most important processes of an organization. These are "key" for success. These contribute in a positive way to the achievement of the strategic goals and business plan of the company/organization.

The results produced by the key process are mainly output and outcome results.

Management

Use of indicators (KPI), objectives, audit, learning, and sharing experiences, and prevention and strategy.

Output and Outcome indicators

Output indicators measure whether the product or service delivered by the process meets the criteria for which it is designed.

An outcome or impact indicator describes whether the product or service meets the needs of the customer for whom it is intended.

For a process to be a Best Practice, both output and outcome indicators must be monitored and validated.

PDCA

The PDCA-cycle consists of four phases: Plan-Do-Check-Act

Process

A chronological order of activities and decisions transforming an input into an output and outcome.

An activity or group of activities that takes an input, adds value to it, and provides an output to an internal or external customer; a planned and repetitive sequence of steps by which a defined product or service is delivered.

SMART	This is an acronym and stands for **S**pecific, **M**easurable, **A**ssignable (Accountable), **R**elevant, and **T**imely executed

Sustainable results

The results are lasting and show a positive trend for a long period (e.g. 10 years).

Systematic

Regular improvement, review, and monitoring of the process.

Index